THE PRESENT STATE OF GERMANY

NATURAL LAW AND
ENLIGHTENMENT CLASSICS

Knud Haakonssen
General Editor

Samuel Pufendorf

NATURAL LAW AND
ENLIGHTENMENT CLASSICS

The Present State of Germany

Samuel Pufendorf

Translated by Edmund Bohun, 1696

Edited and with an Introduction by
Michael J. Seidler

The Works of Samuel Pufendorf

LIBERTY FUND

Indianapolis

11   10   09   08   07   C   5   4   3   2   1
11   10   09   08   07   P   5   4   3   2   1

Frontispiece: The portrait of Samuel Pufendorf is to be found at the Law Faculty of the University of Lund, Sweden, and is based on a photoreproduction by Leopoldo Iorizzo. Reprinted by permission.

Library of Congress Cataloging-in-Publication Data
Pufendorf, Samuel, Freiherr von, 1632–1694
[De statu Imperii Germanici. English]
The present state of Germany/Samuel Pufendorf;
translated by Edmund Bohun, 1696;
edited and with an introduction by Michael J. Seidler.
p.   cm.—(Works of Samuel Pufendorf)
(Natural law and enlightenment classics)
Includes bibliographical references and index.
ISBN-13: 978-0-86597-492-0 (alk. paper)   ISBN-10: 0-86597-492-6 (alk. paper)
ISBN-13: 978-0-86597-493-7 (pbk.: alk. paper)   ISBN-10: 0-86597-493-4 (pbk.: alk. paper)
1. Constitutional history—Holy Roman Empire.
2. Constitutional law—Holy Roman Empire.
I. Seidler, Michael J., 1950–   II. Title.
KK290.P845 2007
342.4302′9—dc22   2006028367

LIBERTY FUND, INC.
8335 Allison Pointe Trail, Suite 300
Indianapolis, Indiana 46250-1684

CONTENTS

INTRODUCTION

Samuel Pufendorf (1632–94) began his academic career at the University of Heidelberg in 1661 in the arts (i.e., philosophy) faculty as a professor of international law (*ius gentium*) and philology. He received this appointment on the basis of his first jurisprudential work, the *Elements of Universal Jurisprudence* (1660),[1] which he had dedicated to the Palatine elector, Karl Ludwig. At Heidelberg, Pufendorf set about the revision of his immature effort, as he later called it, through a series of academic dissertations[2] that culminated in his massive *On the Law of Nature and of Nations* (1672) and its pedagogical distillation *The Whole Duty of Man* (1673), both of which soon made him famous throughout Europe. In 1667, a year before assuming a professorship at the newly created University of Lund, in Sweden, he published the infamous *On the State of the German Empire* under the pseudonym Severinus de Monzambano, a fictive Italian writing to his brother, Laelius, about his travels through Germany. This comparatively slight volume on German constitutional law generated intense interest, and the academic controversy it ignited easily equalled the famous "Scandinavian quarrel" that arose later over Pufendorf's main natural law writings.[3]

Much less known today than these works, the *Monzambano,* as it was soon called, seems like an occasional tract relevant only to the circum-

1. See the bibliography for the original titles of works.
2. *Dissertationes academicae selectiores* (Lund, 1675). This collection was reprinted four more times: in 1677, 1678, 1679 (as *Politica inculpata*), and 1698 (as *Analecta politica*).
3. *Eris Scandica* (Frankfurt, 1686). For a modern edition, see Pufendorf, *Eris Scandica und andere polemische Schriften,* ed. Palladini. On the earlier controversy, see Palladini, "Discussioni sul *Monzambano.*"

stances of its origin. Even so, its influence lasted for more than half a century, and it became part of the historiography that was integral to natural law as a genre.[4] More significantly, though, the piece has a strong philosophical subtext and shares basic features with many of Pufendorf's other writings: the mutuality of theory and practice, a strong empiricism or realism, and opposition to scholastic categorization and argument— all characteristic of his "modern" natural law.[5] Moreover, its historical sweep and detail match Pufendorf's national histories of Sweden and Brandenburg and the broader *An Introduction to the History of the Principal Kingdoms and States of Europe* (1682), which he wrote after 1677 upon leaving academia to become Swedish state historian and, in 1688, official historiographer of Brandenburg. Finally, its controversial remarks on religion and politics point ahead to Pufendorf's *Of the Nature and Qualification of Religion in Reference to Civil Society* (1687) and *The Divine Feudal Law* (1695). It seems appropriate, therefore, that *Monzambano* was both an early and a late work of Pufendorf, the latter in the form of a second edition carefully prepared by him shortly before his death and published posthumously in 1706. It is perhaps the most representative item in his entire corpus.

Background, Political Setting, and Publication Details

Pufendorf's reasons for this description of the empire's history and constitution remain unclear. One explanation found in some early biographies and, through Heinrich von Treitschke, used as the basis of many later accounts must be ruled out: that he wrote the work after being passed over for a position in the more prestigious law faculty at Heidel-

---

4. See Hochstrasser, *Natural Law Theories*, especially pp. 1–39. The *Monzambano* debate became a standard part of many Pufendorf biographies and histories of natural law. For instance, see Glafey, *Vollständige Geschichte*, §125, pp. 203–4.

5. See Tuck, "'Modern' Theory"; Hunter, "Natural Law"; and Haakonssen, "Protestant Natural Law Theory."

berg, attempting to prove that he was in fact the more deserving candidate.[6] There was no such vacancy at the time, and Pufendorf would have been unqualified for and uninterested in it had there been one.[7] Still, this false account of his intentions may have skewed the reception of the work in later periods.

Internal evidence such as the Imperial Diet of 1663 and the dismissal in 1664 of Baron von Boineburg (chief minister in Mainz and an early supporter of Pufendorf's)[8] places the supposed journey of the work's fictive Italian narrator in the period 1663–64. These years also saw a renewed Turkish threat against the empire and a heightening (in 1665) of the so-called *Wildfangstreit* (alluded to several times in the work). This was a bitter, sometimes violent, dispute between the Palatinate and several of its neighbors over the former's vigorous exercise of a historical claim to limited jurisdiction over illegitimate and stateless persons, not only in its own but also in surrounding territories. Given the demographic and financial stakes involved for Karl Ludwig, whose territories had been devastated and depopulated by the Thirty Years' War, Pufendorf and other Heidelberg professors were enlisted in the heated pamphlet war that accompanied the actual hostilities. For his part, Pufendorf issued a short response to a tract by the famous polyhistor Johann Heinrich Bökler, who was in the service of Mainz; and around the same time, he composed the *Monzambano,* which Karl Ludwig was variously said to have encouraged, assisted, or even coauthored.[9] Though mainly a re-

6. Treitschke, "Samuel Pufendorf," 220–21, cites the second (after Gundling's) preface to the posthumous edition, even though there is some doubt that it was written by Pufendorf himself. The story was repeated in other early accounts, including the extended history of the *Monzambano* ("Vorrede des Übersetzers, samt der Remarquablen Historie dieses Buches") preceding Adlemansthal's [i.e., Dahlmann's] 1710 German translation of the work, *Samuels Freyhrn. von Puffendorff . . . Bericht.*

7. See Döring, "Untersuchungen." Also essential for understanding the background of the work are Döring, "Heilige Römische Reich" and "Westfälische Frieden."

8. Both events are mentioned in Pufendorf's 1667 preface. See pp. 5–7 and notes 9, 10, and 12 there.

9. See *Kleine Vorträge und Schriften,* ed. Döring, for the text of Pufendorf's *Prodromus solidae et copiosae Confutationis mox secuturae scripti nuper evulgati* (187–93) and Döring's extensive introduction (158–86). Pufendorf apparently wrote the piece—a

gional dispute, the conflict had broader import because it involved legal claims based on historical precedent, the relations of territorial sovereigns to one another and to the emperor, and appeals to external powers. (The emperor supported Mainz, while Karl Ludwig sought the support of France and Sweden, the formal guarantors of the Peace of Westphalia.) All the while, the empire as a whole confronted a serious, external danger from the Ottoman forces. Although the *Monzambano* did not address the specific conflict directly, it dealt with the underlying structural issues that created it, not just in historical and constitutional terms but also according to the natural law theory developed in Pufendorf's dissertations before and after this period.

Unlike Pufendorf's shorter polemic, the *Monzambano* was controversial because it challenged long-established views that undergirded complex and hard-won arrangements within the empire. Indeed, it can be read as a brusque complaint about the pointlessness or practical uselessness of those views. This perspective, as well as the work's independent, aggressive, and disrespectful demeanor (which many readers enjoyed), meant that it could not be published in Germany and that it was safer to issue it under a pseudonym. So the manuscript went to Paris (in late 1666), where Samuel's brother Esaias, then acting as the Swedish liaison, arranged for a printer. The latter in turn consulted the French historian Mézeray, whose brief response was reprinted by Gundling in the 1706 edition (see below). Mézeray praised the piece, which he called a work of politics, not history, but thought it too dangerous to approve because of passages potentially offensive to the French and certainly to the clergy. Therefore, like other refugees of the age, the book migrated to the Netherlands and was published at The Hague in early 1667 by Adrian Vlacq, who had previously issued Pufendorf's *Elements* (1660).

---

mere *prodromus* (forerunner, preliminary response)—only because he was so ordered. The main task had been assigned to Johann Friedrich Böckelmann, professor primarius of the law faculty, who was more familiar with the dispute and whose promotion to the law chair, supposedly in place of Pufendorf, was said to have motivated the latter to compose the *Monzambano.* On the *Wildfangstreit,* also see Dotzauer, "Kurpfälzische Wildfangstreit"; and Palladini, "Un nemico," 144–48.

Even then it seemed prudent to purport Geneva as the place of publication to mislead anticipated critics.

Despite its irreverent, populist tone, *Monzambano* was immediately recognized as a substantial critique of the empire and its theorists or publicists, as they were called. Since the printer could not meet demand, especially in Germany, the book was frequently pirated. An imperial prohibition and confiscation order, on account of the work's treatment of Austria and Catholicism, merely whetted appetites and increased the circulation. Few works had seen so many editions, according to a 1710 editor, who estimated a total distribution of over three hundred thousand copies.[10] Even if the figure is exaggerated, the book was clearly a seventeenth-century best-seller, achieving a notoriety that lasted for decades. Indeed, even its critics contributed to the book's success by sometimes republishing it with their own commentaries and refutations.[11]

In the broadest terms, the pseudonymous author—whose detailed knowledge of German affairs belied his purported Italian persona—was accused of undermining the empire by attacking its unifying self-conception: that is, critics charged, he lacked patriotism (*Reichspatriotismus*). This was not an anti-intellectual, timid, or merely dogmatic response but a reaction to the boldness of Pufendorf's critique and its

---

10. The figure comes from Adlemansthal [Dahlmann] (1710), "Remarquable Historie." It is also found in Johann Jacob Moser, *Bibliotheca juris publici S.R. German. Imperii* (Stuttgardt, 1729), 550–51, who suggested removing a zero. Salomon, "Einleitung," p. 3, called the figure "substantially exaggerated," while granting the general claim and noting that there were eighteen Latin editions before 1734. In the same work Salomon details the complex publication history, particularly the distinction among the various editions and translations, some of which are unreliable because of unauthorized insertions by others.

11. A well-known example is Philipp Andreas Oldenburger [Pacificus a Lapide, pseud.], *Dominus de Mozambano Illustratus et Restrictus; sive: Severini de Mozambano Veronensis de Statu Imperii Germanici ad Laelium Fratrem Liber unus. Discursibus Juridico-Politicis Explicatus et Restrictus* (1668), which was reprinted for a number of years. For an analysis of Oldenburger's "Discourses" on *Monzambano*, see Palladini, "Discussioni sul *Monzambano*," 116–24. Another edition accompanied Ulrich Obrecht's *In Severini de Monzambano Veronensis De Statu Imperii Germanici Librum, Exercitationum Academicarum Specimen* (1684). Such reprints have sometimes been mistaken by later readers for authorized versions.

concrete implications. Indeed, the outcry against the work was so wide-spread and intense precisely because *Monzambano* took on everyone who had written on the empire; it did not ally itself with any particular interpretation or school but mockingly dismissed them all. This "purely negative criticism"[12] left the work without any established allies and made it seem wholly destructive.

The hunt for the brazen author began almost immediately, with Samuel himself and his brother Esaias, along with Hermann Conring, Karl Ludwig, and von Boineburg on the short list of suspects—the last three because they were favorably mentioned in the book. Boineburg was particularly embarrassed by the suggestion because he seemed to have a motive (dismissal from Mainz, in 1664) and happened, inconveniently, to be in Vienna, the imperial center, after the book appeared.[13] However, more observant minds soon focused on Samuel, not only because of private reports from Heidelberg but also because of similar content in several of his earlier dissertations.[14] Indeed, he confirmed these suspicions by a detailed defense in the following year (1668). *On Irregular States* (*De republica irregulari*) was Pufendorf's first publication at Lund: it provided a systematic analysis of this key notion in *Monzambano* and specific refutations of the book's early critics.[15] From then on his authorship was essentially an open secret, though he denied it until the end of his life.[16]

12. Jastrow, "Pufendorfs Lehre," 381–82.

13. Henrich August Francke, *Notitia uberior variorum sumtibus Gabrielis Trogii*, in *De fatis methodo fine et obiecto iuris publici sac. Rom. imp. celeberrimorum aliquo scriptorum collectio* (Leipzig, 1739), 38, note u; and Moser, *Bibliotheca*, no. 35, 537–43. Boineburg complained to Bökler as late as 1672 about the problems he faced because of his presumed authorship of *Monzambano*. See the 1667 preface, note 12.

14. Christoph August Heumann, *De libris anonymis ac pseudonymis schediasma* (Jena, 1711), p. 122, §XVII. Pufendorf's *De rebus gestis Philippi Amyntae filio* (June 1664) and *De systematibus civitatum* (December 1667) both dealt with regular and irregular states and with state systems or confederations.

15. *De republica irregulari* (Lund, 1668) was reissued several more times by itself, in 1669, 1671, 1673, and 1682, in addition to its inclusion in Pufendorf's *Dissertationes academicae selectiores* (1675). An unattributed German translation, titled *Samuels von Puffendorff Gründliche Untersuchung von der Art und Eigenschaft eines Irregulairen Staats,* was packaged with Adlemansthal's 1710 translation of *Monzambano*.

16. On April 9, 1692, Pufendorf told Christian Thomasius that he had finished

Critiques of *Monzambano* began appearing almost immediately and kept coming for decades. Of varying length and competence, they typically expressed outrage and insult as well as scholarly disagreement. Some addressed specific elements of the work (including factual claims), others attempted broader defenses of positions Pufendorf had panned, and still others offered extensive commentaries on the whole. Most were in the scholastic mode that Pufendorf so despised: merely reiterating traditional categories to schematize the empirical realities of the empire.[17] Their authors ranged from young doctoral candidates still cutting their teeth to accomplished scholars and diplomats.[18] Pufendorf himself continued to engage his critics indirectly until about 1675, when he inserted into the collective edition of his dissertations two lengthy supplements—*Additions*—to *On Irregular States;*[19] and he continued to enjoy the reactions that the work provoked, even as he prepared the second edition.[20]

---

his revision of the *Monzambano* but that he was still not ready to acknowledge his authorship of the work. See *Briefwechsel,* letter 218, p. 340. Also, Gundling (*Samuelis,* ed. Gundling) reports in his preface that Pufendorf ordered the *editio posthuma* to be published anonymously (*sine persona*).

17. In his prefatory "Remarquable Historie," Adlemansthal makes the clever comment that Pufendorf wrote his "monstrous" (i.e., irregular; see below) work against the formulaic views of the scholastics. Jastrow ("Pufendorfs Lehre," 376–79) points to a dissertation by one of Conring's students, Ludolf Hugo's *De statu regionum Germaniae liber unus* (Helmstedt, 1661); and Michael Stolleis ("Textor und Pufendorf") to Johann Wolfgang Textor's *Tractatus juris publici de vera et varia ratione status Germaniae modernae* (Nuremberg, 1667), as other unconventional treatments of the empire with which *Monzambano* had certain unacknowledged affinities.

18. For a detailed analysis of these critiques of *Monzambano,* see Roeck, "Reichssystem," 36–57, and Palladini, "Discussioni sul *Monzambano,*" 111–62. Leibniz's first response to *Monzambano* offers an example of the scholastic, syllogistic method. See "In Severinum de Monzambano" (1668–72), in Gottfried Wilhelm Leibniz, *Politische Schriften,* Reihe 4 of *Sämtliche Schriften und Briefe,* ed. Preussische Akademie der Wissenschaften (Darmstadt: Otto Reichl, 1931), 1:500–502. This brief, private reaction did not become part of the public debate.

19. See notes 2 and 15, above.

20. Christian Thomasius lectured on *Monzambano* at Halle in the summer of 1692. Writing to him on April 9, 1692, Pufendorf relished the thought of his "dangerous Monzambano" now being publicly read and scandalizing some of its earlier opponents. See *Briefwechsel,* letter 218, p. 340.

Conceptual Context

Accused by his enemies in Sweden of defending *Monzambano* and seeking to destroy the German political order, Pufendorf replied that he (i.e., Monzambano) actually sought to preserve the Westphalian settlement and to protect the liberty of the German estates and the security of the Protestant religion.[21] That is, as the additions to the second edition (especially in chapter VIII) make even more apparent, the work was motivated by the very patriotism that its critics found wanting.[22] The empire could not serve its purpose if it misconceived itself and failed to recognize the concrete obstacles to its proper functioning. The title of the book, "On the State [*status*] of the German Empire," is suggestively ambiguous in this respect, by both announcing a description of actual political conditions in Germany and suggesting an assessment of the empire in terms of the general criteria for statehood. The failure of the descriptive and normative aspects to coincide implied not condemnation but the need for meliorative adaptation. That is, any destructiveness at work was thoroughly Cartesian.[23]

21. "Epistola ad amicos suos per Germaniam" [A letter to his friends in Germany] (1676), in *Eris scandica und andere polemische Schriften,* ed. Palladini, 92. Pufendorf had lectured on *Monzambano* at Lund, mocking the German constitutional system to the point that students there called him the "laughing professor." See Modéer, "From Samuel Pufendorf," 8.

22. On Pufendorf's notion of patriotism, see the articles by Horst Dreitzel, "Zehn Jahre 'Patria' in der politischen Theorie in Deutschland"; and Michael J. Seidler, " 'Wer mir gutes thut, den liebe ich,' " in *"Patria" und "Patrioten" vor dem Patriotismus.*

23. Pufendorf was attracted to Descartes because of his antischolastic method, his refusal to accept older authorities without proof. See *Specimen controversiarum circa jus naturae ipsi nuper motarum* (Osnabrug [Leipzig], 1678), in *Eris scandica und andere polemische Schriften,* ed. Palladini, 130–31. Also see Pufendorf's strong defense of Descartes against the Swedish clergy, on similar grounds, in "Unvorgreifflich Bedencken über der Deputirten von der Priesterschafft requeste wegen abschaffung der Cartesianischen Philosophie" (1688), in *Kleine Vorträge und Schriften,* ed. Döring, 433–34. On Pufendorf and Cartesianism, see Döring's introduction to *Kleine Vorträge und Schriften,* 388–431; and Simone De Angelis, "Pufendorf und der Cartesianismus," *Internationales Archiv für Sozialgeschichte der deutschen Literatur,* 129–72.

The great amount of previous theorizing about the empire[24] that Severinus de Monzambano mentions dismissively in the preface had generally taken place within an Aristotelian framework according to which there are three correct forms of state (kingship/monarchy, aristocracy, polity/republic) and three deviant or degenerate ones (tyranny, oligarchy, democracy). Most attempts to characterize and diagnose the empire had used these categories. For example, Jean Bodin (*Six livres de la republique,* 1576) had declared the empire an aristocracy on account of the power of the territorial estates, particularly the electors; so did Hippolithus a Lapide (i.e., Bogislaw Philipp Chemnitz, in *Dissertatio de ratione status in imperio nostro Romano-Germanico,* 1640), whose position is extensively criticized by Pufendorf (VIII.1–3). Others, such as Dietrich Reinkingk (*Tractatus de regimine seculari et ecclesiastico,* 1619), had emphasized the position of the emperor and presented the empire as a monarchy. Although it was clearly not a polity or republic (see VI.3), there were those, such as Johannes Althusius (*Politica methodice digesta,* 1603), who emphasized the popular origins of political power, even in the empire as a whole. However, Althusius himself saw the best state as a combination of all three forms and thus belongs rather to the so-called mixture theorists, who combined different forms in order to explain the phenomena. Simple or mixed, Pufendorf thought all such explanations—including the distinctions invented to make them plausible, such as real versus personal sovereignty or majesty—inadequate to the actual complexities of the empire.

Following Bodin and Hobbes, Pufendorf emphasized sovereignty (*summum imperium*) as the defining characteristic of a state, and he distinguished regular from irregular states in terms of whether sovereignty was unified and effective or not.[25] Whatever particular form a state might

---

24. For the theoretical context of Pufendorf's *Monzambano,* see Jastrow, "Pufendorfs Lehre," 370–88; Riklin, "Gemischte oder monströse Verfassung"; Denzer, "Samuel Pufendorf und die Verfassungsgeschichte"; and Schröder, "Constitution" and "Reich versus Territorien?"

25. Jean Bodin, *Six livres de la republique* [Six books on the state] (Paris, 1576); and Thomas Hobbes, *Leviathan* (1651, 1668), part 2, chapter 22. See Pufendorf's *On*

have was irrelevant so long as king, council, or people had sole and sufficient power to direct the state as a single entity, governed "by one Soul" (VI.8; VII.7). When regular, states could realize their goals: protection of individuals from one another, both singly and in groups, and relief of the general insecurity of human affairs; when irregular, they could not.[26] According to these criteria, which were carefully elaborated in *On Irregular States* and *On the Law of Nature and of Nations,* the empire was an irregular, dysfunctional state. In fact, it did not seem like a state at all, but more like a hybrid or chimera, produced by a gradual, unplanned, and unsystematic devolution from an originally regular state/ status.[27]

One of *Monzambano*'s most notorious passages occurs in chapter VI, which was widely considered the most important in the work and prompted the most criticism. Appealing to his basic notions of moral entities and collective personae,[28] Pufendorf said there that *"Germany is an Irregular Body, and like some mis-shapen Monster, if . . . it be measured by the common Rules of Politicks and Civil Prudence"* (VI.9, first edition). The term *monstrum* was perceived as deeply offensive by many of the empire's apologists, even though it also had a rather ordinary, descriptive sense.[29] In fact, Pufendorf clarified the term as simply

---

the *Law of Nature and of Nations,* VII.4 (on the parts of supreme sovereignty) and VII.5 (on the forms of the state, including regular and irregular states).

26. *On the Law of Nature and of Nations,* VII.1.7–8.

27. In *De republica irregulari,* §1, Pufendorf says that it is valuable to study irregular and imperfect states, just as natural scientists find it useful to study rare and uncommon plants and stones. He may have been influenced in this by Francis Bacon, some of whose works he owned, since one of Bacon's methods of inquiry focused on abnormal specimens of nature.

28. *On the Law of Nature and of Nations,* I.1.12–13; VII.2.13, 21–23.

29. On Pufendorf's notion of *monstrum,* see *De rebus gestis Philippi Amyntae filio* (1664), §3, and *Addenda* to *De republica irregulari,* in *Dissertationes academicae selectiores* (Lund, 1675), 729. Moser, *Bibliotheca,* 548, said that it was unfair to censure Pufendorf for using the term *monstrum,* since this could refer to anything special, unusual, or irregular, including something valued and respected. Thus, one could refer to an unusually learned person as "a monster of erudition." According to Zedler's *Universal-Lexikon* (Leipzig and Halle, 1745), vol. 21, *monstrum* meant "that which is or is born against nature" or "that which hides or changes the true origin of

equivalent to "irregular." Because of the carelessness of the emperors and the ambition of princes and clerics, the empire had degenerated over many centuries from a regular kingdom to the point where it was no longer even a limited kingdom (i.e., a state with limited sovereignty). Nor was it, exactly speaking, a system of independent states united in a league or confederacy. Instead, he claimed, it was "something . . . that fluctuates between these two" and whose irregularity subjects it to "inextricable and incurable Disease, and many internal Convulsions" (VI.9). The original provocation of the term was probably intentional; however, to avoid further misunderstanding or offense, Pufendorf silently omitted it from the second edition, which he tamed in other ways as well.

After criticizing Hippolithus a Lapide's radical cures,[30] Pufendorf tentatively offered some remedies of his own (VIII.4). These are surprisingly modest in view of his dire diagnosis, and they barely go beyond a reaffirmation of the post-Westphalian status quo.[31] Perhaps this is because the empire seemed to him like a harp, as he later observed: even after much tuning, any harmony inevitably devolves into discord again.[32] Nonetheless, Pufendorf acknowledged, the empire contained a balance that needed to be preserved, or reestablished if lost, not least because there was no obvious alternative. Thus, despite the idea's abstract attractiveness, it would be unrealistic and lead "to the utter ruin of the nation" (VIII.4) to attempt a reduction of the empire to a regular monarchy again. Instead, since it already approximated a system or confederation of unequals (VI.9; VIII.4), it was best to accept the fact and, by

---

its birth by assuming a foreign shape." Knoppers and Landes, *Monstrous Bodies,* show how widespread the political use of *monstrum* was, especially in a British context, but seem unaware of the chief instance of that usage on the Continent.

30. Strongly anti-Austrian, Lapide regarded the empire as an aristocracy whose power lay in the collectivity of the estates rather than in the emperor. His "cures" for the empire's ills (VIII.3) were seen by Pufendorf as unrealistic or self-defeating (e.g., complete elimination of grounds for religious controversy, destruction of the House of Austria and confiscation of its domains).

31. Schröder, "Constitution," 971–72.

32. *On the Law of Nature and of Nations,* VII.5.15.

reference to historical precedents and current instances, explore how it might be effectively maintained.[33]

This was both an outward- and an inward-looking strategy, for a functional system protects its members from external threats but also demands from them a strict adherence to cooperative agreements. The weakness in the scheme, as Pufendorf realized, was that it lacked a locus of supreme sovereignty and a reliable source of compulsion to induce the members to compromise and cooperate.[34] This was, of course, the basic problem of the state of nature and how to exit from it—only now on the collective, interstate level that may have been paradigmatic for the notion in the first place. After his early work on systems of states, which preceded *Monzambano*, Pufendorf turned more closely to the internal mechanism of the state, particularly the role of sovereignty. However, if sovereignty within states were to become less feasible or attractive, as it might be already on the international level, the problem of systemic unity would arise again and a return to *Monzambano* might be indicated.

Chapter Synopses

Despite the controversy over *Monzambano* as a philosophical and political work, there was general acclaim for its mastery of German history and its economical portrayal of the complex institutions of the empire. This alone ensured its success, since many, such as the English translator Edmund Bohun, were looking for a clear and comprehensive account. The work consists of eight chapters varying in length. The first five describe the historical origins and concrete workings of the empire and

33. Pufendorf was thinking of the ancient Greek Amphyctionic and Achaean Leagues, which he discussed in *De rebus gestis Philippi Amyntae filio* (1664) and *De systematibus civitatum* (1667), and of the Dutch and Swiss Confederations in Europe.

34. Wrede, "Kaiser," describes the general effect of a principle of "negative integration" (115) in view of the Turkish and French threats to the empire. Even so, Jastrow, "Pufendorfs Lehre," 362, notes the important alteration at VIII.4, between the first and second editions of *Monzambano*: the former still allowed confederates to force a noncompliant member, while the latter—arguably in more dire circumstances—relied on the "intervention of common friends" alone.

thus constitute a unit. The last three focus on more distinctive intellectual questions, albeit not without practical import.

Chapter I traces German origins back to the Franks, and the beginnings of the empire to Charlemagne and his heirs. It also raises the important question of the empire's claimed continuity with ancient Rome. Here, as well as later in the work, Pufendorf rejects the *translatio imperii* (transmission of empire) thesis so dear to monarchists, and according to which Germany—as Rome's inheritor—was the fourth great empire prophesied in the book of Daniel.[35] Pufendorf's dismissal of this idea—consistent with his "secular" approach to history and natural law—deprived the empire of a genetic, historical self-justification, one with religious or apocalyptic warrant. Chapter II reviews the so-called members of the empire, including particular noble families and houses as well as the different ranks of nobility in general, both secular and sacred. Chapter III details the powers and privileges of these so-called estates and how they were acquired over time.[36] This leads to the critical question of the emperor's status and authority vis-à-vis the other estates, as well as the controversial role of the papacy in the appointment or confirmation of emperors (i.e., the "holy" in Holy Roman Empire). These topics are treated in chapter IV, which also describes the transition from a hereditary to an elective imperiate, and the role and privileges of the electors in selecting, deposing, and representing an emperor (during an interregnum). Chapter V (the longest in the work) develops these topics and discusses specific limitations on the emperor's powers, including the so-called capitulars imposed at his election. It also examines the Imperial Diet, the emperor's authority over religious affairs and clergy, and the legal structure and judicial machinery brought into play by disputes at or between various levels of this complex whole.

Chapter VI contains Pufendorf's discussion of the constitutional

35. See Koch, *Europa,* and Lübbe-Wolff, "Bedeutung." The idea had been effectively undermined already by Hermann Conring, who demonstrated in *De origine iuris Germanici* (1643) that the "Lotharian legend" about Roman law's formal introduction into Germany in 1135 A.D. was false.

36. See III.4 and note 7, p. 86, on Pufendorf's controversial *feuda oblata* hypothesis.

form of the empire, in which he argues that it is not a democracy, aristocracy, monarchy (even limited), or some mixed form, but rather an irregular system of sovereign states.[37] This irregular structure entails various specific weaknesses or diseases (in line with the corporative imagery), which are the subject of chapter VII. There Pufendorf describes the geographical, physical, economic, and human resources of Germany in comparison with other European countries (and the Ottoman Empire) and determines that Germany is by no means inferior. Its weakness is due rather to its constitutional structure, which prevents it from using its natural advantages successfully. This chapter served as the foundation of Pufendorf's later work *An Introduction to the History of the Principal Kingdoms and States of Europe* (1682), which greatly expanded these interstate comparisons and their relevance to determining the true "interests" (*ratio,* reason) of particular states. Chapter VIII turns explicitly to the notion of "state interest" or "reason of state" and uses it to explore possible remedies for the empire's maladies. After a detailed critique of the recommendations of Lapide (see above), Pufendorf offers (in VIII.4) his own modest suggestions for reform. The latter, and greater, portion of the chapter (VIII.5–10) addresses the problem of religious diversity and its impact on politics. It compares the political interests and impacts of Lutheranism, Calvinism, and Catholicism, the last of which comes in for special criticism. These controversial comments—ironically placed in the mouths of Catholic clerics and allowed expression by a papal nuncio—were entirely omitted from the second edition of *Monzambano,* partly because of changes in the political landscape of Europe and partly because they had already been treated more extensively by Pufendorf in several intervening works, which also took their origin from *Monzambano.*[38]

---

37. On the distinction between regular and irregular systems, see *On the Law of Nature and of Nations,* VII.5.20, in which Pufendorf says that an irregular system is one in which the majority obligates and compels a minority. Also see Denzer, "Samuel Pufendorf," 303–7; Dufour, "Federalisme et raison d'état" and "Pufendorfs föderalistisches Denken," 109–15; and Schröder, "Constitution," 968–71.

38. *The History of Popedom,* which Pufendorf incorporated (as chapter 12) into *An Introduction to the History of the Principal Kingdoms and States of Europe; Of the*

The second edition of *Monzambano,* which Pufendorf prepared between 1688 and 1692, constituted a substantial revision of the first. Some passages were excised, others inserted, and many others altered. Besides correcting factual errors and reflecting internal developments in the empire since 1666, Pufendorf sought also to address the intervening criticisms launched against the work. Moreover, the international situation had changed significantly, affecting the empire's interests. The Turks were in retreat since 1683, Brandenburg had grown more powerful and Sweden less so, and an overweening France pursued an aggressive annexation policy along the Rhine and seemed, indeed, to aspire to the "universal monarchy" threatened by Austria decades earlier.[39] Strange new alliances took shape, as Brandenburg, Austria, and even the papacy[40] either supported or tolerated the Calvinist William III's invasion of England and the overthrow of its Catholic monarch. Pufendorf revised *Monzambano* to reflect these emergent realities by softening its criticism of Austria and Catholicism and inserting new and harsher language toward France, especially in chapter VIII. Also, the initial preface defining the fictional author's critical and even disrespectful stance toward previous writers was omitted. On the whole, the work's attitude and expression were more temperate, less willing to offend—a change that also made it, at least to some, less able to excite.

Edmund Bohun and His Translation

The publication of Edmund Bohun's (1645–99) *On the State of the German Empire* in 1690 (and 1696) is an indication of the growing famil-

---

Nature and Qualification of Religion in Reference to Civil Society; and *The Divine Feudal Law.* See note 4 on p. 10, below. On the continuity between *Monzambano* and these later works on religion, see Palladini, "Stato, chiesa e tolleranza."

39. On this notion, see Bosbach, "European Debate."

40. Innocent X, pope from 1644 to 1655, had opposed any accommodation of Protestantism during the negotiations preceding the Treaty of Westphalia (1648) and issued the papal bull *Zelo Domus Dei* against the treaty a month after it was signed.

iarity with Pufendorf's work in England from the 1680s onward.[41] Unlike Tyrrell and Locke, however, who were interested in Pufendorf's natural law philosophy, Bohun's attention was drawn to the anonymous author's detailed account of the German empire.[42] (Since the posthumous edition had not yet appeared and Bohun was probably unaware of the *Monzambano* controversy in Germany, he could not know that the work was by Pufendorf.) As he explains in his preface, England's participation in Germany's ongoing wars against France and the Turks made it useful to publish an account that would better acquaint his countrymen with their continental ally. Indeed, one might conclude from his remarks that if England had been allied with China he would have sought an account of Chinese institutions to translate. As in the case of some of his other occasional publications, Bohun had no obvious stake in *Monzambano* other than impact on the domestic scene and revenue. The work is not mentioned in his autobiography, whose nineteenth-century editor lists only the anonymous 1690 edition and not the acknowledged 1696 publication.[43]

This incidental relationship between translator and author does make for some ironies, and it certainly affected the translation itself (see below). For though he came into the world a Dissenter (through his father),

41. Bohun issued a number of his works anonymously, especially in the uncertain period after 1688, but it is unclear why the current translation was among them. Such caution was apparently unnecessary for the work's second printing in 1696, which came out under Bohun's name. See the Note on the Text, p. xxix.

42. James Tyrrell's *Patriarcha non Monarcha: The Patriarch Unmonarch'd,* was published anonymously in 1681 and sought, like Locke's *First Treatise,* to refute Filmer. In it he praised Pufendorf as an advocate of limited sovereignty and translated long excerpts from the latter's *On the Law of Nature and of Nations* (VII.5.14 and VII.6.7–13), since "no man . . . hath writ more clearly of this Subject." Locke's later remark about Pufendorf's *On the Law of Nature and of Nations* being "the best work of that kind" is well known. See Peter Laslett's introduction to John Locke, *Two Treatises of Government,* ed. Peter Laslett (Cambridge: Cambridge University Press, 1988), 75.

43. See *The Diary and Autobiography of Edmund Bohun* (1853) and the introductory memoir by its editor, Samuel Wilton Rix. More recent studies include Stephen, "Bohun, Edmund"; Goldie, "Edmund Bohun"; Thompson, "Bohun, Edmund"; and Kemp, "Bohun, Edmund."

Bohun became a determined Anglican and a Tory propagandist. He was close to Archbishop Sheldon, William Sancroft, and Samuel Parker, and he participated actively in the Filmer renaissance they engineered in the late 1670s and early 1680s. Thus his first published work, *Address to the Freemen and Freeholders of the Nation* (1682–83), advocated a hereditary monarchy and opposed active resistance. His second, *A Defence of Sir Robert Filmer* (1684), was directed against Algernon Sidney, whose contractualist resistance theory, along with the attempt to implement it in the Rye House Plot, led to his execution for treason in 1683. Bohun crowned his contribution to the Tory cause in 1685 with an edition of Filmer's *Patriarcha,* whose preface attacked Tyrrell's critique of Filmer.

Like other Anglicans and Tories, Bohun disliked James II's avid Catholicism as much as Dissent or Whiggery. Therefore, in 1689, after the invasion, he chose the lesser evil and acknowledged William's legitimacy as monarch, thereby turning potential disaster into opportunity. In 1692 he was appointed licenser of the press within the new government. It was an inconvenient post in view of his past publications,[44] and after only five months he was dismissed and briefly imprisoned, the inconsistency between his situation and his views catching up with him. He had rationalized his new allegiance to William not in de-factoist terms but by appeal to the theory of conquest developed by Grotius. This allowed him to maintain his support of divine right, hereditary monarchy, and nonresistance and to reject any kind of contractualism or popular sovereignty.[45] While conquest theory was not unusual at the time and Bohun hardly its only proponent, it was deemed unflattering to the king and dangerous because of the associated baggage that often came with it, as in Bohun's case. So when he unwittingly approved a tract by Charles Blount espousing that interpretation, Whigs accused him of Jac-

---

44. These included not only his works on Filmer but also two pamphlets: *The History of the Desertion* and *The Doctrine of Non-Resistance,* both in 1689.

45. Also in 1689, Bohun translated Johannes Sleidan's *De statu religionis et reipublicae, Carolo Quinto Caesare* (Straßburg, 1555), a general history of the Reformation in Germany. The Lutheran Sleidan (1506–56) was also famous for his *De quattuor summis imperiis* [On the four great empires] (Geneva, 1559), one of the standard sources for the *translatio imperii* thesis.

obitism and engineered his dismissal (in 1693), probably using him as the sacrificial lamb for this kind of argument. Still, after retreating to the country for a while, Bohun managed to obtain (in 1698) the post of chief justice of South Carolina, where his son was engaged in business. Since the colony's constitution had been written by Locke and Shaftesbury in 1669, this final post neatly compounded the ironies of his life.

Bohun probably did not know enough about Pufendorf's views to be guided by them in his translation of *Monzambano*. Therefore, he followed his own royalist leanings instead, particularly when not adhering literally to the Latin text. However, even direct renditions were affected. For instance, though Bohun sometimes translates "citizen" appropriately, often he resorts to "member" or "subject" instead. Likewise, "emperor" sometimes becomes "king"; "empire," "kingdom"; and there are "princes" everywhere, even when the text refers more generally to "estates" (which included the free cities of the empire). As single instances, such substitutions may seem innocuous and unimportant, but repetitively and collectively they can flavor a text and distort its meaning.[46] Pufendorf thought a regular monarchy the best form of government, but he was not an exclusive or absolute royalist; rather, he advocated limited sovereignty, whatever form it took. Moreover, he vigorously rejected divine right justifications, based the origin and legitimacy of political power on contract (two contracts, in fact: association and subjection, and an intervening decree), and allowed that there might be justified resistance *in extremis;* even conquest theory did not legitimize without the eventual implied consent of the conquered. In sum, Pufendorf was far less conservative than Bohun, and it is important to keep this in mind. For while the translator did not consciously distort his author, he was so avidly committed to his own views that, in all likelihood, he did not worry greatly about the risk of doing so.

---

46. See Saunders and Hunter, "Bringing the State to England," which examines another case of translative adaptation of a Pufendorf text in an English context.

Significance of the Work

There has been much discussion about the so-called post-Westphalian order of sovereign states and its continued viability in today's shrinking world. Indeed, the notion of sovereignty as such, as both an internal and external characteristic of states, is being reexamined in view of increasingly complex human dependencies and vulnerabilities. As Pufendorf continues to be historically rehabilitated, he is also gradually being reintroduced into these discussions.[47] A better understanding of the *Monzambano* in the context of Pufendorf's other works can only contribute to this perceived relevance. Indeed, the complexities of the empire, which it theorized, may appear to equal or surpass those of the contemporary world. Thus, our debates about the role of the United Nations, the European Union, and other hemispheric or regional associations, as well as the importance of state systems or alliances—for defense or other purposes—may all benefit from what seems at first an antiquated discussion about an impossible reality. Voltaire is reported to have quipped that the German Holy Roman Empire was neither holy nor Roman nor an empire.[48] Pufendorf himself said as much, but he nonetheless thought it important to examine why others would adopt such a self-interpretation and how it might or might not be conducive to their interests. His recommendations for the problems he diagnosed in the empire were decidedly modest, but in both his world and ours, which confront so many extremes, that very fact may be their most exemplary virtue.

Michael J. Seidler

47. See Hochstrasser, *Natural Law Theories;* Hunter, *Rival Enlightenments;* Boucher, "Pufendorf" and "Resurrecting Pufendorf"; Fagelson, "Two Concepts"; and Hont, "Permanent Crisis."

48. Dufour, "Pufendorfs föderalistisches Denken," 105.

A NOTE ON THE TEXT

Edmund Bohun's translation of Pufendorf's *De statu Imperii Germanici* was issued twice: first by an anonymous "person of quality" in 1690 and then with Bohun's name in 1696.[1] Except for their title pages, the two versions appear exactly the same. The 1696 version, which is reissued here, repeats the licensure page of the earlier printing, with its date of January 31, 1689/90, as well as the prefatory "To the Reader" dated January 24, 1689. Moreover, the table of contents, shoulder (margin) titles and notes, pagination, first and last words on each page, the lack of an index—even Bohun's textual insertions (especially in chapters VII and VIII), which update, expand, or comment on (thus, "continue") Pufendorf's account—all are the same. Neither printing indicates which of the numerous Latin "first" editions since 1667 Bohun used as the basis of his translation. In checking its accuracy, I have consulted one of the 1667 printings (viz., the fourth "Geneva" edition) and also the text issued

---

1. *The Present State of Germany; or, An Account of the Extent, Rise, Form, Wealth, Strength, Weaknesses and Interests of that Empire. The Prerogatives of the Emperor, and the Priviledges of the Electors, Princes, and Free Cities. Adapted to the present Circumstances of that Nation.* By a Person of Quality. London, Printed for Richard Chiswel, at the Rose and Crown in St. Paul's Church-Yard, 1690; and, *The Present State of Germany.* Written in Latin by the Learned Samuel Puffendorff, Under the Name of Severinus de Monzambano Veronensis. Made English and Continued by Edmund Bohun, Esq. London, Printed for Richard Chiswell, at the Rose and Crown in St. Paul's Church-Yard, 1696.

The 1690 version is the focus of Heinz Duchhardt's "Pufendorf in England." Duchhardt mentions the 1696 printing but does not seem to have examined it, for he does not mention Bohun's name or explicitly identify the later version with its 1690 "Vorläufer" (150).

xxix

by Fritz Salomon in 1910, which is based on the very first "Geneva" edition.[2]

When Pufendorf prepared the second edition, which was finished in the early 1690s shortly before his death, he made significant changes in the text. This posthumous edition (*editio posthuma,* or e.p.) was not published until 1706 by J. P. Gundling[3] and was therefore unavailable to Bohun. However, because of the importance of these emendations for an understanding of Pufendorf's development, I have included them in this Liberty Fund edition, thus complementing Bohun's translation with my own renditions of the new material. Indeed, the *editio posthuma*'s many excisions, additions, and revisions (some quite lengthy) made it a thorough reworking of the original text rather than a mere republication with touch-ups. This complicates the identification of variants by requiring judgments of significance. For these I have also relied on Salomon, who reproduced the first edition and indicated (more extensively than Denzer [*Verfassung des deutschen Reiches,* ed. Denzer, 1994]) the variations of the second. However, in all such instances, I have

2. *Severini de Monzambano Veronensis De statu Imperii Germanici ad Laelium fratrem, dominum Trezolani, liber unus* (Geneva: Petrus Columesius, 1667) (Salomon, "Literaturverzeichnis," no. 4, p. 11); and *Severinus de Monzambano (Samuel von Pufendorf) De Statu Imperii Germanici: nach dem ersten Druck mit Berücksichtigung der Ausgabe letzter Hand,* ed. Fritz Salomon (Weimar: Hermann Böhlaus Nachfolger, 1910). Other notable Latin editions include those by Gottlieb Gerhard Titius (Leipzig, 1708), which prefers the *editio posthuma,* and that by Christian Thomasius (Halle, 1714; first published in 1695), which reprints the first edition but considers the *editio posthuma* in the notes. (After Pufendorf's death in 1695, Thomasius, like Gundling [see below], apparently had access to Pufendorf's revised manuscript through his widow.) Both editions are extensively annotated. Geneva was a fictive place of publication; the work was actually published at The Hague by Adrian Vlacq. See pp. xii–xiii of the introduction above.

3. *Samuelis L.B. de Pufendorf De statu Imperii Germanici liber unus,* edited with a preface by Jacob Paul Gundling (Coloniae ad Spream: Rüdiger, 1706). The city of Cölln, in which this edition was published, was located on an island in the River Spree, which flows through Berlin; separately established in the Middle Ages and formally distinct, Cölln was finally absorbed by Berlin in 1709.

The *editio posthuma* left out Pufendorf's original preface, including the pretended Italian persona, and made similar adjustments throughout the text. In its place, Gundling added his own preface to the work, followed by a second preface whose status remains unclear.

directly compared Salomon's text with Gundling's *editio posthuma* as well.

The *Monzambano,* as Pufendorf's work came to be called, was translated into French[4] and German soon after its appearance. One of these early German translations has been reissued recently in a bilingual edition by Notker Hammerstein, in volume 16 of the series Bibliothek der Geschichte und Politik (Reinhart Koselleck, general editor).[5] The *editio posthuma* received an early eighteenth-century German translation by Petronius Adlemansthal (i.e., Peter Dahlmann), which is notable mainly for its accompanying life of Pufendorf ("Vita, fama, et fata literaria Pufendorfiana") and its detailed account of the fierce polemic generated by Pufendorf's work ("Historie von dem wunderlichen Lärmen und Tumult welcher in der gelehrten Welt dieses Buchs wegen entstanden").[6] The nineteenth century saw two more German translations, by Harry Breßlau (1870) and by Heinrich Dove (1877), the latter also using the *editio posthuma* as its base text.[7] More recently, Horst Denzer has provided another parallel edition with a new German translation and the most significant e.p. variants. This appeared first in 1976 (with Reclam) and was reissued in 1994 as volume 4 of Insel Verlag's Bibliothek des Deutschen Staatsdenkens (Hans Maier and Michael Stolleis, general ed-

---

4. Freiherr Samuel von Pufendorf, *L'Estat de l'empire d'Allemagne de Monzambane,* trans. François-Savinien d'Alquié (Amsterdam: J. J. Shipper, 1669).

5. *Monzambano, eines Veronesers ungescheuter offenherziger Discurs, oder Gründlicher Bericht von der wahren Beschafenheit und Zustand des Teutschen Reichs. Geschrieben an seinen Bruder Laelium von Monzambano, Herrn zu Trezolan . . . ins teutsche übersetzt durch ein ungenantes Glied der hochlöblichen Fruchtbringenden Gesellschaft,* 1669; in *Staatslehre der frühen Neuzeit,* ed. Notker Hammerstein (Frankfurt am Main: Deutscher Klassiker Verlag, 1995), 568–931. (The Fruchtbringende Gesellschaft ["fruitbearing society"] had been formed in 1617 to foster the use of German as an academic and literary language.) Also see Hammerstein's long essay in "Staatslehre der frühen Neuzeit," 1013–1115, which helps to contextualize Pufendorf's work.

6. *Samuels Freyhrn. von Puffendorff . . . Bericht von dem Zustande des H.R. Reichs Teutscher Nation . . . ,* von Petronio Harteviggo Adlemansthal [i.e., P(eter) Dahlmann] (Leipzig, 1710; reprinted 1715).

7. *Severinus von Monzambano (Samuel von Pufendorf), Über die Verfassung des deutschen Reiches,* trans. with an introduction by Harry Breßlau (Berlin: L. Heimann, 1870); and *Die Verfassung des deutschen Reiches von Samuel von Pufendorf,* trans. Heinrich Dove (Leipzig: Philipp Reclam [1877]).

itors).[8] It remains the most accessible edition and translation of Pufendorf's *Monzambano* and has done much to redirect attention to the work.

As noted, although Bohun's 1690/1696 text did not include them, I have added Pufendorf's important preface to the first (1667) edition, wherein he (as Monzambano/Samuel) dedicates the work to his brother (Laelius/Esaias), and the second preface to the *editio posthuma* (1706), even though it may be by someone else. The latter includes a short assessment of the work by François Eudes de Mézeray (1610–83), official French historiographer (after 1648) and secretary of the Académie Française (1675),[9] who had been approached for his opinion by the Paris printer to whom Esaias Pufendorf first brought the manuscript to be published. Like the other *editio posthuma* insertions, these pieces appear here in English for the first time.

In addition, there are other, minor, changes to Bohun's text (made in the interest of readability), though the translation and punctuation remain substantially intact. In all cases, corrections, clarifications, and alternative renditions are clearly noted, appearing in the text between special symbols, and in the footnotes at the bottom of each page. The following markers are used:

{...}	= e.p. (*editio posthuma*) deletion
<...>	= e.p. insertion
|[...]|	= e.p. variant
SMALL CAPS	= Gothic script (in Latin original)
[...]+	= language added by Bohun (pleonasm, periphrasis, elaboration)
//...\\	= longer additions by Bohun, originally in brackets or parentheses
[...]	= editor's corrections, clarifications, alternative renditions
/	= editorial divider (used in footnotes)

---

8. Samuel von Pufendorf, *Die Verfassung des deutschen Reiches,* ed. and trans. Horst Denzer (Frankfurt: Insel Verlag, 1994).

9. See note 5 of the Preface to the Second Edition.

Editorial footnotes are of two kinds. Lettered notes deal with textual matters; numbered notes clarify content. Some notes also contain editorial explanations, placed there to avoid having two notes at the same spot in the text. Bohun's shoulder (margin) notes (six in all), which were originally indicated in the text by single asterisks, have been moved to the footnote area and the asterisks replaced by lowercase Roman numerals in parentheses (e.g., $^{(i)}$). The shoulder headings are Bohun's; however, all paragraph divisions, except for numbered sections, are mine (often following previous editions and translations). I have also expanded abbreviations, standardized internal numerations, added numbers (i.e., §1) to the first section of each chapter (to match the remaining sections), and corrected obvious typographical errors. Page breaks in Bohun's text have been indicated by the use of angle brackets. For example, page 112 begins after <112>.

In-text editorial emendations have been tailored to the diction, structure, and flow of Bohun's text. However, some of Bohun's run-on sentences have been subdivided, typically by substituting periods in place of colons or semicolons and then capitalizing the next word in the text. Shorter clarifications or corrections to Bohun's archaic and sometimes confusing translation have been placed in the text (within brackets); longer ones, in effect alternative renditions, appear in the footnotes (preceded by "Rather:"). These new translations, like the two prefaces and the e.p. insertions, do not attempt to imitate Bohun's style or terminology but aim at accuracy, clarity, and usability by contemporary readers.

In general, Bohun's translation is loose, his choice of terminology insufficiently consistent and attentive to philosophical and political nuance, and his understanding of Pufendorf and the German context in which *Monzambano* first appeared quite limited. His royalist inclinations are evident throughout, not only in the selection of terms ("princes," "kingdom," "rabble," etc., for "estates," "empire," "common people," etc.) but also in the occasional tendency to complete, color, or emend—according to his own views.[10] The translation is hasty, often

10. There are three main viewpoints at work in the text: Pufendorf's (German,

lazily stacking subordinate clauses in the same order as the Latin (where the practice is less unwieldy), occasionally omitting phrases or clauses, and sometimes translating the same term differently in the same paragraph. Moreover, careless rendition of crucial prepositions or conjunctions sometimes obscures the logic of the original. On the other hand, Bohun often gets it right, and he can be quite sharp in capturing the meaning of the Latin. His intention was to further an English audience's general acquaintance with the Germany that had recently (1688) assisted William III in acquiring the English throne, and whose affairs would involve England in continental wars for at least another decade. This simply did not require the precision of a work within the German natural law and public law contexts.

Therefore, as with all translations, caution must be exercised when resting an interpretation or argument on specific language, and the Latin original should be consulted.[11] Also, when quoting from the current reprint, it seems advisable either to use Bohun's original wording as is or else to quote the emended or alternative translation provided in the text or footnotes. Of course, either policy should be clearly noted.

Lutheran), Monzambano's (fictionalized Italian, Catholic), and Bohun's (Anglican, royalist). Moreover, in the first edition Monzambano attributes some of the more controversial remarks (in chapter 8) to yet other speakers. Pufendorf drops the Monzambano pretense entirely in the *editio posthuma,* and Bohun generally ignores it before that.

11. A new Latin edition will appear as volume 8 of Samuel Pufendorf, *Gesammelte Werke,* Wilhelm Schmidt-Biggemann, general editor (Berlin: Akademie Verlag, 1996–).

ACKNOWLEDGMENTS

My initial debts are to the special collections units of the research libraries that have generously supplied microfilms or expertise. These include the University of Chicago Library, the New York Public Library, Vanderbilt University Library, Kungliga Biblioteket (Stockholm), the British Library, and the Herzog August Bibliothek (Wolfenbüttel). I first encountered Adlemansthal in the old reading room of the British Library and then revisited it and other texts years later in the library's new facility. Two recent summers in Wolfenbüttel gave me direct access to many of the early histories of natural law and to works by Pufendorf's critics. Both experiences were wonderfully stimulating and productive, and I am grateful to the staff of each institution for their professional help and gracious accommodation.

Knud Haakonssen has been an invaluable editor, advisor, and friend. My deepest thanks to him for inviting me to participate in this series and for his flexible and responsive assistance throughout, especially at the final stages. Indeed, I have learned much just by watching him help me. Åsa Söderman graciously volunteered her research assistance in Stockholm and obtained a number of microfilms there on my behalf. For this too I am very grateful.

More locally, it is a pleasure to acknowledge the substantial contribution of my own institution, Western Kentucky University, which has long supported me with release time and research funds. Despite its primary commitment to classroom teaching, the university has consistently facilitated and recognized my scholarly work, and I am deeply in its debt for its essential assistance.

I want also to express my sincere appreciation to Fiammetta Palladini. Though she had no specific connection with this project, her important work on Pufendorf as both editor and scholar has been of immeasurable help to me over the years. Moreover, her personal advice, encouragement, and conversation have greatly enhanced the sociability of the enterprise.

Finally, I would be remiss if I did not thank my family for putting up with my many absences, in both body and mind, while working on this and other projects. Scholarship inevitably exists in a context of physical and social needs, which are as essential as they are ordinary. In this sense, those who surround us in our work are as much its authors as we ourselves. Thankfully, all achievements are ultimately shared.

THE PRESENT STATE OF GERMANY

PUFENDORF'S PREFACE TO
THE FIRST EDITION OF 1667[1]

To Laelius of Monzambano, Lord of Trezolano,
Severinus of Monzambano sends many greetings![2]

You have asked me in many letters, dearest brother Laelius, about my
intentions and thoughts while traveling around Germany for so long,
and I want now to explain these to you in a few words as I am finally
drawn homeward by your insistent requests. For our nation is otherwise
known for its disinclination to traveling about, because we believe that
our talents shine forth by virtue of their own natural goodness and do
not need external refinement. Among those beyond the Alps [i.e., Ger-
mans], however, one acquires a certain reputation for wisdom if one has
so much as seen Italy from the highest mountains.

You know how the matter which I crossed the Alps to accomplish
detained me at the Bavarian court longer than expected. There, in my
eagerness to relieve the boredom, I began to read more carefully the
things written by one or other of us [Italians] about the German [Thirty
Years'] War. For the Germans themselves have more faith in these authors than in their own citizens, who are either clearly partial toward one
or other side, or afraid to tell the whole truth; and their most prominent

---

1. This first English translation of the preface is based on Monzambano, *De Statu
Imperii Germanici,* 1667, which is no. 4 in Salomon, "Literaturverzeichnis," 11.

2. Read S.P.D. (*salutem plurimam dicit*) for S.P.Q. See *Severinus,* ed. Salomon,
27, and Louis-Alphonse Chassant, *Dictionnaire des abréviations latines et françaises*
(Hildesheim: Olms, 1989; reprint of 5th ed., Paris, 1884), 155. Christian Thomasius
(*Severini,* ed. Thomasius, 1, note a) speculates that Pufendorf assumed an Italian
persona so that he would be read by Roman Catholics.

book about that war, spread over many volumes, deserves more than the
Chaos of the ancients to be called "an unfinished and disorderly heap."[3]
As I read it I was overcome by astonishment at the great exertion brought
bear, at the number and horrors of the battles waged, and at how a land
which its citizens no less than outsiders had labored to destroy for thirty
years could survive such great disasters. Hence my mind was filled with
a desire to examine more closely the strength and wealth of this nation
[*gens*], the variety of its peoples, and also the kind of connection holding
so immense a body together.

I demonstrated great patience in this task, almost more than could be
expected from a fastidious Italian. For in addition to learning the German language (which surpasses all European languages in difficulty) required for that end, I began also with the conviction that the state [*status*]
of Germany could not be thoroughly known except by one who had
examined from head to toe all writers of that nation [*nationis*] who have
treated of *public law,* as they call it. Therefore, I asked a certain coun-
cillor with a library well-stocked in that field, somewhat presumptuously,
to supply me with the authors whom he thought most appropriate for
my purpose. This person, seeking to be as accommodating as possible
but also to exhibit his extensive holdings, used two strong servants groan-
ing under the weight of several carrying trays to fill my chamber with
books, to the point that there was hardly any room left for me. And, he
added, these were just an appetizer for the time being, to prepare my
stomach for the proper meal that would soon follow. Here I was stunned,
like one who has stepped upon an unexpected snake among sharp bram-
bles,[4] and groaned over the many torments that I had voluntarily

3. The language is from Ovid, *Metamorphoses* I.7, and the reference to Johann
Phillip Abelin[g], author of *Theatrum Europaeum, oder Beschreibung aller denkwür-
digen Geschichten, die hin und wieder, vornehmlich in Europa hernach auch an anderen
Orten der Welt, sowohl in Religion als Polizeiwesen von J. Christi 1617 sich zugetragen,*
21 vols. (1635–1738). Abelin died before 1637 and was responsible for only the first two
volumes (through the year 1633), though the work was continued through 1718 by
various others. Abelin also wrote an *Arma Suecica,* on the wars of Gustaphus Adolphus (published 1631–34, in 12 parts), and an *Inventarium Sueciae* (1632).

4. Virgil, *Aeneid* II.379–80.

brought upon myself. For it did not seem appropriate, on the one hand, that I should be exhausted by a mere glance after having shown such eagerness to learn; yet, on the other hand, the expression of curiosity about another country [*respublica*] did not seem so great a crime that I deserved to die so cruel a death.

As I stood there sweating, I was finally relieved by something I once heard from one of our native [Italian] scholars: that *Germans are infected by an incurable writer's itch*[5]—even though very few of them can produce anything capable of evoking the applause of their refined contemporaries by virtue of either its inventive cleverness or creative charm. Nonetheless, [he said,] lest they be too sparing of paper, which perishes anyway, most of them combine randomly gathered bits and pieces into a mass to which hardly a grain of judgment has been added. Nor do they consider it plagiarism to sell as new, works of others which have [only] been touched up in a few places. Some of them, finally, believe that they deserve a place among authors because they have reduced a more extensive work to a compendium or—God willing—to tables, as a mnemonic aid or to relieve stupidity. And so, to be honest, I rather expected that by knowing one of these writers I would know the lot of them, because most [also] regard themselves as legal experts, among whom it has become a rule to copy one another faithfully.

Having steeled my mind in this way, I proceeded patiently to read through from the beginning one of these works that was more conspicuous than the rest on account of its bulk, and that I had heard especially commended by many people.[6] It was one, as well, about which I correctly

5. This comment echoes that of the Venetian ambassador to Germany, Gasparo Contarini (1483–1542), who had written home to his senate that "the Germans, more than any other nation, are addicted to writing." See Monzambano, *Über die Verfassung,* trans. Breßlau, 24, note 1. This is an initial example of the work's method of concealment, its use of anonymous third parties to express controversial views, which is especially evident in the discussion of religion in chapter 8.

6. Probably a reference to Johannes Limnaeus (1592–1663), whose five-volume *Ius publicum Imperii Romano-Germanici* (vols. 1–3, Straßburg, 1629–34; 2 vols. of additions, Straßburg, 1650/1660) offered the first systematic examination of the empire's constitution. See Monzambano, *De Statu Imperii,* ed. Thomasius, 14–15, note

believed that, as a compilation of all previous works, it had been treated similarly by those that followed it. In this author, that which could have made me indignant in the case of others somehow seemed like a relief. For the more impertinent things were stuffed randomly into the account, the more quickly I seemed to be carried [through it] toward the end. Now it was certainly possible in this way to gain a sufficient familiarity with the German Empire's external appearance. It seemed quite absurd, however, that though the author displayed everywhere a feverish knowledge of the Civil [i.e., Roman] Law and attached to it whatever he had ever read or heard, I found nothing there which revealed even a mediocre understanding of sound politics. For annotating those prior works requires only a moderate diligence, and no intelligence, and those who rush before the public in order to explain the structure of so irregular a state [as the German Empire], while barely cognizant of their country's [Germany's] history and of civil science, might rightly be described as *asses playing the lyre.*[7]

Now after I had made it through that tedious reading and discovered, as well, that most authors go astray playing the same tune, I decided that I should take a different path; and [so], putting aside the inanities of worthless little books, I began rather to examine whatever seemed doubtful by asking men who had been tested in practical affairs. The fruits I derived from this undertaking were not inconsiderable. For beside the fact that I learned many things which you would seek in vain in books, that curiosity also earned me much good will from a people already well

---

q. Thomasius borrows here from Hippolithus a Lapide (i.e., Bogislaw Philipp Chemnitz). On Lapide, see VI.7, note 6, p. 169.

7. Thomasius (Monzambano, *De Statu Imperii,* ed. Thomasius, 16, note t) says here: "By civil science and solid politics he [Pufendorf] understands not Aristotelian politics, and the vulgar or useless questions customarily treated here, but the obligations [*nexum*] of rulers and ruled in individual states [*respublicas*], a knowledge of the human race and its affects, and of the nature of human affairs." History, especially recent or modern history recounting actions motivated by reasons of state, provided one of the empirical foundations of Pufendorf's politics and natural law theory.

The sarcastic image of *asses playing lyres* occurred in Erasmus's *Adages* (1502–) but went back further to a version of Aesop's fables by Gaius Julius Phaedrus (ca. 15 B.C.– ca. 50 A.D.), which was reissued in the fifteenth century by Nicolo Perotti.

inclined toward outsiders. They were especially pleased to find in me none of that revulsion toward their affairs that is so familiar in most [other] outsiders. And the more boldly and frankly they saw me dealing with them, the more generously they embraced me as an imitator, as it were, of the candor for which they themselves so enjoy being praised. So I finally decided to make more use of the good will thus offered to me by this people.[8]

Having finished the business in Munich to my satisfaction, I therefore betook myself to Regensburg at a time when the recent fear of a Turkish war had drawn many princes there.[9] Here it was quite easy to behold the character [*ingenium*] of German affairs with one glance, and [to see] how loosely that structure [i.e., the empire] hangs together. But with my Bavarian friend preparing the way, I was also able to get to know a man whose equal I have hardly ever met in Germany, who was then in charge of the court at Mainz and highly regarded by most Germans.[10] He received me with the greatest kindness, such as an unknown traveller could hardly expect from a man whose favor the learned often thought it honourable to seek even through public flattery. And, indeed, this man's support not only gained me many friends in Regensburg, but when I had indicated to him my intention to travel through a part of Germany he also equipped me with letters to various courts which, like friendship tokens, generated for me a most gracious hospitality.

Next I followed the Danube down to Vienna where several of my

---

8. This is ironic, of course, since the work's irreverent frankness about the real condition of the empire actually set off a firestorm of indignant protest and eager refutation—as Pufendorf must have anticipated.

9. The *Reichstag* (Imperial Diet)—from the German verb *tagen*, to meet or assemble "for a day"—was the periodic (albeit irregular) convention of the estates of the German Empire; it remained in permanent session after its 1663 meeting at Regensburg. That session dealt largely with the emperor's appeal for help against the Turks, who were defeated the following year at St. Gotthard, in Hungary. See Schindling, "Development of the Eternal Diet."

10. Johann Christian Freiherr von Boineburg (1622–72), minister to the elector of Mainz (Johann Philipp von Schönborn) 1652–64. On Pufendorf's relation to Boineburg and their important correspondence in 1663, see Hochstrasser, *Natural Law Theories*, 47–60. Boineburg was also instrumental in advancing Leibniz's career by suggesting that he dedicate his *Nova Methodus* (1667) to the elector.

countrymen, whose fortune there had been very favorable, saw to it that I was not regarded as a foreigner. Then something advantageous happened, in that a certain Imperial minister with whom I had already become friends was sent off to the Electors of Saxony and Brandenburg. I was quite pleased to join him as a companion when he invited me, especially once he had assured me that the reputation of Italian sobriety could protect me from drowning in wine because of excessive politeness. For according to that nation's customs, it is generally regarded as cowardly to value one's own health over the customary libations thereto.

After leaving Berlin I was received at the court of the Duke of Braunschweig. There, beside other things, I was most pleased to converse with a professor from a neighboring university whom I had already heard highly recommended in Regensburg for his knowledge of German affairs.[11] For he also agreed with me in most respects concerning the state of Germany and readily shared with me his writings, which reveal a much different character than that other heap of books. In them, although much was stated freely enough, it was nonetheless quite clear that he had concealed more than a few things so as not to offend the powerful or incite the complaints of dullards against himself. From that time on, I first thought of setting these things to paper, because I hoped that perhaps the truth would be more readily accepted if it came from a stranger lacking in partiality, or not suspected of currying favor or exacting revenge.

Having come thus far, it seemed lazy not to visit the Netherlands. This would have detained me longer if your insistent letters, as well as affairs at home, had not brought me to think seriously about returning to our fatherland. Therefore, ascending along the Rhine, I experienced at Düsseldorf the same kindness previously shown to me at Neuburg [in Bavaria]. Nor was Bonn any less hospitable. I seemed less welcome at Mainz because I had, through imprudence, greatly praised the services

---

11. Hermann Conring (1606–81), professor of natural philosophy, medicine, and politics in Helmstedt. On Conring, see Constantin Fasolt's introduction to Conring, *New Discourse,* ix–xxii; and for his relations with Pufendorf, see Hochstrasser, *Natural Law Theories,* 47–60.

of that minister who had, in the meantime, been dismissed from their employ for I know not what reasons.[12] Despite being in a hurry, I was compelled to halt in Heidelberg by a desire to see the Palatine Elector,[13] whose character and wisdom—many people had told me—are unequalled among German princes. And, indeed, though the fame he enjoys for his praiseworthy qualities is not slight, he seemed so to live up to his reputation that I consider it among the chief fruits of my travel through Germany to have called on that prince and seen his endowments close up. The pleasantness of my stay there allowed me to devote only a few days' time to Stuttgart, though I do not regret having visited it as well.

You see now, dearest brother, how I spent my time among the Germans, and how valuable it has been to have partaken so substantially of the hospitality extended by this very forthright nation. I can offer it no other thanks now except a true depiction of its Empire. I trust, at least, that this little work will not be unappreciated by my own countrymen, because it also sets forth most of the things into which they themselves usually inquire when seeking to know the countries of outsiders, presented with a disciplined brevity to satisfy the fastidious.

I gladly dedicate it to you, dearest brother, not only to make up for the delay which has caused you no small bother in taking care of my affairs, but also to assure you that there was something in Germany to exercise my curiosity. For, otherwise, both your favors toward me and the mutual affection between us are too great to be adequately expressed, even in part, by such a small token.[14] Farewell.

12. Boineburg fell out of favor and was dismissed in the spring of 1664, placing Monzambano's account after this time. Döring, "Untersuchungen," 198–99, suggests late 1665 or early 1666 as the date of composition, based on the work's relevance to the *Wildfangstreit* during summer/fall 1665. See pp. xi–xxii of the introduction.

13. Karl Ludwig, elector of the Palatinate (1649–80), had brought Pufendorf to Heidelberg in 1661. He encouraged the present work and may have helped shape it— see the 1706 preface, p. 10, and the introduction, p. xi. Pufendorf's singling him out for praise was regarded as evidence for his own authorship of the pseudonymous work.

14. The Severinus/Laelius relationship reflected Samuel's ties to his supportive older brother, Esaias, with whom he remained close even when their political views began to diverge in the 1680s. Pufendorf's *Dissertationes academicae selectiores* [Select academic dissertations] (Lund, 1675) was formally dedicated to Esaias.

PREFACE TO THE
SECOND EDITION (1706)[1]

To the Benevolent Reader, Greetings

This small book lays aside its mask now that the author has been removed from human affairs and no longer fears men's hatreds. It was written in an impulse of indignation when a professorship which the author believed he deserved was snatched away by another.[2] Its publication followed the assessment and approval of the prince whom the author then served, and whose views and feelings are here and there expressed [in it].

In its youthful boldness, the work did not weigh sufficiently how dangerous it is for a private person to criticize the powerful. So later, in his maturer years, the author reviewed the book and expunged from it the things included there by a different sentiment, or without sufficient forethought, and elided here and there, by changing a few words, some things to which others had objected. It [also] seemed appropriate to omit the things that had been added toward the end of the book concerning religion,[3] because that argument was more extensively and forcefully de-

---

1. This new translation is based on *Samuelis L.B. de Pufendorf, De Statu Imperii Germanici*, ed. Gundling, the so-called *editio posthuma*, or posthumous edition.

2. Pufendorf died in 1694. The story about his supposed ire at losing a coveted law professorship at Heidelberg to another candidate, and then writing the *Monzambano* to prove himself, became part of Treitschke's (1886–97) influential nineteenth-century account ("Samuel Pufendorf," 200–21). However, Döring, "Untersuchungen" (especially 185–95), has shown convincingly that it is not accurate. In fact, there is some doubt about whether this preface to the *editio posthuma* is even by Pufendorf himself.

3. See VIII.5–10.

veloped afterwards in the author's other writings.[4] For the work's chief aim was to inquire about the form of the German republic,[a] whose irregularity will be the more easily acknowledged the more deeply one sees how this vast mechanism [*machina*] is governed.

The author initially published the book under a fictitious name because, even though the Palatine censor approved of the work in itself, he nonetheless recommended that it be printed elsewhere. It was therefore sent to the author's brother, Esaias Pufendorf, then the Swedish *chargé d'affaires* at the French court. When the latter had given it to a certain typographer to be printed, a proofreader caught the words, in [Ch. I] §.3, "the inappropriate conceit of certain Frenchmen," and had it submitted to the noted historian, Mézeray,[5] for review. Since the latter did not dare to approve its printing in Paris, it was published soon thereafter by Adrian Vlacq at The Hague, without a scruple. It is worthwhile here, however, to append Mézeray's judgment.

a. That is, *respublica* / Pufendorf also refers to the empire as a state [*status*] and as *imperium*. This variation of terms itself indicates the difficulty of conceiving the empire in terms of traditional forms of the state. [Ed.]

4. Specifically, in *Basilii Hyperetae* [a pseudonym] *Historische und politische Beschreibung der geistlichen Monarchie des Stuhls zu Rom* [Historical and Political Description of the Spiritual Monarchy of the Chair at Rome] (Leipzig and Franckfurt, 1679), translated by John Chamberlayne as *The History of Popedom* and incorporated (as chap. 12) into Pufendorf's *Einleitung zu der Historie der vornehmsten Reiche und Staaten so itziger Zeit in Europa sich befinden* (Frankfurt, 1682). The latter work was translated by Jodocus Crull as *An Introduction to the History of the Principal Kingdoms and States of Europe*, a title that will also appear in the Natural Law and Enlightenment Classics series, published by Liberty Fund. Already published by Liberty Fund are Pufendorf's *De habitu religionis christianae ad vitam civilem* as *Of the Nature and Qualification of Religion in Reference to Civil Society*, and *Jus feciale divinum, sive de consensu et dissensu Protestantium* as *The Divine Feudal Law; or, Covenants with Mankind, Represented*, which present Pufendorf's views on the state-church relationship and the possibility of religious unification (among Lutherans and Calvinists).

5. François Eudes de Mézeray (1610–83) was official historiographer of France and a member of the Académie Française (since 1649). He wrote histories of France and of the Turks.

A Letter of Monsieur Mézeray Concerning the Manuscript
On the State of the German Empire,
Written to a Bookseller of Paris.[1]

I have read the manuscript which you sent me concerning the present state of the German Empire. In my view, it is a work of politics, not history. The author is a man of much reflection in full command of his subject, which he advances considerably. The book well deserves to be published, but, as for me, I would not dare to give that permission. For, first of all, there is a small passage offensive to France, and as you know the times are very delicate. Second, priests and monks are badly treated there. This is very well done, to be sure; but they would lay the blame on me and damn me in this world—as for the other one, I don't fear them there and would, if we met face to face before a tribunal, have more of a case against them than they against me.

So, what is to be done about the matter? Tone down anything offensive to France, and have the permission to publish requested by one of these gentlemen, or someone acting in their stead, who has no knowledge of Latin or, at least, of the world of letters, so that the Lord Chancellor does not reproach him for having published a book in which he should have found some fault. This I advise you, telling you also that the book would do much better in French than in Latin. For our language is better equipped for these kinds of arguments than Latin, at least it is more elegant. Inform these gentlemen of what I have told you, [and also] that, if one so desires, I will provide you with a good translator. I am, etc.

This 19th of August, 1666.

---

1. Gundling's version of this letter in the *editio posthuma,* which includes Mézeray's advice on how to revise the book to improve its chances, is dated some six months after another version (on February 28, 1668) provided by Marcus Detlef Friese, a close friend of Pufendorf's, which was addressed to Esaias. See Döring, "Untersuchungen," 198.

THE PRESENT STATE
OF GERMANY.

Licens'd *Januar.* 31. 1689/90.

J. Fraser.

THE

Present State

OF

GERMANY.

Written in Latin
By the Learned *SAMUEL PUFFENDORFF,*
Under the Name of

Severinus de Monzambano Veronensis.

Made English and Continued
By *EDMUND BOHUN,* Esq;

LONDON,

Printed for Richard Chiswell, at the
Rose and *Crown* in St. *Paul's* Church-Yard. M DC XCVI.

I need not pretend to apologize for the publishing this small Piece at a time when the continued Victories of the Emperor of *Germany* over that once so formidable Enemy the *Turk,* and the present War with the *French,* has made that Nation the Subject of all our Conversation and Discourse for so many years: and our present Union with those Princes in a War that is of so great consequence in the event, be it what it will, is like to make this Country more the Subject of our Hopes and Fears now, than ever it was before.

It is natural for men to be very desirous to know the Circumstances of those they are concern'd with; and there is nothing excites our Curiosity so much, as the considering our own Happiness or Misery is wrapt up in the <vi> Fate of another. Our Regards for the Empire of *China* are very languid, and we read their Story and Descriptions with little more attention than we do a well-drawn Romance, because be they true or false, we are nothing concerned in the Fortunes of that remote Empire, which can have no influence upon our Nation.

If the World desires it, it will not be difficult to give a more particular account of the Electors, and of the other Princes and Free Cities of *Germany,* but without that, this will be sufficient to shew the general State of *Germany,* which is the thing we *Englishmen* are most desirous and concerned to know.

I shall make no other Apology for it, because I am beforehand resolved to be wholly unconcerned for its fate; the Reader is left entirely to his own liberty, to think and speak of it as he himself please.

January the 24th.
1689.

THE CONTENTS[1]

<vii>

CHAP. I.

1. The page numbers in the Contents are those from the present Liberty Fund edition.

CHAP. II.

Of the Members of which the present German *Empire is composed.*   49

CHAP. III.

CHAP. IV.

a. Bohun (or his printer) mistakes this midsection shoulder title for the beginning of a new section, thus suggesting there are ten such divisions in the chapter instead of nine. However, since there is also a numbering error in the text itself, where the section numbers skip from §3 directly to §5, the final portion of the chapter is designated §10, thus unwittingly coinciding with the numeration in the table of contents. See note a on p. 101. [Ed.]

CHAP. V.

CHAP. VI.

Of the Form of the German *Empire.* 159

CHAP. VII.

CHAP. VIII.

CHAPTER I

Of the Origine of the German *Empire.*

1. *GERMANY* [*Germania magna*] of old was bounded |[to the East by the *Danube,* to the West by the *Rhine*]|,[a] towards *Poland*[1] it had then the same bounds it has now, and all the other parts were washed by the Ocean; so that then under this Name, *Denmark, Norway,* and *Sweden* were included, with all the Countries to the *Botner* Sea;[2] which three Kingdoms [*partes*] were by most of the ancient Writers call'd by the name of *Scandinavia.* < This is still so in the case of Scania,[3] the province first encountered by those coming from the Continent and, for this reason, first frequented by outsiders, whose name seems to have been extended to the whole peninsula. > But then, I think, the Countries on the East of that Bay [of Bothnia], were not rightly ascribed to, or included in, the bounds of the ancient *Germany;* for the <2> present *Finlanders* have a Tongue so different from that spoken by the *Swedes* and other *Germans,* as clearly shews that Nation to be of another extraction. To

The ancient Bounds of Germany.

a. Rather: to the East by the *Danube,* to the South by the *Rhine* / e.p.: to the south by the Danube, to the west by the Rhine / These directions were mistaken in editions prior to the e.p., probably intentionally in order to support the pretense of foreign authorship. Bohun has already substituted "west" for "south" in regard to the Rhine, though he leaves the Danube in the "east." [Ed.]

1. *Sarmatia* was an old name for eastern Europe beyond the Vistula River and the Caspian Sea; the Sarmatians were sometimes considered the ancestors of the Poles.

2. The Gulf of Bothnia separates Sweden from Finland.

3. Scania, the southern tip of Sweden, was claimed by Denmark until it was annexed by Sweden in the Treaty of Roskilde (1658). Lund was located in this disputed area.

this I may add, that what *Tacitus*[4] writes of the Manners of the most *Northern Germans,* will not all agree with the Customs of the *Finlanders,* but is wonderfully agreeable to those of the *Laplanders,* who to this day live much after the same manner. It is probable therefore, that the *Finni* mentioned by the Ancients were the *Estoitlanders* in *Livonia.*[5] Nor is it any wonder that *Tacitus* should not write very distinctly of this People, they being then [the most Northern Nation that was ever heard of, and]＋ known only by an obscure Fame or general Report.

These Northern Countries have however for many Ages been under distinct Kings of their own [ruled separately], so that *Germany* has been taken to reach only to the *Baltick* Sea; and even here the King of *Denmark* has deprived it of a considerable part of the Promontory of *Jutland* [*the Cimbrian Peninsula*], which he claims as a part of his Kingdom, tho' it lieth on this side of the *Sound* or Mouth of the *Baltick* Sea.[6]

The present Bounds. But then [as if] by way of Reprisals she has enlarged her Borders to the South-East, beyond the *Danube,* to the Borders of *Italy* and *Illyrica,*[7] and beyond the *Rhine,* to the West and North [*cis Rhenum*],[8] she has gained [both the *Alsatia's, Lorrain,* and the 17 united Provinces, which last were formerly called *Gallia Belgica*].[a] <Yet a significant portion thereof has recently been joined by the French to their kingdom again.>[9]

a. Rather: a large tract formerly belonging to Belgian Gaul

4. Tacitus, *De origine et situ Germanorum* [On the origin and region of the Germans], or *Germania* (98 A.D.).

5. The area along the Gulf of Riga, between Lithuania and Estonia, now known as Latvia.

6. The strait connecting the North and the Baltic Seas, and separating contemporary Denmark from Sweden.

7. *Illyricum* was the general Roman name for the area along the eastern Adriatic Sea.

8. Since *cis Rhenum* means "on this side of the Rhine," this too must be an intentional mistake by Monzambano. For, as Thomasius (*Severini,* ed. Thomasius) notes, from an Italian perspective the term should be *trans Rhenum* ("on the other side of the Rhine"). Bohun uses geographical directions to avoid such complications.

9. The 1681 French occupation of Straßburg was acknowledged by the empire in the Truce of Regensburg (1684) and formally confirmed by the Treaty of Ryswick (1697).

2. This vast Tract of Land was in those early times possessed by various The ancient Peoples <3> and Nations, who were much celebrated on the account of State of it. their numbers and valour; yet each of them [was under a distinct Regiment, very different from that used by their Neighbours],[a] but then [except that] they had one common Original, and the same Language; and there was a great similitude in their Manners. The greatest part of them were under popular Governments; some had Kings, but that were rather to perswade their Subjects by their Authority, than to command them by the Soveraign Power [*jubendi potestate*];[10] for that Nation was never able to brook an Absolute [total] Servitude.[11] This Ancient *Germany* was never reduced into one Empire [or Kingdom][+], wherein it was like the rest of her Neighbours, *Italy, France, Spain, Greece,* and *Britain,*[b] before they were conquered by the *Romans.* [But then, as *Germany* never was reduced by a Conquest, so it retained more lively traces and marks of the Primitive State of Mankind, which from separate and distinct Families by degrees united into larger Bodies or Kingdoms.][c]

But then, tho' [this Independent Knot of States and small Kingdoms, The old *Ger-* by reason of its freedom, was very grateful to the *Germans* of those *man* state dangerous & times],[d] yet it was absolutely necessary they should frequently be en- weak

a. Rather: constituted a separate state [*civitatem*] that was distinct from the rest / The Latin speaks of "peoples" (*populi*), not "nations." [Ed.]

b. Rather: *Italy, Spain, France, Britain,* and *Greece*

c. Rather: [Indeed,] this kind of state [*status*] still retained more expressly the traces of that first origin of states [*civitatum*], when separate families coalesced little by little into one body. / See *On the Law of Nature and of Nations,* II.2.4 and VII.1.7. Pufendorf's state of nature was not among Hobbesian individuals but among extended families, similar to the condition still characterizing interstate relations. Thus, he argued not that there is no sociality before the political sphere is established, but that it is not sufficient to contain humans' unsocial tendencies. [Ed.]

d. Rather: such autonomy, marked by an exceptional kind of liberty, was most flattering to those ancient peoples

10. See Tacitus, *Germania,* 11.5–6.

11. On the other hand, Pufendorf (*Introduction to the History,* VIII.19, p. 306), said later about the Germans: ". . . they are not easily stirr'd up to raise Tumults, but commonly are willing to remain under the same Government where they are Educated."

gaged in mutual and destructive Wars, when they were so many and so small. This again exposed them to the Invasions of their neighbour Nations, though [they were a warlike People],[a] because their scattered Forces were not united in one Empire for their defence. Neither had the <4> greatest part of these small States so much Politicks [foresight] as in due time to unite in Leagues against the dangers of their potent Enemies; but they perceived the Benefit of such a Concord, [only] when it was too late, and they by fighting separately for their Liberty, were one after another all conquered.[12]

The *Franks* the first Conquerors of *Germany*, of an unknown extraction.

3. The first that reduced *Germany* from that ancient state were the FRANKS, which Nation is of so controverted an Origine, that it is not easie to determine whether it were of *Gallick* or of *German* extraction.[13] For, tho' we should grant that all those Nations which the *Greeks* comprehended under the title of *Celtae*, that is, the *Illyrians, Germans, Gauls,* [*Old*]+ *Spaniards,* and *Britains,* did as it were, flow from the same Fountain, yet it is very notorious [well known], they afterwards much differed each from the others in Language and Manners, so that no man that is any thing versed in Antiquity, can in the least doubt of it.

The foolish Pride of some of the *Gauls* [i.e., French] occasioned this difference [controversy], who being ignorant that many of the *Gallick* People in the first Ages had ambitiously boasted they were of *German* extraction, [did in the later times envy *Germany* the honour of having

a. Rather: they were quite strong in other respects

12. This remained Pufendorf's worry about the empire in his own time. See VIII.4, especially pp. 218–20.

13. This was more than a theoretical question for Pufendorf, since current French expansionism was partly defended with historical claims about the supposed French nationality of Charlemagne and other predecessors. Indeed, there was an active pamphlet war on the matter waged between French and German authors at the time of *Monzambano's* first publication (*Verfassung des deutschen Reiches,* trans. Dove, 136–37, note 2). On the importance of Charlemagne's nationality at this time, also see Monzambano, *Über die Verfassung,* trans. Breßlau, 31, note 1, which observes the appearance in 1667 of a work, by Sieur Aubery, basing Louis XIV's claims to large areas of Germany on Charlemagne's supposed title thereto as king of France (not Holy Roman Emperor).

been the Mother of the FRANKS].[a] These men pretend, that great multitudes of men out of *Gaule* invaded *Germany* in ancient (but unknown) times [formerly], and passing beyond the *Rhine,* possessed themselves of all the Countries upon [the area around] the River *Mayn,* to the *Hercynian* Forest,[14] and that after [this they returned, and conquering the Parts on the West of the <5> *Rhine,* recovered][b] the possession of their ancient Country, but so that a part of their Nation still inhabited on the *Mayn,* and left their Name[15] to that Country [the surrounding region]. For the confirmation of this Opinion, they cite *Livy, lib.* 5. *c.* 134. *Caesar de bello Gallico,* lib. 6. *Tacitus de moribus Germanorum,* c. 28.[16]

4. But to all this the *Germans* may truly reply, That the Testimony of these Latin Writers is not without just exceptions, because they testifie very faintly [hesitantly] of a thing which hapned long before their times, and concerning a [foreign] People too whose Antiquities were not preserved in any written Records. Nor is it at all probable, when the (1) *Trebocci,* (2) *Nemetes,* (3) *Vangiones,* & (4) *Treveri,*[17] and some other [People who in those times lived on the West side of the *Rhine,* and yet owned themselves to be of *German* extraction; That the *Franks* should on the contrary pass the *Rhine,* and out of *Gaul,* make a Conquest in *Germany*].[c] And yet, after all, though we should grant, that the *Franks*

The Franks *were a German* People.

1. Trebocci, Alsatia, the chief Towns of which were *Breuco-magus, (Bruomat)* and *Elcebus,*

a. Rather: disdained to acknowledge the Germans as authors of the French race [*Francorum generis*]

b. Rather: they had traversed or occupied the region lying on the right [east] bank of the Rhine, up to where it forks, they crossed back over and recovered, as it were,

c. Rather: peoples closer to the Rhine boasted about their German origin, that an area quite distant from them should have been occupied by a Gallic people

14. Old designation for the Thuringian Forest and the Erzgebirge.

15. Franken, or Franconia; also, Frankfurt-am-Main (that is, place where the Franks forded the Main River).

16. Livy, *Ab urbe condita,* V.34; Caesar, *De bello Gallico,* VI.24; Tacitus, *Germania,* chap. 28.

17. The Tribocians settled in Alsace and the Palatinate, the Nemetes originally in the Palatinate, whence they were moved by Caesar to Speyer; the Vangiones lived around Worms, and the Treverians in Belgian Gaul. The Chaucians (see p. 30) were a tribe on the North Sea coast between the rivers Ems and Elbe. All are mentioned by Tacitus, *Germania,* chaps. 28 and 35.

were at first a *Gallick* Colony, yet seeing they lived about 800 years in *Germany,* and both in their Language and Customs differed from the *Gauls,* and in both these agreed exactly with the *Germans,* they are for that cause to be reckon'd amongst the *German* Nations<; at least, their descendants have no reason to be ashamed of their German origins>.

This is certain in the mean time, that [till about 300 <6> Years after Christ],[a] there is scarce any mention of the *Franks* made in any ancient History. |[From hence there arose two very different Opinions: whilst some believe those People, who are by *Tacitus* call'd the (5) *Chauci,* changed that name in after times, and call'd themselves the *Franks;* [and others][b] think, that a number of *German* People, or some parts [a coalition] of them, united in this name, and [out of a vain affectation of][c] Liberty, took up the name of FRANKS: for in the German Tongue FRANK signifies *free* [*a free man*]. And to this purpose they produce the Testimonies of *Francis* I, and *Henry* II, Kings of *France,* who in their Letters to the *Diet* of *Germany* say, they are of German Extraction. Tho' it is very well known at the same time, to all wise men, to what purposes such ancient and overworn Relations of Kindred are for the most part pretended.]|[d]

a. Rather: before the third century after Christ's birth / That is, till about 200 A.D. [Ed.]

b. Rather: others

c. Rather: to show their exceptional desire for / Bohun's language reveals his own political opinions. [Ed.]

d. E.p.: Hence it is a very probable opinion that, around the third century, several German peoples situated between the Rhine and the Elbe assumed that name in order to exhibit their exceptional desire to preserve their liberty against the Romans, who threatened repeatedly from Gaul to impose their yoke on Germany as well. For in the German Tongue FRANK signifies *a free man.* Still others think that the first beginnings of the French [*Francici*] kingdom among the Sygambrians and other surrounding peoples, up to the Isère River, should be more carefully explored. And to this purpose they produce the Testimonies of *Francis* I, and *Henry* II, Kings of *France,* who in their Letters to the *Diet* of *Germany* say, they are of German Extraction. Though this testimony alone does not exhaust the matter, since wise men have no difficulty determining the purpose for which such faded relations are sometimes pretended.

5. But however this [may] be, the *Franks* for certain first passed the *Rhine* upon [among] the *Ubii,* [or Inhabitants of the Archbishoprick of *Cologne,*]+ and after they had conquered the far greatest part of *Gaul,* [(now call'd *France*)]+ <they founded the famous kingdom of France. Its kings, called Merovingians after its first dynasty,> turning as it were the course of their victorious Arms back again, [and having crossed the Rhine once more,] they conquered the greatest part of *Germany,* and subdued all the Countries between the *Mayn* and the *Danube,* and went Northward as far as *Thuringia:* After this *Charles* the Great extended his Conquests much further by subduing the *Saxons,* and *Tassilon* King of the *Bavarians;* [18] so that not only the Countries possess'd by the old German Nations [*populis*] were all reduc'd <7> under his Obedience, but all those that lay upon the *Baltick* Sea, and that part of *Poland* which lies on the West of the *Vistula,* which was then inhabited by the *Sclaves* [Slavs]; for History saith, They also were either Tributaries to that Prince, or *majestatem comiter coluisse,* [i.e.,] were Homagers to his Crown.

The Franks conquer Gaul, now France, and after it Germany.

6. The greatest part of the German Writers have very fondly [anxiously] endeavoured to have it believed he was their Countryman, as being born at *Ingelheim,* a Town in the Bishoprick of *Mentz,* but now under the Elector *Palatine;* and in an ancient Charter of the Abby of *Fuld* [a], the Lands upon the River Unstrut in *Thuring,* are call'd *The Lands of his Conception:* And that he us'd the German Tongue,[a] is apparent by the names of the Months used in his time, which {are still retained in *Germany,* and} are thought to have been introduced by him.

Of what Nation Charles the Great was.

But |[if the *Germans* would suffer me, (a Foreigner) to pass my judgment in this [their] Affair, tho' I am not at all disposed to favour the *French* in their other pretences[, to the damage of the *Germans*]+; yet I would perswade them here freely and willingly to renounce their Pretences to *Charles* the Great, and the rather, because it can bring no injury [*fraudi*] to their present Empire. For it is certain, the *Franks* placed the

A Frank

a. *lingua Germanica* / e.p.: *lingua Teutonica*
18. Duke Tassilo III (ca. 742–94), deposed by Charlemagne in 788.

Seat of their Empire in *Germany* [*Gallia*]]|;[a] and it is no less certain, that
By his Father, the Father of *Charles* the Great was King of *France* [*Franciae*], and all
his Progenitors had for many Ages lived in great Honour, and managed
And born in great Employments in that Kingdom. Besides, those parts of *Germany,*
France. <8> which lie on the West of the Rhine,[b] and were then subject to the
Crown of *France,* were possess'd by them [only] as Accessions acquired
to that Kingdom by Conquest, and were looked upon as conquered Provinces. And every man is esteemed to be of the same Nation his Father
was, and in which he has placed the Seat of his Fortunes and Hopes after
[passed down by] his Father and Ancestors.[19] The sole consideration, That
a man was born in this or that Country [*locus*], will hardly be allowed to
make a man of a different Nation from his Father; |[unless we can [really]
believe, that if the present King of *Sweden* had been born in *Prussia,* he
had to have been esteemed a *Prussian,* and not a *Swede*]|.[c] Nor was that
part of *Germany* which lieth on the West of the *Rhine,* esteemed a part
of *France,* till under *Charles* the Great it was united to that Kingdom:
[And in the first times that followed],[d] when his Posterity had divided
their Ancestor's Dominions amongst them, the Historians [also] frequently [begin to] distinguish between the Latin or Western *France,* and
the German or Eastern *France,* which is the same with [*Greater*] Germany:[e] And it is observed [Although it seems], that after the times of the
Otho's,[20] that name of *Germany,* by degrees, grew out of use.

a. E.p.: it can be maintained, on the contrary, that the Franks established the seat
of their kingdom in Gallia [Gaul], which was at the time still separated from Germany
by the Rhine / *Gallia* is Gaul or France, not Germany. [Ed.]

b. *Transrhenanae* / e.p.: *Cisrhenanae* [east of the Rhine] / Likewise, later in the
paragraph. See note 8 in this chapter. [Ed.]

c. E.p.: although, if we suppose the Rhine as the border, Ingelheim [Charles's
birthplace] is situated in Gallia [Gaul]

d. Rather: For then, especially

e. *Germania magna, seu Transrhenana* / e.p.: *Cisrhenana*

19. The notion of "fatherland" (*patria*) was already associated with one's fortunes
or patrimony in Pufendorf's dissertation *De obligatione erga patriam* [On the obligation toward one's fatherland] (Heidelberg, 1663), §11; in *Dissertationes academicae
selectiores* (1675), 20.

20. Otto III died in 1002 A.D. Otto IV, son of Henry the Lion, became king in
1198, emperor in 1209; he died in 1218.

The objection made on the account of the use of the German Language by *Charles* the Great, may be thus easily answered. The *Gauls* having been long subject to the *Romans,* by degrees lost their own Tongue, and embraced that of their Conquerors; so that at last there were scarce any footsteps of the old *Celtick* left amongst <9> them: But then the *Franks*[, when they entered Gaul,] brought their German [*Teutonicam*] Tongue along with them, and without doubt did not presently forget it. But then, as the *Franks* neither destroyed nor expelled the [ancient] *Gauls;* but only assumed the Government and Soveraignity of the Country, [from whence it]ᵃ came to pass, that those who were descended of the *Franks,* were employed in the great Affairs, and the [ancient] *Gauls,* as a conquered People, were kept under. But then as two Rivers of different colour, uniting in one stream, may for some time preserve each his proper colour, [but at length the greater stream will certainly change the lesser into its own colour];ᵇ so in the beginning the *Gauls* had their Tongue, and the *Franks* theirs, till in length of time a third was made out of both mixed and twisted together, in which yet the *Latin* is the predominant. The plain cause of which is, That the *Gauls* were more numerous than the *Franks,* and it was much harder for them to learn the *German,* than it was for the *Franks* to learn the *Gallick* Latin{; for with what difficulty Foreigners learn the German Tongue, I my self know by experience}. From hence it proceeds, that [the most ancient Writers of this Nation]ᶜ call the vulgar Latin the Rustick or Countryman's Tongue, because the Nobility and Gentry still used the German, whilst the Countrymen and the rest of the [ancient] *Gauls* had no knowledge of any other than the Latin. And thus we see it is in our own times, in *Livonia* and *Curland,* where the old Inhabitants are by the *Germans* <10> reduced into the

Tho' he used the German Tongue.

a. Rather: it

b. The Latin *donec tandem paulatim majus in minori suum perdat* seems to require: "until at last the greater gradually loses its own [color] in the lesser." Either *majus* and *minus* are mistakenly reversed here, or they have a qualitative sense (in conjunction with the preceding passage, where the conquering Franks are said to rule the Gallic majority) rather than a quantitative one (as in the subsequent elaboration of the metaphor). [Ed.]

c. Rather: even the most ancient writers about Frankish affairs

condition of meer Rusticks; for all the Nobility, and the Inhabitants of the Cities, speak the *Sclavonian* [*rusticanam*] Tongue, and the *German,* but the Countrymen do scarce understand one German word of ten.

Thus *Charles* the Great might easily understand the German Tongue, because the *Franks,* [who were a German Nation,] + had not quite laid aside the use of it; and also because the *Franks,* before his time, had conquered a great part of *Germany,* and he went on with the work, and reduced all the rest under his Dominion. Nor was it possible in that unlearned Age to converse with the *Germans* in any other than their own Language.

|[But then he that observes, that [here] there is [are] two very different Questions confounded into one [by most people], will very accurately determine this Controversie]|;[a] for if the Question be, Whether *Charles* the Great were of a *Gallick* or a *German* Original? without doubt it will be answered, That he was not a *Gaul* but a *German,* or which is all one, a FRANK. But if the Question be, [What Countryman][b] he was? *France* [*Gallia*], and not *Germany,* is to be assigned him, and therefore in this respect he was no *German,* but a *Gaul,* or [rather a] *Gallo-Frank.*

{I fear I shall make the Reader think I take him for a stupid person, if I should dwell any longer on so plain a thing; and yet I will presume to give the *Germans* a known example:} If you fall upon a Nobleman of *Livonia* [among them], and ask him what Countryman [*cujas*] he is, he will reply a *Livonian,* and not a *German;* but then, if you still insist, and ask him of what Lineage, <because Livonia is inhabited by two nationalities [*duplex natio*],> <11> he will say, he is descended of the *Germans,* and not of the *Livonians.*

The Titles of *Charles* the Great to his several Dominions.

7. This Prince (*Charles* the Great) had under him divers Nations [*regiones*], which he had acquired by very different Titles: He enjoy'd *France* as his Inheritance, devolved to him from his Father by [right of] Succession. For though we read in their Histories, that the ancient *Franks* had lodged in the Nobility and People of that Nation, some

a. E.p.: One must be careful here, however, not to confuse different questions
b. Rather: of which fatherland [*patria*]

Authority in the constituting their Kings; yet I conceive, it was rather
[like] a solemn Ina[u]guration, and an acknowledgment of their Loyalty
and Obedience to the new King, than a Free Election;[21] for they rarely
departed from the Order of a Lineal [*sanguinis*] Succession, but when
there were Factions, or the next Heir in the Line was wholly unfit for
Government.

A part of *Germany* was, before this time, united [by Conquest] + to
the Crown of *France*, and the rest of it was subdued by the victorious
Arms of *Charles* the Great. Whether any part of this Country freely and
willingly submitted to him out of Reverence to his Greatness, is very
uncertain. He also by his Arms conquered the Kingdom of the *Lombards*
in *Italy*, the Pope of *Rome* affording him a Pretence for it; after which,
he was by the Pope and People of *Rome* saluted *Emperor of Rome*, and
Augustus. Now, what he gain'd by this Title, we shall by and by inform
you.[22]

8. Thus, under *Charles* the Great, *Germany* became a part of the Kingdom of *France*, and was [sufficiently subject to the][a] Absolute Empire
or Soveraignty of those Princes. <12> During this state of Affairs, it was
divided into divers Provinces, which were governed by [prefects called]
Counts or *Earls*, and *Marquesses*, who were for the most part of French
extraction. Yet [in these times] + the *Saxons* enjoy'd a greater shew [re-
tained a fuller kind] of Liberty, because *Charles* the Great had not been
able to reduce them without a long and tedious War, and was at last to
perfect the Work, and establish his Soveraignty, necessitated to admit
them to a participation of the Priviledges [*jura*] enjoy'd by the *Franks*,
and to unite them into one Nation with their Conquerors. That he
might further assure himself of this fierce Nation, which was so impa-
tient of Servitude; he call'd in the assistance of the Priests, who were
ordered to teach them the Christian Faith [*religione*], and to inculcate
into them how much they were obliged to those who had shewn them

Germany a
part of the
Kingdom of
France.

a. Rather: subject to what seems quite an
21. See IV.1.
22. See I.12.

the way of obtaining Eternal Life. On this account many Bishopricks and Abbies in *Germany* [were founded by *Charles* the Great].ᵃ

Germany was in the same estate [condition] under Saint *Lewis* [Louis the Pious,] the Son of *Charles,* but that the Authority [and power] of the Prefects or Governours of the Provinces began to grow greater<, and the clergy, their wealth swelled by the Princes' indulgence, grew considerably haughtier as well>.²³

The Children of St. *Lewis* divide their Father's Kingdom. 9. But afterwards, when the Children of this *Lewis* had divided their Father's Kingdom amongst them (which was the first and principal cause of the Ruin of the French [*Francicae*] Power, and of the *Caroline* Family) *Germany* became separated from the [rest of the] French Empire, and was a distinct Kingdom under *Lewis* II. Son of St. *Lewis.*ᵇ <And although soon, under Charles the Fat [*crassus*], it was combined with the rest of France [*Francia*] again, a short time later, when Arnulf was king, it was torn away once more and henceforth maintained its own separate affairs as Germany.> To it was afterwards added a great part of the *Belgick France* [*Galliae*], [(or of <13> the *Low Countries,* as it is now called)]⁺ which lies towards the *Rhine,* which for the most part was inhabited by German Nations [Teutonic peoples], [and] which from *Lotharius* another of the Sons of St. *Lewis,* was then called [the Kingdom of]⁺ *Lorrain,* though at this day only a very small part of that Kingdom retains the old name.

During the destructive Wars, which followed after these times, between the Posterity of *Charles* the Great, not only the German Nobility [*procerum*] gained exorbitant Power, but the very Family of *Charles* was at last totally extinguished, or at least deprived of the *Crown* of *France,* (for to this day [the Dukes of *Lorrain* <and others>, and the Electors *Palatine,* pretend to be descended of that Family)]ᶜ and the *Germans*

a. Rather: acknowledge Charles as their founder
b. Rather: Louis, son of Louis the Pious
c. Rather: the Counts Palatine upon the Rhine, and the Dukes of Lorraine<, and others>, trace their line back to Charles)
23. This is an interesting addition to the e.p., which generally tones down the anticlerical remarks of the first edition.

chose themselves Kings out of the Nobility of their own Nation; from which times *Germany* [became again a free State, and had no dependance on the Crown of *France*].^a

Now, because the *German* State [*respublica*] is commonly call'd the *Sacred Roman Empire,* I think it will be worth my pains to enquire [briefly], How it first obtained this Title? what it has gained by it? and by what Right it now enjoys that Name? for the clear understanding of which it will be necessary shortly to recapitulate the state the [ancient] Roman Empire [in the West]⁺ was reduced to before the times of *Charles* the Great.

10. It is very well and commonly known after what manner the People of *Rome,* after they had by the Success of their Arms subdued the noblest part of the then known World, were at last, by the ambition of a <14> few over potent Citizens engaged in Civil Wars, and at length brought under the Dominion of a single person. But then *Augustus* the Founder of the Roman Empire (or Monarchy) when he had by the assistance of the Army gained the Empire, [perswaded himself, that he should easily keep it by the same way].^b Therefore tho' from thenceforward he seemed to leave some of the Affairs of the State to the disposal of the *Senate,* that it might still seem to have a share in the Government; yet he wholly kept in his own hands the Care and Government of the Army[, indicating the same by his adoption of the title *Imperator*]. But then it was his principal care to conceal from the Rabble of the Army, [as if it were the most important state secret, involving the most careful disguise,] That the Souldiers were the men who could set up and pull down the Emperors; which Secret, when it was once discovered, the State of the Empire became as miserable as the Condition of the Emperors.

[F]or the Empire being weakened by frequent intestine Wars, found it self also often exposed to the worst of men by a covetous and turbulent Rabble, [which oftentimes most wickedly murdered her best Princes, to

a. Rather: managed its affairs separately and did not form a common empire together with France

b. Rather: easily perceived that he could [only] thereby keep it for himself

her great damage and sorrow]:[a] Nor could any of her Emperors after this entertain any hopes of firmly settling the Empire in their Families, but [was necessitated to be contented with a precarious Title amongst a parcel of mercenary Souldiers]:[b] So that in truth the whole power of making the Emperors, was in the Army, (which is the common Attendant of all Military Monarchies, [or] where a strong and perpetual Army is kept together in any one <15> place), and the *Senate and People of Rome* were weak and vain Names, made use of to delude the simple common People, as if the free and voluntary consent of the whole Body [*universorum*] had constituted the Emperor.

That Kingdom [*regnum*], thus founded on a Military Licence, as it was unfit for continuance, was by *Constantine* the Great and *Theodosius* hastened to its fatal period: the first of these making *Byzantium* [(now called *Constantinople*)][+] the Seat of the Empire, and withdrawing the [strongest] Armies, which had till then been maintained on the [East of the *Rhine* <and the Danube>, for its preservation];[c] and the lat[t]er by dividing the Empire between his two Sons *Arcadius* and *Honorius,* soft lasie Princes, and neither of them fit for such a Command<, who were also much weakened by the dishonesty of traitors>. From thence forward there were two Kingdoms for one, and this Division was no way useful, but only for the fitting the Western part by separating it from the Eastern, to be the more easie Prey to the barbarous Nations.[24] And accordingly, not long after this, an end was put to the Western Empire, and *Rome* was taken and sack'd by the <Herulians and> *Goths* which [i.e., Rome] before that had been deprived of all her Provinces by as

a. Rather: and often lamenting the premature loss of its best leaders through some immense crime

b. Rather: they were always necessarily beholden to those who could be purchased with money [*inter venales*]

c. Rather: on the bank of the Rhine <and the Danube>, to the east

24. Arcadius and Honorius were in fact young and ineffective leaders, and the empire's two halves were mainly controlled by ambitious praetorian prefects who distrusted and undermined each other and failed to present a joint front against the Visigoths under Alaric.

good Right as she had got them, and now, in her turn, lost her beloved [own] Liberty, and became a part of the *Gothick* Kingdom.

11. After this, the *Gothick* Power being entirely ruin'd, *Rome* and a considerable part of *Italy* returned under the Obedience of the Greek Emperors, tho' on the account of her former Majesty, and [for that *Constantinople* <16> was considered as the Metropolis; *Italy*]ᵃ was rather treated by them as an Ally [or equal] than as a subject Province. But however [in fact], the Supremacy was acknowledged to be in the Emperor of *Greece* who exercised it in *Rome* and those other parts of *Italy* which were under his Jurisdiction by his *Exarchs*. But by degrees the *Popes* became weary of this *Greek Empire* [as well]. They lay the blame however on the Misgovernment [wilfullness] of the *Exarchs*, and because some of the Greek Emperors were too severe against Images,²⁵ which they [i.e., the Popes] yet judged a most useful Tool to instruct the *Many* [uneducated populace] in the Superficial Rites of Religion, which [i.e., the Many], as they said, was become incapable of receiving or bearing a more solid Piety; nor was it so profitable to the Priests, to let the People know, a good and holy Life would certainly please God. Perhaps also it was believed, the Church would be very much exalted in her Authority [*splendoris*], if the Pope could by degrees gain the Secular Empire, as he had already, in a good degree, assumed the Supremacy in Ecclesiastical or Sacred Affairs throughout the World. And in truth, it did not seem fit that he should live in subjection to the Slave of a Greek Emperor, (who sometimes was deprived of his Virilities)ᵇ whom God had in-

Rome for some time under the Greek Emperors.

---

a. Rather: because she was considered the mother-city [i.e., metropolis] of Constantinople, she / Despite the patrilineal determination of political identity in terms of worldly place and success (cf. I.6. above), the ancient relation of colonies to their city of origin was conceived more organically in terms of a mother-offspring relationship. [Ed.]

b. Denzer, Breßlau, and Dove translate this passage abstractly, as referring to the attenuated state of the Eastern Empire. However, it is more likely a literal reference to the eunuchs who were often in charge of state affairs in the Eastern Empire (*Verfassung des deutschen Reiches*, ed. Denzer, 1994, 39; Monzambano, *Über die Verfassung*, trans. Breßlau, 35; *Verfassung des deutschen Reiches*, trans. Dove, 22). [Ed.]

25. The Byzantine iconoclastic periods were in the eighth (730–87) and ninth (813–43) centuries A.D.

trusted with such Power [authority], as his own *Vicar* in the World, that
he being freed from the Care of the Church, [might be at the better] [a]
leisure to attend the Civil Affairs of the World, [and that they too had
been delegated by God to the Pope], [b] if it had not been apparent, that
the holy <17> minds of these Bishops [prelates] were so taken with the
Pleasures of Divine Affairs, that they wholly declined the being concerned in these prophane Employments. [26]

The *Lombards* feared by the Popes.
But then, though the Greek Emperor was not much feared, both on the
score of his distance, and also because he had enough to do to defend
himself against the *Saracens,* [which then from the East fiercely and successfully attack'd the Empire]; [c] yet the Power of the *Lombards* was more
dreadful, and hung like a mighty Tempest over all *Italy,* and had almost
made themselves Masters of the *Suburbs* of *Rome.* And the Pope not
being able alone to grapple with this Enemy, could bethink him of no
body that was able to succour the See of *Rome* in this exigence, but the
King of *France;* and he too was very much disposed to it by the Prospect
of that Glory which would attend the rescuing from Injury [of] that
Person, who like an unexhaustible Fountain dispensed to all Christian
Souls the Waters of Divine Grace. The Pope also had before-hand very
much obliged *Pipin* the Father, and *Charles* the Son, by his ready con-
senting, That *Chilprick* King of *France* should be shaven and turn'd into
a Monastery: [27] Which could never be equally recompensed by those

a. Rather: was at
b. Rather: which [affairs] would also have been delegated to him
c. Rather: whose power was growing then throughout the Orient
26. The sarcasm in this passage contributes to its obscurity. Pufendorf is suggesting that the popes' ecclesiastical authority as God's vicars (substitutes) on earth
was so great (and effective) that they needed something else to fill their time (such as
wielding secular power, in addition to their religious role), and that God would have
explicitly given them such powers if their supposed piety had not made them averse
to profane tasks. The passage is also interesting because it shows again that not all
passages critical of Catholicism were stripped from the e.p.
27. The last Merovingian ruler, Childerich III, was dethroned by Pippin (the
Younger), his minister, after the latter had induced Pope Zacharias to say (in reliance
on the recently discovered "Donation of Constantine") that he who had the actual
power of the kingdom in his hands, rather than one with a mere title, was more

Princes, who might otherwise have had painful Scruples of Conscience to perswade themselves, That a Subject might lawfully shave his Prince, and make him, of a Monarch, become a Monk, who was guilty of no other fault, but his having committed more Power to a Potent Minister, than was consistent with the safety <18> of his Crown and Kingdom. And in this the FATES strangely befriended the *French* in giving them so plausible a pretence of invading and possessing {our}ᵃ *Italy,* which has alwaies [been courted by the *Ultra-montane* Kingdoms].ᵇ

12. After then that *Charles* the Great had subdued all that part of *Italy* which was before subject to the *Lombards,* the Pope (who had a good share of the Prey) that he might shew his gratitude, and assure himself for the future a *Potent Defender,* declared *Charles* Emperor and *Augustus,* with the Approbation of the People<, at least as first citizen and head of that city's clergy, which commonly participates in such inaugural activities>.

Charles the Great Subducs the *Lombards,* and is made Emperor,

Now it is not easie to conceive what *Charles* got by this Title; in truth *Rome* long before this was not the Seat of the ancient Roman Empire,[28] being made first a Part of the *Gothick* Kingdom, and after that of the Eastern Empire. And therefore the *Romans* could not give that to *Charles,* which heretofore belonged to the Western Empire: for all that [Right was determin'd by Conquest and the Right of War, by Cession and Desertion, and was now for a long time in the peaceable possession

---

worthy of the throne. Childerich was deposed in 751 A.D. at the Imperial Diet of Soissons, shorn of his long hair (a Merovingian symbol of strength), and relegated to a monastery. See *Verfassung des deutschen Reiches,* trans. Dove, 137, note 4.

    a. Bohun usually omits Monzambano's first-person references. [Ed.]

    b. Rather: inflamed the desire of those beyond the Alps

    28. According to Pufendorf, the crowning of Charles did not signify the establishment of a western Roman Empire. Yet the German emperor was so perceived throughout the Middle Ages, and no one challenged his claim to rule the world [*imperium mundi*]. Indeed, Otto III and Henry VI saw the empire's reestablishment as the task imposed by their imperial crowns (Monzambano, *Über die Verfassung,* trans. Breßlau, 36, note 1).

of others].[a] And even *Rome* her self was not *sui juris* [independent], and therefore could not give her self to another: And therefore *Charles* was at first in doubt, whether he should accept the Title, till he had made an agreement with the Greek Emperor, and obtained his consent. The Emperor of *Constantinople* who {was then weak, and} needed the Friendship of *Charles* yielded the point without any difficulty, to preserve *Calabria,* and those other [Ports he had yet left him in *Italy*].[b]

|[So that upon <19> the whole, *Charles* the Great, under the splendid Title of *Emperor,* borrowed from the ancient State of *Rome* (but in a very different sense) was made the Supreme Defender, Protector, and Advocate of the See of *Rome,* and of the States [properties][c] belonging to it, either by the Usurpation of the Pope, or the Liberality of others. Now whether this Defence and Protection included in it a Supreme Empire or Dominion [*summi Imperii*] over that See, as some *Civilians* [*politicis*] have said, seems a doubt to me, and I should rather think there was a kind of unequal League only entred between *Charles* and the See of *Rome,*]|[d] That he should defend her [and her possessions] against all

Or rather Protector and Advocate of the See of Rome.

a. Rather: had by right of war, by cession and dereliction, long ago come under the control of others

b. Rather: strategic places [*opportuna loca*] in Greece he still retained / Calabria, at the southern tip of Italy, was originally a Greek colony and, until the Roman conquest, a part of "greater Greece" (*Graecia magna*); it belonged to the Byzantine (or Greek) Empire in the ninth century A.D. [Ed.]

c. That is, *bonorum* [goods, *Güter*]. [Ed.]

d. E.p.: But whatever right over the city of Rome and its surrounding regions belonged to Charles, it was in the end not derived from that acclamation but acquired before, by right of war over the previous holdings of the Langobards, or by the voluntary submission of those seeking a strong defender for themselves. Thus it appears that hardly anything substantial was or could have been conferred on Charles at the time, except that the Pope and people of Rome bestowed on the new prince the splendid title of Emperor and *Augustus,* from the ancient Roman state, in order to flatter him or signify their respect. As for Charles's subsequent right over the city of Rome and its environs, there is disagreement among writers according to their respective allegiance to Emperor or Pope. One thing is unquestioned: that Charles gave the Church or Seat of Rome many lands and a certain power over that city itself. But it is unclear whether Charles reserved sovereignty over these to himself, conferring only their income and a lesser jurisdiction upon the Pope and the Roman Church, or whether he conferred a full dominion over those things on the Seat of Rome, while himself retaining only the function of defender, protector, or advocate. In effect there

Invaders, or [and] by his Authority compose all internal Commotions, which might tend to the damage or dishonour of that See [the Church]; and on the other side, [That] the See of *Rome* should pay a due respect to his [Charles's] Majesty, {and not undertake any thing which was of great consequence, without his Authority or Leave:} and in the first place, that no man should be admitted Pope against his will.

|[From whence it will appear, that the See of *Rome* from thenceforward became a particular State [*civitatis*], and, properly speaking, was not united [to the Kingdom of *France*].ᵃ And that *Charles* the Great was not the Master of the See of *Rome,* and the States [properties] belonging to it, nor did he exercise a Soveraign Dominion [*vim imperii*] over her, by making Laws, imposing Tributes, creating Magistrates, or exercising any Jurisdiction, or the like. For [But] all these things are not above the Pretences of an Advocate, *viz.* To expel a Pope that entered by ill Arts, to reduce into <20> Order such as designed the Ruine of the Church, or any other signal damage [dishonor], or to subdue the *Romans,* or any other who should rebel against the Pope.]|ᵇ

[Moreover,] *Charles,* and some of his Posterity, tho' they seemed fond enough of the Titles of Emperors and *Augusti,* and on that account took upon them the Priority amongst the other *European* Princes, who will- However, neither he nor any of his Successors would

---

scems to be little difference here. For princes who have once given anything to the Church seem to retain no other rights over it than those pertaining to its defense and preservation. It is the task [*munus*] of a defender and advocate, however, . . .

a. Rather: with the kingdom of the Franks into one commonwealth [*rempublicam*]

b. E.p.: Thus the right of a defender or advocate does not go beyond expelling those admitted to the Papacy through devious means, bringing into line those engaged in activities that subvert or disgrace the Church, or restraining those, in Rome or elsewhere, who rise up against the Pope, by using the Church's own means for the expenses incurred in this matter. But those who insist on maintaining that the Pope, along with the city of Rome and all the possessions that belong to the See of Rome, were subject to Charles and that he exercised full sovereignty over them, as in passing laws, imposing tributes, appointing magistrates, serving justice, and other similar activities, let them see how to reconcile these claims with the donation made by Charles. It seems, much rather, that since that time the See of Rome has been constituted as a special sort of state [*peculiaris instar civitatis*], and that properly speaking it did not coalesce into one commonwealth [*rempublicam*] with the kingdom of the Franks.

suffer *France*
to be taken for
a part of the
Empire. ingly yielded it to them on that score; yet after all, for ought that appears
to me, we shall never read, that [any of the Line of *Charles* the Great,
call'd the Kingdom of *France* by that Name].[a]

The Fall of
the *Caroline*
Race, the Rise
of the King-
dom of *Ger-
many* under
Otho I. 13. When the *Caroline* Family began to decline, and the *Germans* had
divided themselves from the Kingdom of *France,* and *Italy* was afflicted
with great Commotions, there sprung up other States out of the Ruins
of this House [the older powers], and amongst them *Otho* the First, King
of *Germany,* who having overcome *Berengarius,*[29] and reduced the Kingdom of *Italy,* the Popes (who [could not trust to their States])[b] thought
fit to put *Otho* in possession of [nearly] the same Power [*jure*] [as de-
fender] that had been enjoyed by the Family of *Charles* the Great, and
consented, That for the future the Protection of the See of *Rome* should
be united to the Kingdom of *Germany,* so that whosoever enjoyed that
Kingdom, should [be the Protector of that See].[c]

But then, after many of those old German Kings had [couragiously
executed that Office upon][d] the See of *Rome,* and in the mean time the
Wealth and Power not only of the See of *Rome,* but of the Bishopricks
of *Germany,* was become very great, the Popes of *Rome* began to grow
weary <21> of this German Protection too. The Causes of this were,
1. The Aversion common to all Nations, against a Foreign Dominion.
2. The Indignity which was offered hereby, to the *Italick* People, who
having ever been celebrated for Civil Prudence {(it would be cowardly
not to acknowledge that which outsiders attribute to us)},[e] were by this

a. Rather: under any of the line of Charles the Great, was the kingdom of the
Franks designated "the Roman Empire"

b. Rather: could not yet be sufficiently confident about their state [*statui*] amid
those commotions

c. Rather: immediately acquire the right [*ius*] to protect that See as well / The
German *Schutzrecht* is more revealing since it indicates the fact that this relationship
involved not only obligation but also privilege and opportunity. [Ed.]

d. Rather: vigorously exercised that sort of right toward

e. Bohun does not translate the material in parentheses, which Pufendorf later
omitted in the e.p. [Ed.]

29. Berengar II was installed as king of northern Italy by Otto I in 952 A.D. but
removed by him in 961 because of his misrule and conspiracy with Pope John XXII.

kept under the Tutelage [wild rule] of the {less-politick [uncultivated]}
Germans. 3. Besides, it was very uneasie to the Vicar of *Jesus Christ* to
be any longer under the Guardianship of another, whose [the Pope's]
fingers [had long] itched to be giving Laws to all Princes. Therefore for
the shaking off this Yoke, they [the Popes] took this course, *viz.* They
found out ways, [by the means of the Bishops, to imbroil the Affairs of
these Kings, sometimes in *Germany,* and at others in *Italy,* and the Pope
seconded them with his Fulminations or Censures, which in those Ages
were wonderful terrible].ᵃ

Thus by degrees the Kings of *Germany* grew weary of *Italy,* and being
content with their own Kingdom, left the See of *Rome* to the sole management [*arbitrio*] of the Popes, which they [these] had sought so many
Ages, and by such a variety of Arts, to the embroiling [of] all *Europe.*
After this the Kings of *Germany* {a long time omitted the being crowned
at *Rome,* yet they} retained the old Titles of *Emperors of Rome;* and when
they entred upon the Kingdom, the Defence of the See of *Rome* was in
the first place enjoin'd them; from which care the *Protestant Electors* have
since given the Emperor a Discharge.

14. By all that has been said, it will appear how {childishly} they are mistaken, who think the Kingdom of *Germany* has succeeded in the <22>
Place of the old Roman Empire, and that it is continued in this Kingdom; when in truth, that Empire which was seated at *Rome,* was de-
stroyed many Ages before *Germany* became one Kingdom. |[And that
Roman Empire which was given to *Charles* and *Otho*]|ᵇ (which was
nothing but the Advousion [defense] and Protection of the See of *Rome)*
in length of time fixed its Name upon that Kingdom of *Germany,* tho'
the States [*ditiones*] of the Church [in *Italy*]⁺ never were united into
one and the same Polity [*civitatem*] with the Kingdom of *Germany,*

The Kingdom
of *Germany*
has not suc-
ceeded in the
*Roman
Empire.*

---

a. Rather: to stir up the affairs of the German kings, sometimes in Italy and sometimes in Germany itself, with the assiduous assistance of the bishops; occasionally
they also issued bans against them, which were still greatly feared in those ages
   b. E.p.: The title of Roman Emperor, however, which was conferred on Charles
and Otto

much less did either *Charles* or *Otho* submit their proper [own] King-doms to *Rome,* as the Metropolis or Seat of the Empire. In the mean time, because it was believed the very Title of *Emperor of Rome,* upon the account of the Greatness of that ancient Empire, had something of Majesty and Grandeur in it, it was frequently given to the Kings of *Germany* [only].[a] And the consequence of this was, that *Germany* [too] was afterwards call'd the *Roman Empire,* by way of Honour. But the different Coronations [and inaugurations] which belong to them do not obscurely shew, that there is a real difference to be made between the Roman Empire and the Kingdom of *Germany;* and the later Emperors, since *Maximilian* I. after the Title of *Roman Emperor,* expresly subjoin that of *King of Germany.* The *Germans* also at this day do commonly call {their State}, *The Roman Empire of the Teutonick Nation;* which form of Speech seems to contain in it a contradiction, seeing it is very certain the present State of *Germany* [*modernam Germanorum rempublicam*] is not one and the same with the ancient Roman Empire. <23> Yet the Kings of *Germany* retain the Title which has been received, tho' they have for a long time omitted the Reception of the *Crown* of *Rome,* and use very little of the ancient Rights of an Advocate, which belonged heretofore to them, because Princes do more easily part with the things in dispute, than with the Titles to them. Now, whether that Right they once had, is by the lapse of time expir'd, or preserved by the use of the Title only, we shall hereafter, when occasion is offered, enquire.[30]

a. Rather: by itself / That is, "only" refers to the bare title (*solo nomine*), not to the German kings in comparison to other kings. [Ed.]

30. On the bestowal of esteem, including titles, as one of the prerogatives of sovereigns, see *On the Law of Nature and of Nations,* VIII.4 and I.I.18, in which titles are characterized as moral qualities that "designate the varying importance and status of persons in communal life. . . . they indicate the humanly imposed rights, authority, and function of those to whom they are attributed. And so it is not much ado about nothing if men fight heatedly over titles now and then. . . ." The quotation is from *The Political Writings of Samuel Pufendorf,* 106.

15. But in the mean time the Title of the Empire of *Rome* is so far from being any advantage, that it is manifest, it has been the cause of great Mischief and Inconvenience to *Germany*. Priests are <almost [*fere*]>[a] alwaies ready to receive, but never part with any thing. And whereas all other Clients dispose their Masters to favour them by their Presents [services], if a Priest be not fed with new Presents, he presently snarles, and imputes his Blessing as a wonderful [boundless] Obligation.[b] I should think, that the ancient Princes heaped their Bounties upon the Clergy of *Germany*, principally because they were made [to] believe [that] God [expected they should][c] provide plentifully for that Order of Men.

And what has been spent by *Germans* in Journies to *Rome*, for [obtaining] the Imperial Crown? What Treasures and Men have been consumed in *Italick* Expeditions, in composing the Commotions stirr'd up by the Popes, and in protecting them against refractory men that have attack'd them, is not to be conceived. Nor has any Foreigner got much by attacking [occupying] <24> *Italy*, {the *Spaniards* excepted, who have stuck so many years in the Bowels of our[(i)] Country, that we have never yet been able to repell them.} Lastly, no Princes were oftner fulminated [banned] by that See than the German Emperors; nor was any of them more exercised by the frequent Seditions of the Churchmen than they. The principal cause[s] of all which misfortunes seem to have arisen from [hence, *That they thought these Princes, who had this Title from the See of* Rome, *in which they took such pride, were obliged by it, above all other Men, to promote the Affairs of that See*]:[d] Or otherwise, because that Order of Men [is above all others unwilling to be subject to the Soveraignty

(i). *The Author, tho' a* German, *pretends to be an* Italian.

a. An important qualification in the e.p. [Ed.]

b. The suggestion is that priests consider themselves slighted because they are not suitably rewarded for the great blessings they bestow (i.e., they regard themselves ahead in the exchange of benefits); indeed, they consider secular powers in their debt, thus reversing the patron/client relationship. [Ed.]

c. Rather: had imposed on them a very powerful injunction to

d. Rather: the belief that the chief obligation of those who prided themselves over others on account of that title was to justify their actions before the See of Rome

of another, and with Mother-Church, is ever seeking how to shake off the hated Secular Authority].[a]

{Yet I would have this understood with *Salva reverentia sanctissimae sedis,* [a saving the Reverence and Respect due][b] to that most Holy See, to whose Judgment I most devoutly submit all this.}

a. Rather: [i.e., the clergy], which cannot bear the sovereignty of another [*alienus*], has [always] kept the hated secular authority from its mother [the Church]
b. Rather: with due reverence

Of the Members of which the present German *Empire is composed.*

1. After the *German* Nation [peoples], by the help of the *French* [*Franks*], became one Body, it has in all times been thought one of the strongest States in *Europe;* and at this day it is not less regardable, on the account of its bulk, though great parts of it have been ravished <25> from it, and either annexed to other Kingdoms, or formed into separate and independent States.[1] How much the German Empire is now less than it was anciently, has been [thoroughly] shewn by *Hermannus Conringius,* a most skilful man in the German Affairs, in his Book, *de finibus Imperii Germanici, concerning the Bounds of the German Empire.*[2] But it will be enough for us to observe what she has at present.

Germany a potent State, tho' much diminished as to its extent.

The principal Members then of this Body are designed [designated] by the Title of *The States* [*Estates*] *of the Empire,* who have, as we express it, a Right to Sit and Vote in the *Diet.* Tho' many of these are opposed [excluded] by others, |[or whose Right to be immediate States is disputed by other more potent States, who pretend they ought to represent them in the *Diet*]|:[a] The occasion of these Controversies is, because these Po-

---

a. E.p.: that is, they are represented at the Diet by other, more powerful orders [*ordines*], either by a right that is publicly conceded by all concerned or by one that remains ambiguous, in that the latter's challenge to the former's unmediated status, and their attempt to exempt [exclude] them, is opposed by the former [themselves] as well as by the Empire

1. Both Switzerland and the Netherlands, which formerly belonged to the empire, were recognized as independent states in the Treaty of Westphalia (Hammerstein, "Kommentar," 1187).

2. Hermann Conring, *De finibus Imperii Germanici libri II* (Helmstedt, 1654).

49

tent States would make those that are controverted Members of their own Provincial |[States]|,[a] and not of the general *Diet*.[3] But then, as to the Families of the Princes, it is to be observed, that there regularly belongs to each House a certain number of Votes in the *Diet*<, according as the powers it possesses have customarily entailed a right to vote>; as some Houses have only one Vote, some two, some three, some four, and some five. In some Principalities the eldest Brother enjoys the whole Estate [*ditio*], and all the younger must be content with an *Apanage*,[4] and in others, they have all a share, though not an equal one, with the eldest. Where the first of these is observed, the eldest [alone] represents the Person of the whole Family; |[where the latter, they may all come to the *Diet*, but they <26> have altogether but one Vote, of which they must all agree amongst themselves]|.[b]

Which are the Members of the Empire.

2. To prove a Person a Member of the States of the Empire, two things are commonly thought sufficient, 1. if his Name is in the Catalogue or *Matricula* of the |[States]|;[c] and 2. if he is obliged to pay what he con-

---

a. E.p.: *Ordines* / The e.p. as a rule replaces "states" or "estates" [*status*] with "orders" (*ordines*). [Ed.]

b. E.p.: or rather, their concerns are not taken into account. But in the latter instance, where several are in undivided possession of a territory entitled [*capax*] to one vote, they can come to the Diet as individuals but may cast only one vote, about which they must agree among themselves. But where the individuals have been separately invested with their rightful portions of a seat, they also vote as individuals / See V.25. [Ed.]

c. *Ordinum* / e.p.: *Statuum*

3. So-called exempt (excluded) or mediate estates were those whose primary obligation was to other intermediaries, who sometimes assumed their obligations to the empire and thus claimed to speak for them, rather than directly (immediately) to the emperor or empire as such. Understandably, the empire frowned on these relationships, and the Treaty of Westphalia (VIII.3) proposed to reinstate these mediate or exempt estates at the next diet. See *Verfassung des deutschen Reiches*, trans. Dove, 138–39, note 6; and Haberkern and Wallach, *Hilfswörterbuch für Historiker*, "Exemption," 1:187, "Immediat," 1:300–301, "Reichsunmittelbar," 2:529.

4. An *apanage* was a restricted grant (land, stipend, or office) for maintaining noninheriting (male) members of a family.

tributes to the Publick, to the Empire, and not into the Exchequer or Treasury of any other [subordinate]^a State. [Tho' the plainest Proof is, to alledge the Possession of this Priviledge.]^b [For] some pretend they have by mistake paid their *quota* into other inferiour States [another's treasury]; and others say, [on the contrary,] that some others, by meer Usurpation [presumption], have passed by the Provincial Treasury [to which they belonged of Right,] ⁺ and have flown with their share to the publick Treasury; and these Allegations are made, as men endeavour to [acquire or deprive others of the Right of being Members of the *Diet* respectively].^c Nor was there ever yet any *Matricula* extant, in which nothing was wanting or redundant [excessive],^d and about which there was not some Controversie; |[tho' those that were published in the year 51, 56, 66. of the last Century, are thought [the most]⁺ authentick]|.^e But I should however think, that the most ancient *Matricula*'s which represent many as Parts of the States of the Empire, who have been long since excluded out of the *Diet,* are [better than the latter, because they are nothing but Lists of those who were then in the *Diet,* when publick Instruments were made by publick Authority; and therefore from thence undoubted Arguments may be made for both the <27> contending Parties].^f But in the mean time, from this variety in the *Matricula*'s I may safely conclude, That in the most ancient times the number of the States of the Empire was never fixed and certain, [and that all that were enabled by their Wealth or Prudence, to contribute any thing to the Welfare of

a. That is, subordinate to the Empire. The term is added by Bohun. [Ed.]

b. Rather: Though this is plainly to appeal to [the fact of] possession [alone].

c. Rather: to be included among, or to exclude others from, the [Imperial] orders [*ordines*]

d. That is, in which either too few or too many estates were listed. [Ed.]

e. E.p.: though that which was established in the year 1521 at Worms, by the common agreement of Emperor and the Estates, and was supplemented in 1551, 1556, and 1566, may be considered authentic

f. Rather: [merely] lists of those then present at the Diet, rather than authorized public records from which convincing [*indubia*] arguments may be made for either side

their Country, had liberty to be present in]ᵃ the *Diet.* Afterwards the
Poorer [not being able to attend the *Diet,* by reason of the Expence and
Charge, remained willingly at home];ᵇ and [that in after-times others,
who would willingly enough have been there, were excluded by others,
who were too powerful for them to contend with],ᶜ till the States were
by degrees brought to the number we now see them.

It were too tedious for us to transcribe here a [whole] *Matricula,* but
yet I shall represent the Principal of the States [the chief estates], as a
thing absolutely necessary to the forming a Judgment of the Magnitude
of this whole Body.

An account of 3. Amongst the Secular Princes, we give the first Place to the House of
the House of *Austria,* not so much for its Antiquity, as on the score of the greatness
Austria. of its Dominions, and because it has now for some Ages possess'd the
Imperial Throne. This unusual Clemency of the Fates has raised this
Family from a very mean original, to an invidious greatness.

Its Rise. *Rudolphus*⁵[, the first of these, who obtained the *Imperial Dignity,*]⁺ was
Count of *Hapsburg,* and possessed a small Estate, nothing above his
Condition and Title in the Borders [vicinity] of *Switzerland,* but then
he was a good Souldier, and a man of Valour: |[There having been in
his times an *Interregnum* <28> of about 20 years, the State of *Germany*
was in great confusion and disorder. [So] the principal Princes of *Germany* met, and to put an end to these Calamities, resolved to elect
[*creato*] an Emperor. *Wernerus,* then Bishop of *Mentz,* mentioned *Rudolphus,* who had civilly waited upon him in one of his Journeys to
Rome, from *Strasburg* [*Argentina*] to the *Alps,* and he much extolled his
Prudence and Courage [magnanimity], and the Electors of *Cologne* and

---

a. Rather: but that anyone who thought himself of any importance in the state
[*republica*], in terms of either power or prudence, was free to attend
b. Rather: whose care for their private affairs did not leave them any time for public
matters, stayed away on their own
c. Rather: others were excluded by the more powerful
5. Rudolph I (of Hapsburg), 1218–91 A.D.

Trier soon joined with him. Now he that is any thing well acquainted with the Temper of the Churchmen, will, without any difficulty, conjecture what occasion'd this great desire in the Bishop of *Mentz* to raise this Gentleman. [He concluded, he]ᵃ would be the more obnoxious or compliant to him[self], because [the Nobility of his extraction]ᵇ did not [yet] encourage him to act with that freedom another would have used; and besides, he would [in greater degree be obliged to him]ᶜ for his preferment. But then it might seem a wonder that none of the greater [other] Princes should aspire to the Imperial Throne, except we consider the confused state of things in *Germany,* at that time, which made them all [some of them] fearful they might not be able to reduce it into order; and perhaps others of them were not of sufficient age and experience to effect so difficult a Work. Thus the Secular Electors complied with the Spiritual. But then the Elector of *Saxony,* and the Burgrave of *Norimburg* [*Nuremberg*], would not give their Votes for him till he had promised each of them a Daughter in Marriage; and the same was asked by the Duke of *Bavaria,* who [was then present],ᵈ and granted. Thus *Rudolphus* <29> [immediately] became allied to the best Families of *Germany,*]ᵉ which in the beginning was both an honour and a support to this House.

The Imperial Dignity gave him also afterwards opportunity of obtaining a considerable Patrimony for his Posterity; |[for when any Fee [fief] became vacant, none could better pretend to it than one of his own Sons, for to take it to himself, would have been very invidious

---

a. Rather: To wit, he hoped that the latter
b. Rather: his modest family status
c. Rather: be obliged to him alone
d. Rather: then collaborated with those princes
e. E.p.: Deemed suited by the Electors' votes to repair the very confused state of Germany after an interregnum of nearly twenty years, he not only arranged the state [*rempublicam*] in an excellent way but was no less fortunate and industrious in solidifying and expanding the power [*res*] of his own house. For he also linked himself with the first families of Germany through the nuptials of his daughters, / The e.p. version tones down the implied challenge to Austrian claims. [Ed.]

[aroused much ill will]. Thus that House]|[a] obtained *Austria, Stiria* [*Styria*], *Carniola* [*Carinthia*], and the Marquisate of *Vindish* in *Carniola* [*the Wendian March*], and some other Territories <which he [Rudolph] took from the vanquished Ottokar, king of Bohemia, who had [previously] seized them>. |[And in process of time many others were added, by the Bounty of other Emperors, as the Opulent are more frequently obliged [courted] with such Favours than the Poor.[b] Being thus enriched, it became very easie for this Family to match into the best Houses; and because Ladies are not only won by Riches, but dazzled sometimes with the glittering of a new and extraordinary Title, [a Son might easily gain in that case, from a less yielding Father, some new additions, which might][c] set him above the other Dukes.

And yet even here the Prudence [skill] of the House of *Austria* deserves commendation.]|[d] It would have been very invidious [given rise to great jealousy] for this new Family to have taken a *Place* in the *Diets,* above the more ancient; and yet it did not become it to follow the rest[, now it was possessed of the Empire] [+]. Therefore they took the first place amongst the *Spiritual Electors* [*Ecclesiastical Princes*], who have a Bench distinct from the *Secular Princes;* for these [being for the most part descended of lower Families],[e] did without any reluctance yield the first place to this Family. {And yet this their modesty went <30> not unrewarded: for} on this account they [the house of Austria] obtained that Employment or Honour which they call the *Directory* in the Colledge

a. E.p.: for since he was permitted to bestow vacant Fees [fiefs] on others, no reasonable person faulted him for also taking his own family into consideration. Thus his son, Albert,

b. That is, the emperors favored already well-to-do members of their own family by bestowing vacant properties on them. [Ed.]

c. Rather: a son could easily get for himself from an otherwise strict father, the addition of a special title [e.g., archduke] that would / This hereditary title was first assumed by Duke Ernest the Iron around 1414, in accordance with the *privilegium maius.* See II.4 and notes 7 and 9, p. 56. [Ed.]

d. E.p.: To these, many other territories were later added through marriages, in which respect no other family is said ever to have been more fortunate. Since they surpassed the remaining princes in wealth, it was also fair that they exceed the rest of the dukes [*duces*] in the splendor of their title.

e. Rather: having for the most part ascended to princely rank from a lower lineage of the Princes, to be exercised by turns with the [Arch]bishop of *Salsburg*.[6] {These things are so far from deserving the blame of any wise man, that it would have been the utmost degree of stupidity to have done otherwise.}

Thus the House of *Austria* [gained to it self]ª the greatest part |[of the Eastern Countries of *Germany*. After this, they got [In addition, they possess] the Crown of *Hungary*, by almost an Hereditary Title, which amongst other advantages serves as a Bulwark to their other Dominions against the Irruptions of the *Turks*, and gives the *Austrians* many pretences of draining the Moneys of *Germany* [to maintain its Wars against that dreadful Enemy].b]|c

4. We ought well to consider [also not only that the House of *Austria* has continued its self so long in the Imperial Dignity, that there is scarce any other House in *Germany*, which has a Revenue sufficient to bear the Expence of that [splendid] Station; but that they have also found]d means in the interim so to order their Dominions, that without any difficulty they can erect them into an Independent separate State or Kingdom, if any other Family [someone else] should happen to be advanced to the Imperial Crown. For they have procured such Priviledges, that whenever they shall not be pleased to acknowledge the Authority of another Emperor, they may [immediately] say, *They have no business*

This Family has long possessed the Imperial Throne.

---

a. Rather: encompasses within its terrains

b. Rather: through fear of a Turkish war

c. E.p.: of Germany toward the south and the east, which is composed of the Kingdom of Bohemia and the Austrian Provinces properly speaking. Add to this the Kingdom of Hungary, also by hereditary right now that a great portion thereof has been seized from the hands of the barbarians [Turks] by Emperor Leopold's military successes. / The Turkish threat had diminished since the first edition of *Monzambano*. After their defeat in 1683 at the battle of Kahlenberg, the Turks were gradually pushed out of Hungary, a situation formally affirmed in the Peace of Karlowitz (1699). [Ed.]

d. Rather: that the House of Austria has continued its self so long in the Imperial Dignity, not only because there is . . . Station; but also because they have found . . .

6. The Council of Princes (*Reichsfürstenrat*) contained both clergy and laity, the former on account of their ecclesiastical land holdings. It was the second college at the diet, after that of the electors.

with the Empire of Germany, *their Dominions are a separate State [civi-tatem]<, or they acknowledge the Emperor's authority only at their discretion and insofar as it pleases them >.*[7] Which would not only wonderfully [significantly] maim the Empire by depriving it of <31> so great a part of its body, but would also set a dangerous Example to other powerful Princes [for others] to do the like, especially if they conceive they are able to preserve themselves without the assistance of the Empire. Yea, if this example were once given, [even] the meaner and lesser Princes would not continue in the state of Subjects [would reject their lower status]. And thus *Germany* would soon be brought into the same state [condition] with *Italy;* but then it seems to me to be very doubtful, whether [it could so well preserve it self as *Italy* doth].[a]

That I have not rashly feigned all this, will be easily granted, if any one is but pleased to consider, That the Kingdom of *Bohemia* has very little concern with the Empire [rest] of *Germany,* {besides its Vote in the Election of the Emperor;}[8] or if he will but reflect [a bit more carefully] on the greatest part of the Priviledges of the House of *Austria.* It will to this purpose be sufficient to represent [excerpt] a few Heads of the Immunities given by *Charles* V.[9]

The Priviledges granted to this Family by *Charles* V. In the very entrance of this Grant he is pleased to acknowledge, that Men naturally [most of all] desire the welfare of their Families. Then he decrees, [1.] That *Austria* shall be a perpetual Fee of this Family, which

---

a. Rather: it [Italy] will be able to preserve itself in that same manner in the future

7. The broadest of these privileges (*Freiheitsbriefe*), the *privilegium maius* (a spurious counterpart to the *privilegium minus,* issued by Emperor Frederick I in 1156), was actually a mid-fourteenth-century (1359) forgery commissioned by Duke Rudolph IV in order to gain for Austria the electoral rights specified by the Golden Bull (1356). Although Petrarch advised Charles IV not to confirm it, the Hapsburg Emperor Frederick III did so in 1453. Its falsity was not conclusively established until 1856.

8. Bohemia lost its status as an independent kingdom after 1620 and became an imperial crown land. It regained a vote in the Electoral Council of the diet in 1708 (Monzambano, *Über die Verfassung,* trans. Breßlau, 44, note 1).

9. Charles V confirmed the *privilegium maius* in 1530, the year he was crowned emperor by Pope Clement VII.

no future Emperor shall deprive it of. 2.[a] That the Duke of *Austria,* [for the time being,] + shall be such a Counsellor of the Empire, as without his knowledge nothing shall be determined. And yet, 3. He declares his Dominions free from all Contributions to the Empire. 4. And yet obligeth the Empire to the defence of them; so that in all Advantages it [Austria] is a Member, in all Charges it is not. 5. The Duke of *Austria* shall not be obliged to demand the Investiture of his Dominions out of the Bounds <32> of them, but it shall be offered to him in his own Territories; to wit, [because for a naked acknowledgment of the Tenure, he will not confess himself |[subject to the Empire]|;[b] or as if he were to be intreated to own himself a Vassal of the Empire].[c] And then the [Ornaments that are allowed him in this action],[d] do also sufficiently argue, that he is to be treated |[like an Equal, and not like a Subject]|.[e] {6. If he please, he may come to the *Diet;* and if he please, he may forbear.}[10] 7. The *Emperor* has no Author[it]y to rectifie any thing done by him in his own Dominions. 8. The Emperor [Empire] can dispose of no Fees within the Dominions belonging to the House of *Austria.* 9. His Subjects shall not be drawn out of his Dominions to answer in any other Courts. 10. From his Sentence there lies no Appeal. 11. He may without any danger receive such as are put under the BAN of the Empire, so [provided] that he take care to do Justice to the Party injured [the accuser]; but then those that are banished by the Duke of *Austria,* shall be absolved by no other Prince, nor in any other place than in *Austria.* 12. He may lay new Tributes or Taxes [on his own Vassals],[f] at his own pleasure. 13. [Likewise] he may create Earls, Barons, and Gentlemen [nobles] within his own Dominions, which was heretofore [is otherwise]

---

a. The explicit enumeration is Bohun's. [Ed.]

b. E.p.: subject [*obnoxium*] to the Emperor

c. Rather: he is unwilling to confess himself subordinate [*inferiorem*] to the Empire for a bare feudal acknowledgment, but acts, instead, as if he were a vassal of the Empire only per request / That is, he must be asked, and must consent. [Ed.]

d. Rather: insignia that he bears when accepting his fief

e. E.p.: more as an Equal than as a Subject

f. Rather: in his own dominions

10. This privilege was pointless after 1663, when the *Reichstag* began to meet in permanent session at Regensburg.

thought one of the Acts of Soveraignty [in Germany]. 14. Lastly, [to perfect his Power],[a] it is decreed, That in case the Male Line fail in this House, the Estates [dominions] belonging to it shall devolve to the Female Issue; and if there be no Females, neither, the last Possessor shall give or dispose [*alienare*] of them as he thinks fit.

It is to no purpose to add any more, seeing these are sufficient to <33> convince any [moderately] wise man|[. So that the man must be very silly who doth not perceive the *Sham* designed [perpetrated on] the Empire by *Charles* V. when he submitted his 17 Provinces [*Belgium suum*] to the Empire, with a magnificent Promise, that they should pay as much as any two of the Electors paid to the Charges of the Empire. For he well considered that all was to be spent on the *Turkish War,* and the Preservation of the *Austrian* Dominions: and when [since] the Accounts of the Moneys expended in the *Turkish War* were to be in the hands of the Princes of this *Austrian* Family, [the *Low Countries* were not likely to be overcharged, nor to be very ill treated, if they proved slow in the payment].[b] So that it was easie [for an Italian] to observe, That *Charles* V. by this Promise only encouraged the *Germans* to spend their Treasures [*res*] the more freely in the defence of his [someone else's] Territories, when they saw him so freely consent to bring his own Patrimony under the same Burthen.

The Low Countries united to the Empire by Charles V. and why.

[T]ho' perhaps there might be another reason too at the bottom of it, *viz. That whereas his son* Philip *then aspired to the Empire, it might not be objected against him, that he had no Dominions in the Empire, those belonging before* [in Germany] *to the House of* Austria, *being then assigned to his Brother* Ferdinand:[11] Or, perhaps, that the *Germans* might think themselves the more obliged to defend these Provinces, if they were at any time invaded by the French King.[12]

a. Rather: to remove any doubt that he does not grant the Empire any right over his own dominions

b. Rather: the tax collectors in Belgium were not going to be treated too harshly if they were a little sluggish in collecting their portion

11. Ferdinand succeeded as Holy Roman Emperor after Charles's abdication in 1556, while Philip (II) became king of Spain and inherited the Dutch provinces.

12. Six circles of the empire were established at the Diet of Worms in 1495; the

At this time that Line is reduced to two Males, *Leopold* Emperor of
Germany, [(who has, since our Author wrote, had a Son named *Joseph*)] +
and *Charles* King of *Spain* [, who has no Issue]:[a] I have heard many of
the *Germans* wish this Prince [Leopold] a numerous Male Posterity,[b]
out of meer fear that the failing of the Line in <34> this Family may
cause dreadful Convulsions in *Europe* [may require costly funeral
games].[13]][c]

---

number was increased to ten in 1512. The Burgundian Circle including the Dutch
provinces became nominally independent from the empire in 1548, though it retained
certain financial obligations in return for the empire's protection.

13. Charles II died childless in 1700, which led to extinction of the Hapsburg line
in Spain. Shortly before his death he had designated as his heir Philip of Anjou,
grandson of Louis XIV, whom the latter duly acknowledged as Philip V of Spain
(thereby revoking his formal renunciation of 1660, a condition of his marriage to the
Spanish infanta, Maria Theresia). Since Leopold I also claimed the Spanish crown
because of his marriage to a younger sister of Charles II, this led to the War of the
Spanish Succession (1702–13). Leopold had two sons: Joseph I (1678–1711) and
Charles VI (1685–1740), the former of whom reigned 1705 to 1711, and the latter from
1711 to 1740.

a. Rather: whom few people expect to live much longer

b. The passage is written as Bohun saw the situation in 1690, not as Pufendorf
saw it in 1667, when he wrote: ". . . wish that other prince [i.e., Leopold] a marriage
rich in male offspring." [Ed.]

c. E.p.: who knows how easy it is to elude the specious legal vocabulary flaunted
so fervently by academics [*Scholasticis*], when one may safely disregard another's
strength.

These things are by no means meant to create ill will toward that house [of Haps-
burg], since it surely deserves praise for its skillful exploitation of fortune's favors in
order to consolidate its position. However, there are also those who do not like this
interpretation because[, they say,] those privileges were bestowed on the Austrians
by Frederick I. long before the Hapsburgs acquired Imperial rank, and so before they
could entertain any thought of using them to secure it for themselves. Others add
that though those privileges were acquired by a disputed [*oneroso*] legal title, they
have brought Germany much good. For Henry, Count [*Markgraf*] of Austria, gave
up [for them] his claim to Bavaria, over which he had been engaged in dispute with
Henry the Lion of Saxony, to the disturbance of all Germany.

However, since Frederick I. granted the privilege [i.e., *privilegium minus*] to
Count Henry for a particular reason, it could not go beyond his own person and
family. By no means was it bestowed on the province of Austria as such, so that
whoever later on controlled it should enjoy that privilege no matter what, apart from
any right derived from Henry. For the claim to Bavaria had been given up by Henry
in his capacity as Count [*Marchio jure*], not by the Estates of the province of Austria.

The Counts
Palatine of
the *Rhine*, and
the Dukes of
Bavaria.
5. The Family of the Counts *Palatine* of the *Rhine,* and of the Dukes of *Bavaria,* are [is], as to Antiquity, equal to the best, and it enjoys a vast Tract of Land, which extends from the *Alps* to the River *Moselle,* <though dotted here and there by the territories of others,> and two

---

Much less do the reasons adduced by Frederick I. [for bestowing the privilege] pertain to the family of the Hapsburgs, which never had a right to Bavaria and therefore could not be compensated with the privilege for restoring peace to Germany by yielding it. Nor could it claim for itself, upon assuming control of those provinces after the prior Austrian family's extinction, the special privileges granted to that family, unless they were later bestowed on it by its own Emperors [i.e., of its own line].

The latter did not arouse ill will by granting their family members what had already been obtained by earlier possessors of that province [Austria], especially since no one could be found to object to that bestowal. Nor is it any objection to say that the intentions of those who initially granted or received the privilege differed from those of later parties who knew how to apply it in ways not previously envisioned. Of course, if Frederick I. could have foreseen such an interpretation and effect of that privilege, he would have gravely violated the Imperial office by granting it, and taken the first step toward the destruction of the Empire. For if all princes enjoyed such a privilege—which, as far as I know, no other Emperor has given to any of the Estates [*Ordinum*]—Germany would long ago have come apart at the seams. As it is, it cannot fall to any of them unless a particular Emperor wishes, as it were, to marry the Imperial dignity to his own family.

Still more loosely joined with Germany [than Austria] are the Belgian provinces [Netherlands], which Emperor Charles V. linked to the Empire under the name of "the Burgundian Circle," promising that they would carry as much of the public burden as two Electors. The chief reason for this move, it seems, was to make the Germans believe that they should send aid to those conjoined with them by that name, if those provinces were ever attacked by the French, and to involve Germany in all the wars which the House of Austria is almost continually waging with France. Perhaps he wanted also in this way to make the Estates more willing to contribute money to the Turkish war, for which most taxes were sought at the time, by showing that the Emperor was calling upon his own territories to carry their part of the burden. And, is it possible that he also sought to preclude objections to the Imperial aspirations of his son, Phillip [of Spain], because the latter had no territories in Germany after the Austrian patrimonial lands had been given to Ferdinand [of Austria]? Whatever reason moved him, that association had no other effect than the vote cast in Burgundy's name in the Diet. For the liberty [independence] of the Belgians was so amply provided for that that entire incorporation was limited to the mere payment of taxes deemed necessary for the common safety of Germany—which the Belgians still refused to pay. And on the other hand the German Estates never deemed themselves obligated to participate in the Belgian Wars, [acting] as if these did not matter to them.

Dukedoms in the Borders of the *Low Countries* [*Belgii*]. It is divided into two Lines, the *Rudolfian* and *William*[*ite*]. One of these [the latter] is possess'd of the Dukedom of *Bavaria,* and has ever been thought very   *Bavaria.* Rich, and in the [last tedious Civil War it got also the Electoral Dignity from the *Palatinate* Family].[a] And for almost an hundred years it has possessed the Electorate of *Cologne* [(Prince *Clement,* who was lately chosen, being likely still to continue it in this Family, tho' powerfully opposed by the King of *France*);[14] his Predecessor also possess'd the Bishopricks of *Liege* [*Lüttich*] and *Hildisheim*].[b]

The *Rudolfian* Line is divided into many Branches, |[the Principal [at   The *Palatine* the head] of which is the Elector *Palatine,* and it [who still] enjoys   Family. the *Lower Palatinate* on the *Rhine,*[15] a Country [region] which for its strength, pleasantness, and fertility, was equal to the best parts of *Germany*[, before the French with Fire and Sword barbarously laid it desolate, not only demolishing, but burning down to the Ground the

---

Today the male line of that house, which had been reduced to two, has been, as it were, reinvigorated by Emperor Leopold through [his sons,] Joseph and Charles, while King Charles of Spain has not been blessed with the offspring he hoped for.

a. Rather: last war its booty included the Electoral Dignity as well as the upper Palatinate [*Oberpfalz*], which it had seized from its relations / e.p.: Thirty Years' War . . .

b. Rather: in addition to which the current Elector [*modernus*] also has the Bishopricks . . . / Pufendorf (in 1667) meant Max Henry of Bavaria, archbishop of Cologne from 1650 to 1688. The material in parentheses was added by Bohun in 1690, when he could render *modernus* as "predecessor." [Ed.] / e.p.: as well as other adjoined bishoprics [*Praesulatibus*]

14. Joseph Clement (1671–1723), a brother of Max Emanuel, elector of Bavaria, was appointed in 1688 (at the age of seventeen) by Pope Innocent III to succeed the Francophile Max Henry to the archbishopric of Cologne, one of the spiritual electorates of the empire. This move was supported by Emperor Leopold I and most other European rulers (including William of Orange) because it frustrated the efforts of Louis XIV to expand his influence in northern Germany through his own candidate, Cardinal Wilhelm Fürstenberg, then bishop of Straßburg.

15. The lower (*inferior,* western) Palatinate refers to the *Kurpfalz* (or *Rheinpfalz*), which includes Heidelberg. The upper (or eastern) Palatinate (*Oberpfalz*) is still a region of Bavaria, adjacent to Bohemia or the modern Czech Republic.

greatest part of its Towns, Cities, Palaces, and Churches].[a] The Count

Palatine of *Newburg* possess'd heretofore [still possesses] the Dukedoms of *Juliers* [*Jülich*] and *Montz* [*Berg*], and some Dominions on the *Danube*. [And in the year 1685, *Charles Lewis* the last Elector dying without Issue, *Philip William* of the House of *Newburg*, succeeded in the *Electorate* too, which in the year 1688, he resigned to his Son *John William*,

being grown very old, and <35> sorely oppressed by the French.][b] Besides these, there are the *Palatines* of *Sultzback*, *Simmeren*, *Deuxpont*, or *Zuibrucken* [*Zweibrücken*] [(as the *Germans* call it)][+] *Birkenfield* and *Lawtreck* [*Lautereck*][, all with modest domains]. The Family of *Deuxpont* [also] produced *Charles Gustavus* King of *Sweden*, who [whose son,

Charles, though still a minor] now reigns in that Kingdom,[16] [and] who by the Peace of *Osnaburg* has obtained in *Germany* the Dukedoms of

Breme[*n*], *Ferden* [*Verden*], and the upper [western] *Pomerania*, together with *Stetin*, the Principality of *Rugen* [*Rügen*], and the Barony of *Wismar*.

This Family [enjoys now also Princes of great worth and virtue].[c] For

a. Added by Bohun. / The French incursions in the Kurpfalz began in 1688–89. Actually, the region had already been devastated earlier that century, when Elector Friedrich V lost his electoral status to Maximilian I, Duke of Bavaria, whose troops looted Heidelberg in 1623 and sent its precious library (the so-called *Biblioteca Palatina*) to the Vatican, where most of it remains today. Friedrich's son, Karl Ludwig, regained the electoral status in 1649, but Maximilian kept his as well. [Ed.]

b. Added by Bohun. / After Karl Ludwig died in 1680, he was succeeded by his son Karl II, who died in 1685 without issue. With the extinction of the Calvinist Pfalz-Simmern line, the Palatinate went to the Catholic line of Pfalz-Neuburg, first to Philipp Wilhelm (1615–90) and then his son Johann Wilhelm (1658–1716). Louis XIV contested the Neuburg succession on the grounds of the marriage of his brother, Philippe of Orleans (in 1671), to Karl Ludwig's daughter (Charlotte Elizabeth, or Liselotte) and destroyed Heidelberg (1693) during the War of the Palatine Succession (1688–97). [Ed.]

c. Rather: also flourishes today on account of the fame of its highly praised princes

16. Charles X, or Charles X Gustav (1622–60), was the son of John Casimir, Count of Pfalz-Zweibrücken, and Gustav Adolphus's sister, Catherine. He succeeded to the Swedish throne in 1654, after Christina abdicated, and was succeeded in turn, after an interregnum, by his young son, Charles XI (1655–97), who assumed full powers in 1672. Pfalz-Zweibrücken went to Charles XI in 1692, after John Casimir's death, and it remained Swedish until the death of Charles XII in 1718.

as the *Bavarian* Line are celebrated for their great Piety, so the [Electoral Family have been much esteemed for their Prudence];[a] which character will belong equally to the House of *Newburg*. The last of this Family was on that account thought worthy of the Crown of *Poland*, tho' he was no way related to the Families that had worn it.[17] And Prince *Rupert*, [a Branch of the elder House of the *Palatinate*, who died in *England*, was a Person of great Valour and Worth,][+] and famous over all *Christendom*, for the Wars he had managed by Sea and Land]|.[b, 18]

6. The Dukes of *Saxony* possess almost the [entire] middle parts of *Germany*, to whom belongs *Misnia* [*Meißen*], *Thuring*, and a small Country [region] on the *Elbe*, called the *Upper Saxony*, *Lusatia* [*Lausitz*, *Łużyce*] and in *Franconia*, the Dukedoms of *Coburg*, and the Earldom of *Henneburg*, [overall] a Country celebrated in some parts for its Fertility, and in others for its Mines.

The House of
Saxony.

a. Rather: Palatine Elector [Karl Ludwig] is regarded, on account of his rare wisdom and other virtues, among the ornaments of his nation [*nationis*] / See Pufendorf's 1667 preface and its note 13. [Ed.]

b. E.p.: [and] now possesses, after the extinction of the previous [Simmerian] line, beside the lower Palatinate—one of the most fertile and pleasant parts of Germany—the duchies of Jülich and Berg, along with the small territory of Neuburg on the Danube. The duchy of Zweibrücken fell [in 1692] to Charles XI, king of Sweden, though the French have laid a sophistical claim to it as a fief of Metz. Other Palatine counts include those of Lautereck or Veldenz, Sulzbach, and Birkenfeld, some of whom have also been hard pressed by their French neighbors

17. Pfalz-Neuburg's claim to the Polish succession rested on Philipp Wilhelm's (first) marriage, in 1642, to Anna Katharina Konstanze (d. 1651), a daughter of Sigismund III of Poland.

18. Prince Rupert (1619–82) was a younger son of Frederick V of the Palatinate and Elizabeth, daughter of James I, and thus a brother of Karl Ludwig. Imprisoned for three years by the emperor for continuing to press his father's cause, Rupert came to England in 1636 and fought vigorously in the English civil war on behalf of his uncle, Charles I, acquiring a reputation as leader of the Royalist cavalry. After the demise of the Royalist cause, he became a buccaneer in the Caribbean (where he attacked English shipping), returned to England after the Restoration, and finally became director of the Hudson's Bay Company. The city of Prince Rupert, in British Columbia, is named after him. The eight words Pufendorf gives him here understate his reputation throughout Europe. See Rebitsch, *Rupert von der Pfalz* (2005), and Kitson, *Prince Rupert: Soldier* (1994) and *Prince Rupert: Admiral* (1998).

This Family is divided into two Branches, *viz. Albert* and *Ernest:* |[the last [first] of these is in possession of the *Electorate,* and the second Son [among the three remaining brothers] is to be Bishop [Archbishop] of *Magdeburg* [for life];[19] of the first [latter] <36> are the Dukes of *Altenburg, Gotham,* and 4 Brothers of the Family of *Wimar* [*Weimar*], and a numerous Posterity besides]|.[a]

The House of
Brandenburg.

7. Next these are the Marquesses of *Brandenburg,* the Head of which Family is one of the *Electors,* who has large Dominions in *Germany.* Besides *Prussia,* which is placed now out of the [Roman] Empire, which also he lately obtained from the Crown of *Poland,* he has *Mark,* [the further [eastern] *Pomerania* gained from the *Swedes,* tho' it belonged to him by Inheritance, upon the death of the last Duke without Issue; *Halberstad, Minden,* and *Camin,* three Bishopricks, given him as an Equivalent for the hither [western] *Pomerania;* and he was also to have that of *Magdeburg* after the death of *Augustus* the present Possessor of the House of *Saxony.*][b] These Dominions are large and fruitful, yet some

a. E.p.: The former divided itself into four branches through the sons of Johann Georg I; the latter diffused itself through William of Weimar and his four sons, and through Ernest of Gotha and his seven sons, as well as through numerous grandsons. / Altenburg belonged to Weimar since 1672 and is not mentioned separately in the e.p. [Ed.]

b. Rather: the further [eastern] *Pomerania* [i.e., *Hinterpommern*], the duchy of Crossen in Silesia, the duchy of Cleve, [and] the territories of Mark and Ravensberg. Also, in place of the [western] part of Pomerania [i.e., *Vorpommern*], which was ceded to the Swedes, and which would otherwise have fallen to him after the extinction of the ducal family of Pomerania, he received as an equivalent the bishoprics of *Halberstadt, Minden,* and *Camin,* and, after the death of *Augustus* of *Saxony* [in 1680], the archbishopric of *Magdeburg.* / Bohun omits some important lands (viz., Cleve, where Locke encountered the Great Elector in 1665–66) and partially obscures the distinction between eastern and western Pomerania. Much to the chagrin of Frederick Wilhelm, the latter went to the Swedes as part of the peace settlement of 1648 and did not come to Brandenburg until 1720. [Ed.]

19. Bohun confuses this passage. The Albertine branch included Johann Georg I, elector of Saxony from 1611 to 1656, and his three brothers, the second eldest of whom (August) was administrator of the archdiocese of Magdeburg until his death in 1680. After that, Magdeburg went to Frederick William of Brandenburg, the Great Elector. Pufendorf takes note of this in the e.p. revision.

believe he would have chosen the two *Pomerania*'s entire, before all the rest.

{I remember when I was in my return from *Germany*, being at an Entertainment at *Padoua* [*Padua*], in which were present some *Italian* and *French* Marquesses, I had an occasion to say the Marquess of *Brandenburg* could travel 200 German miles in his own Dominions, without lying one night in any other Prince's Country (though in some places it was indeed interrupted [by intervening territories]) whereupon many that were present, began to suspect I was guilty of the common fault of Travellers, [i.e., exaggeration] and my Faith [credibility] was much questioned [by my countrymen, who for some reason hardly ever leave their native land], but that an old Souldier [officer], who was present, and had served long in *Germany*, and had been one of my Acquaintance[s] in that Prince's Court, delivered me from their Suspicions [supported my statements]. They could not but <37> blush thereupon, when they considered, that some [many] prided themselves in this Title [Marggrave] in *Italy* and *France*, who were scarcely Masters of Two Hundred Acres of Land: So little did they understand, that [our]+ German MARG-GRAVES are [much] more considerable than their [our] *Marquesses*.}

There is another Branch of this Family in *Franconia*, who (if I am not mistaken) possess the old Inheritance of the *Burggraves* of *Norimburg* [*Nuremberg*], and are divided into two Lines, that of *Culemback* [*Kulmbach*], and that of *Onolzbeck* [*Onolzbach, Ansbach*].

8. Next after the Electors follow some other Princes, whose Houses are still extant; and because amongst these there are various Contests for the Precedence, I would not have the Order I here observe, give any prejudice to any of them in these their {vain} Pretences [those disputes].

Of the other Princes of the Empire.

The Dukes of BRUNSWICK and LUNENBURG possess a very considerable Territory in the Lower *Saxony*. They are divided into two Branches; |[to the first of these belongs the Dukedom of *Brunswick*, now enjoyed by an ancient Gentleman;[20] two Brothers have divided the Dukedom of

The Dukes of Brunswick and Lunenburg.

---

20. Herzog August the Younger (1579–1666) of Braunschweig-Wolfenbüttel, who built up the famous library collection in Wolfenbüttel.

Lunenburg between them, one of which resides at *Zel* [*Celle*], the other at *Hannover,* and the third Brother is now Bishop of *Osnaburg*]|.[a, 21]

Mechlenburg. The Dukes of MECHLENBURG have a small Tract of Land belonging to them, which lies between the *Baltick* Sea and the River *Elbe;* and this Family |[is now]|[b] divided into two Branches, *Swerin* [*Schwerin*] and *Custrow* [*Güstrow*].

Wurtemburg. The Duke of WURTEMBURG has in [*Franconia*][c] a great and a powerful Territory; his <38> Relations have also in the extreamest parts of *Ger-*
Montpelgart. *many* the Earldom of MONTBELGARD [Montbéliard] in *Alsatia.* The
Hassia. *Lantgrave* of HASSIA [Hessen] has also a large Country, and is divided
Baden. into the Branches of CASSEL and DARMSTAD. The Marquesses of BA-DEN have a long but narrow Country on [the right bank of] the *Rhine,* and are also divided into two Lines, that of *Baden,* properly so called, and that of *Baden Durlach.*

Holstein. The Dukes of *Holstein* possess a part of the Promontory of *Juitland* [the Cimbrian peninsula], which by reason of the Seas washing its East-

a. E.p.: Wolfenbüttel and Celle, whose domain has been bifurcated up to now, with one brother [Georg Wilhelm] residing at Celle and the other [Ernst August the Older] at Hannover. The latter also obtained the bishopric of Osnabrück for his lifetime, and later on the Electoral dignity

b. E.p.: was formerly / This variant was probably introduced by Gundling, since Pufendorf died in 1694 and the Güstrower line of Mecklenburg did not end till 1695 (*Severinus*, ed. Salomon, 58, note 5). [Ed.]

c. Rather: Swabia [*Suevia*] / Although both are now partially in Bavaria, Franconia and Swabia had separate histories as circles of the empire. [Ed.]

21. The two brothers were Georg Wilhelm (1624–1705) of Lüneburg-Celle, and Johann Friedrich (1625–79) of Lüneburg-Calenberg. The third brother, Ernst August the Elder (1629–98), became secular "bishop" of Osnabrück in 1662. After Johann Friedrich's death, his holdings went to Ernst August, who became elector of Hannover (the empire's ninth electorate) in 1692; and then to the latter's son, Georg Ludwig (1660–1727), in whose hands—after Georg Wilhelm's death—all of Lüneburg was finally united. Since Ernst August's wife, Sophie (sister of Karl Ludwig), was a daughter of Frederick V and Elisabeth Stuart (daughter of James I), Georg Ludwig as her oldest son became George I of England in 1714, according to the English Act of Settlement (1701).

ern and Western sides, is very Rich. That part of *Holstein* which belonged to the Empire, is possessed [governed] by the King of *Denmark* and the Duke of *Holstein Gothorp;* |[which last]|ᵃ has also the Bishoprick of *Lubeck.* The Dukedom of *Sleswick* doth not belong to [is not dependent on] the Empire. <There are still other lines of the Dukes of Holstein sprung from their descendants, whose numerical increase has gone beyond the bounds of their modest territory.> The Duke of Sax[ony]-Lawemburg |[has a small Estate [territory] in the Lower *Saxony*]|,ᵇ and almost equal to that of the Prince[s] of Anhalt in the Upper *Saxony.*

Lubeck.

Sax-
Lawemburg.

9. These are the ancient Princes of the Empire. For the Dukes of Savoy and Lorrain, though Fees depending on the Empire, and so having Seats in the *Diet,* yet by reason of the Situation of their Countries, they are in a manner separated from the Empire, and have different *Interests.*

Savoy and
Lorrain.

Ferdinand II,²² who, as many believe, designed the subduing [of] the Power of the *German Princes,* and to gain an Absolute Authority [*Imperium*] over them, amongst other Arts by him imployed, [brought into the *Diet* many Princes, which]ᶜ depended entirely on <39> him. He intended by their Votes to equal, if not overballance, the Suffrages of the ancient Princes, if he should be at any time forced to call a [general] *Diet,* which yet he avoided as much as was possible; or that he might shew at least, that there was no reason why the ancient Princes should so much value their Power [be so proud of their status], seeing he was able, when he pleased, to set as many as he pleased on the same Level with them. And the Princes of the old Creation [the eminence of the old families] had without question been very much endangered, if the Emperor could have created Lands as easily as he could give Titles.

Ferdinand II.
increased the
number of the
Princes.

a. E.p.: whose house
b. E.p.: formerly had a small region in Lower Saxony on the Elbe / The Lauenburg line died out in 1689 (*Verfassung des deutschen Reiches,* ed. Denzer, 1994, 71, note 14; *Severinus,* ed. Salomon, 59, note 1).
c. Rather: elevated to the order of Princes many who
22. Ferdinand II (1578–1637), Holy Roman Emperor from 1619 to 1637.

Amongst those however that then gained Places in the *Diet,* [albeit with some resistance,] <and only upon the condition that, if they did not yet have them, they would later acquire goods worthy of a Prince's rank,>

The Titles of Eleven of his creation.

are [so far as I know] these; the Prince[s] of *Ho[h]enzolleren, Eggenburg, Nassaw-Hadmar,* <*Sigen,*> *Nassaw-Dillenburg, Lobkowitz, Salm, Dietrichstein, Aversberg,* and *Picolomini*<, Schwartzenberg, Portia, East Frisia, Fürstenberg, Waldec, Oetingen>.[23] But then this Project of *Ferdinand* miscarrying, and the Estates [means] of the new Princes bearing no proportion with that of the ancient Families, their advancement to this Dignity has never been found as yet of any use to them [vis-à-vis the latter]. {And they have also been much exposed to the Reproaches [ridicule] of the ancient Princes (as the new Nobility is ever slighted by the old) [and they have taken it up as a Proverb against them,]a *That they have got nothing by this Exaltation, but of Rich Counts,* (or Earls) *to be made Poor Princes.* Yet it is to be considered, That the most ancient Nobility had a beginning [was new once], and that these Families in time may get greater Estates.} |[Though]|b the easiest way <for surrounding themselves with wealth> is <40> now foreclosed against them, [by restraining the Emperor from disposing of the vacant Fees as he thinks fit].c

The Ecclesiastick States,

10. The Next Bench [of princes] in the *Diet* belongs to the Bishops of *Germany,* and Abbots. Though this Order consists of men of no very great Birth, as being but Gentlemen, or [at best]+, the Sons of Barons or Earls, and advanced to this Dignity by the Election of their Chapters;[24] yet in the *Diet,* and other publick Meetings, [for the most part,

a. Rather: who say

b. E.p.: Especially since

c. Rather: because the Emperor may not confer vacant fiefs of any importance on whomever he pleases

23. These e.p. additions had been elevated to princely rank since the preparation of the first edition. See II.12, note 30, p. 73.

24. Minor nobility, as well as noninheriting children, often saw the church as their only way to worldly advancement. Indeed, the church absorbed many such social misfits, as it were, and thus relieved the pressure otherwise placed on secular institutions.

they are placed]ᵃ above the Temporal Nobility: For since the Fortune of the Churchmen in these latter Ages has [been so vastly different from what it was in the beginning of Christianity],ᵇ it were very absurd to expect they are now bound to observe those [obsolete] Laws of Modesty our Saviour at first prescribed [them];ᶜ and perhaps those Laws too were by him designed only for the [those] Primitive Times: For in truth, it would have been ridiculous for Fishermen and Weavers ambitiously to seek the Precedence of Noblemen [a higher place]; who were to earn their [daily] Bread with the labours of their Hands, or to subsist on voluntary Contributions.

Now [though] the Authority and Revenues of the Churchmen is very great [quite respectable] [in all those Countries that ever were under the Papacy];ᵈ yet their Riches and Power are no where so great as in *Germany,* there being few of them [in the Empire] ⁺ whose Dominions and [domestic] Equipage is not equal to that of the Secular Nobility. And <41> their Power [jurisdiction] and Authority over their Vassals [subjects] is of the same nature. And many of them are also more fond of their *Helmets* than their *Miters,* and are much fitter to involve their Country in Wars, and their Neighbours in Troubles, than to propagate true Piety.²⁵ [But however],ᵉ in these later Ages there are more than there were in former times, who are not ashamed to take Orders, and [only] once or twice in a year to shew the World how expert they are in expressing the Gestures, and representing the Ceremonies of the most August [holy] Sacrifice [i.e., the Mass].

Once very rich and powerful.

a. Rather: they are placed almost
b. Rather: departed so immensely from the meager circumstances of the ancient clergy
c. Rather: to that order of men
d. Rather: throughout the whole of Christendom where Catholic rites are in effect
e. Rather: Indeed
25. Perhaps a reference to the aggressive Christoph Bernhard, Freiherr von Galen (1606–78), Catholic prince-bishop of Münster (1650–78), who imposed an absolute rule on the city in 1661. The Dutch Republic made some moves to assist the city but stopped short of direct intervention. In response, von Galen undertook hostilities against the Republic on two subsequent occasions, as he did against the Turks, the French, and the Swedes.

Now much
diminished.

But then, whereas of old their Estates equalled, if not exceeded, that [the domains] of the Secular Princes, the Reformation of Religion, which was embraced by the greatest part of *Germany,* and <whose seizure of ecclesiastical goods was confirmed by the Treaty of Passau, the Peace of Augsburg, and later by> the Peace of *Westphalia* [in the year 1648],[a] have strangely [considerably] diminished them; for in the Circles of the Upper and Lower *Saxony* the Churchmen have very little left: But then, in the Upper [southern] *Germany* (if you except the Dukedom of *Wurtemburg*) [they escaped better].[b] Now the reason of this is this; The *Saxons* being more remote, did not fear the Efforts of [Emperor] *Charles* V. so much as the other Princes, who were awed by his Neighbourhood to them, and oppressed by his Presence: Besides, in *Saxony* their [Churchmen's] Dominions were intermixed with [those of] Potent Secular Princes, and consequently lay exposed to their Incursions; but in the Upper [southern] *Germany* <and in Westphalia> they were seated nearer one another <and better suited for rendering mutal assistance>,

They possess
the greatest
part of the
Lands on the
Rhine.

and [especially] on the *Rhine,* which is the most fruitful part of *Germany,* they <42> were possessed of the whole Country, except what belongs to the Elector *Palatine,* which[c] as it interrupts that beautiful Chain of Church-Lands, {has for that reason alone, I perswade my self, been looked on by them with an evil Eye.} //This their Neighbourhood has in the mean time contributed very much to the preserving them from the Reformation, one of them assisting another to expel that dangerous Guest, till the *French* at last, by a just Judgment of God, (though a Catholick Nation, as they call it) came in to revenge their Contempt of the True Religion, and has laid the far greatest part of these populous well-built fruitful Countries in Ashes twice or thrice within the Memory of

a. Added by Bohun. / The Treaty of Passau (1552) and the Peace of Augsburg (1555) legitimated Protestantism (i.e., Lutheranism) in the empire, with the latter also establishing the principle that each ruler could determine the official religion within his own territories (*cuius regio, eius religio*). The seizure of ecclesiastical holdings may also allude to the so-called ecclesiastical reservation. See V.10–11, notes 8–11, pp. 129 and 131. [Ed.]

b. Rather: there was less booty [for secular princes]

c. Rather: who / That is, it was the elector himself who was looked at with the evil eye. [Ed.]

Man, and now especially in the year now current 1689. But to return to our Author.)\\[26]

11. Ecclesiastick States, which are [not yet][a] come into the hands of the Protestant Princes, are these: The three Archbishopricks of *Mentz, Trier,* and *Cologne,* which are three of the Electors, and the Archbishopricks of *Saltsburg* and *Besanzon* in *Burgundy*{; for, as for *Magdeburg,* it is [now] a meer Lay-Fee}.[27] The inferiour [simple] Bishopricks are, *Bamberg, Wurtzburg, Worms, Spires* [*Speyer*], *Aichstad* [*Eichstätt*], *Strasburg, Constance, Au*[*g*]*sburg, Hildisheim, Paderborn, Freisingen, Ratisbone* [*Regensburg*], *Passaw,* {*Trent*}, *Brixen* [in *Tirol*][+], *Basil* [*Basel*], *Liege* [*Lüttich*], *Osnaburg, Munster, Curen* [*Chur*] [in *Curland*].[b] The Master of the *Teutonick* Order[28] has the first Seat amongst the Bishops. And we must observe too, that in our times there are sometimes two or more Bishopricks united [in the same Person][+], either <43> because the Revenues of one single Diocess were not thought sufficient to maintain the Dignity and Splendor of a Prince's Court, or that they might by that means be rendred more formidable to those that hated them [their rivals]. The Bishoprick of *Lubeck* is very little better than a part of the

The Ecclesiastick Electors.

Mentz, Trier, and *Cologne.*

The Bishops.

a. E.p.: not / This small change signifies Pufendorf's later resignation to the status quo and his more positive view of the united empire (containing both Protestants and Catholics) as a necessary bulwark against French expansionism. [Ed.]

b. Added by Bohun. / Chur is an old city in the canton of Graubünden in Switzerland, while Kurland or *Curonia* was a Baltic province in Livonia and became part of Latvia after World War I. [Ed.]

26. Bohun speaks as an Anglican: the Catholic French are God's instrument for punishing these Catholic regions for rejecting the "true religion" (i.e., Protestantism). The reference to 1689 as "the year now current" indicates that Bohun's 1696 edition was in fact a reprint of the 1690 edition, prepared already in 1689.

27. See note 19 in this chapter. The archbishopric had been secularized as a duchy in 1648 and was occupied by the Great Elector's troops already after 1666, even though the Great Elector did not formally take possession of it until 1680.

28. A German order of knights [*equites*] (like the Hospitallers and Templars) established by the pope at the end of the twelfth century. After their military and charitable activities in Palestine had ended, the Teutonic Knights became, as it were, Christian mercenaries in eastern Europe, establishing themselves especially in eastern Prussia, which its grand masters ruled as a Polish fief until 1660, when it became a part of Brandenburg.

Patrimony of the Duke of *Holstein,* and all the Country has also embraced the Protestant Religion. Amongst the [Abbies which are called
Prelates],[a] are these; *Fuld[a], Kempten, Elwang, Murback, Luders,* the
Master of [the knightly order of] St. *John, Berchtelsgaden, Weissenburg,
Pruym [Prüm], Stablo,* and *Corwey.* The rest of the Prelates, who are
not Princes, are divided into two Benches, that of the *Rhine,* and that
of *Schwaben* or *Suabia,* [one of each of which has a][b] Vote in the Diet,
and they are esteemed equal to the Counts or Earls of the Empire.

Mitered Abbots

The Prelates that are not Princes but vote in the Diet.

12. The Estate [condition] of the Counts, or Earls; and Barons [*Frei-
herren*] of the Empire, is also much more splendid and rich than that
of men enjoying the same Dignities in other Kingdoms. For they have
almost the same Priviledges [rights] with the Princes, and the ancient
Earldoms had [have] also large Territories belonging to them; whereas
in other Kingdoms a small Farm or Mannour shall dignifie its owner
with that Title. Yet the Division of the Estate amongst the Brothers has
damnified [hurt] many of the German Families, [and][c] is only to be
admitted in *Plebeian* Families, for its Equity and Piety sake. Some others
have been equally ruined by the [Carelesness and Luxury <44> of their
Ancestors],[d] and their prodigal Expences.

The Earls and Barons of the Empire

At this day, the Earls have four Votes in the Diet, one for *Wetteraw,*
another for *Schwaben,* a third for *Franconia,* and the fourth for *Westphalia.*
The Earls which are known to me, are these; NASSAU, {OLDENBURG},[29]
FURSTEMBERG, HOHENLOHE, HANAW, SAIN [SAYN], WIT[T]GEN-
STEIN, LEININGEN, SOLMS, WALDECK, ISENBURG, STOLBERG,
WIED, MANSFELD, REUSSEN [REUß], OETINGEN, MONTFORT,
KO[E]NIGSECK, FUGGER, SULTZ, CRONBERG, SINTZENDORF,

Have 4 Votes.

Their Names.

a. Rather: abbots or prelates with princely rank
b. Rather: each of which has one
c. Rather: this is a great ill for illustrious houses and
d. Rather: lazy management of their patrimony
29. Oldenburg went to Christian V of Denmark in 1676, after its count left no
descendants.

WALLENSTEIN, PAP[P]ENHEIM, CASTELL, L[O]EWENSTEIN, ER-
BACH, LIMBURG, SCHWARTZENBURG [SCHWARZBURG], BENTHEIM,
{OSTFRI[E]SLAND, (who is now made a Prince)}[30] [RHINE, and
WALTS],[a] RANTZOW, and perhaps many other[s], whose Nobility is not
to be prejudiced by my silence. And as to those I have named, I pretend
no skill in the marshalling of them according to their proper Places.
There are also many Earls and Barons [in the Hereditary Countries be-
longing to the Emperor, who being of late Creation, or subject to other
States, have no Place or Vote in the *Diets* of *Germany,* and therefore are
not to be mentioned here].[b]

13. There is also in *Germany* no small number of Free Cities, who are
subject to no Prince or State [estate], but are immediately under the
Emperor and the Empire, and are therefore called IMPERIAL CITIES. In
the *Diet* they constitute a particular *College,* which is divided into two
[classes, commonly called] BENCHES, that of the *Rhine,* and that of
Schwaben. The Principal of these are, NORIMBERG, AUGSBURG, <45>
COLOGNE, LUBECK, ULM, {STRASBURG [*Argentoratum*],} FRANK-
FORD, RATISBONE [Regensburg], AIX LA CHAPELLE, or AKEN [Aa-
chen], <and Straßburg, which awaits its return to the Empire;> [of lesser

The Free Cities make a College in the Diet.

a. Rather: LIPPE, the RHINE- AND FOREST-COUNT / *Rheni et Sylvarum;* translated as *Rhein- und Wildgraf* in *Verfassung des deutschen Reiches,* ed. Denzer, 1994,
77. This difficult expression refers to the honorary titles *Wildgraf* (*comes silvester*) and
Raugraf (*comes hirsutus*) attached to territories in Nahegau that devolved on the Palatinate (on the Rhine) in the seventeenth century, and that Karl Ludwig bestowed
in 1667 on his morganatic wife, Marie Louise von Degenfeld, and the thirteen children he had with her. [Ed.]

b. Rather: in the hereditary domains of the emperor, or only recently been elevated to that rank, who have no place in the Diet since they are subject to other estates.
It is not worth our effort to enumerate them / e.p.: , both in other parts of Germany
and, in great numbers, in the hereditary domains of the emperor, who, whether they
are more ancient or only recently elevated to that rank, have no place in the Diet
since they are subject to other estates. It is not worth our effort to enumerate them

30. The e.p. includes East Frisia among the newer princes admitted to *Reichstag*
in 1667. See II.9 and note 23 in this chapter.

status are] [METZ]+, WORMS, SPIRE [Speyer], {COLMAR},[31] MEM-
MINGEN, ESLING [Eßlingen], HALL in SCHWABEN [Schwäbisch-Hall],
HEILBRON, LINDAW, GOSLAR, MULHAUSIN [Mühlhausen], NORTH
HAUSIN. The rest have reason rather to pride themselves in their Liberty
than in their Wealth.

[In the former Ages the conjunction of two or three of these Cities
together made a great Power, and they were terrible to the Princes],[a] but
now [their Wealth is much][b] reduced, and we may probably enough
conjecture, they will [one after another be all reduced][c] under the Yoke
of the Princes: At least, the Bishops threaten those very much in which
their Cathedrals are.

There |[are also some potent Cities which preserve]|[d] their Freedom,
though (perhaps) not very well grounded [*non ita liquido jure*]. |[For the
Hamburg.   Dukes of *Holstein* pretend a Right over HAMBURG, which this most
wealthy City of all *Germany* will not submit to; and [but] it is thought
[the Strength of it and]+ the Jealousie of the neighbouring Princes (who
envy the King of *Denmark* the possession of this fat Morsel) will preserve it.[32]

The King of *Sweden* has such another Dispute with the City of
Breme.   *Breme*[*n*], without which he can never secure that Dukedom;[e] and perhaps the Kings of *Sweden* have too much reason [are right] to suspect
that [that] City was admitted into the *Diet,* in the year 1641, [among the

a. Rather: One or two hundred years ago the power of these cities was great and
formidable, even to princes
b. Rather: the wealth of many has been
c. Rather: sometime be brought entirely
d. E.p.: were formerly . . . preserved
e. That is, the province containing the city. [Ed.]
31. The German cities of Colmar and Straßburg, in Alsace (Elsass), were occupied
by France in 1673 and 1681, respectively. Colmar is not mentioned in the e.p., but
Pufendorf is still hopeful there that Straßburg will return to the empire. This did not
happen, and the French possession was formally acknowledged in 1697.
32. Christian V's attack on Hamburg, in 1686, was foiled by the intervention of
Saxony and Brandenburg. See VII.5, page 189, below. Holstein was historically associated with Denmark, though not formally a part of its territory.

free cities,] when [they began to suspect those Princes]ᵃ would become Masters of this Dukedom[, on purpose to keep it out of their hands, and deprive them of this <46> convenience and security].ᵇ

The City of BRUNSWICK doth strangely [greatly] weaken and disfigure the Dukedoms of *Brunswick* and *Lunenburg,* and by its Site interrupt their otherwise well compacted Territories: And yet they will never suffer the Bishop of *Hildisheim* to take possession of that City [Hildesheim].³³ The Elector of *Brandenburg* is not very favourable to [an excessive liberty of] the Cities in his Dominions, [as is well known,] and therefore it is not improbable, the City of *Magdeburg* may [suffer the loss of her Liberty]ᶜ after the death of *Augustus,* of the House of *Saxony.*³⁴   *Brunswick.*   *Hildisheim.*   *Magdeburg.*

They of *Erford,* weary of a doubtful Contest for their Liberty, submitted, and for their Folly and Cowardice were thought worthy to lose their Liberty. Wise men wonder also that the Dukes of *Saxony* have not seized the Citadel of *Thuring* [for themselves instead].³⁵   *Erford.*

[A]nd I suppose, by this time, the *Hollanders* [*Batavos*] are made sufficiently [sensible they ought to have defended]ᵈ the Inhabitan[t]s of *Munster* against their Bishop; seeing it would the better have became   *Munster.*

a. Rather: it was already becoming clear that they
b. Rather: in order to defraud them of it / Even though the archbishopric of Bremen was secularized and assigned as a duchy to Sweden in 1648, the city of Bremen refused to submit. After two wars, the relationship was finally settled by the Treaty of Habenhausen in 1666: the city could remain in the empire, but without attending the Imperial Diet and while paying taxes to Sweden. [Ed.]
c. Rather: experience a change in government
d. Rather: regretful that they did not assist the
33. The city of Hildesheim was Catholic, while the surrounding territory, administered from Brunswick-Wolfenbüttel, was Lutheran.
34. See notes 19 and 27 in this chapter.
35. Erfurt, which is located in Thüringen, was conquered by troops of the archbishop of Mainz in 1664.

them who took Arms against their own Prince, for their Liberties, to have assisted their Neighbours in a like Attempt.]|[a, 36]

The Knights of *Germany*

14. The Knights of *Germany* are not all in the same condition, part of them being immediately subject to the Emperor and the Empire, and another part being under the subordinate States, who are their Lords. They that belong to the first of these *Classes,* call themselves the *Free Nobles of the Empire,* and [the *Conjunct,*][b] *Immediate, and Free Nobility of the Empire.* These, according to <47> the respective Circuits [districts] in which their Estates are, stand divided into three Classes, of *Franconia, Schwaben,* and the *Rhine,* which are again subdivided into lesser Divisions. They have of their own Order certain *Directors* and Assessors,[37] who take care of those Affairs, which concern the whole Body of this Order; and [occasionally,] if any thing of great moment happen, they call a general Convention. But then they have no Place in the [Imperial] *Diet,* which they look on as a Priviledge for the saving of the Expences necessary in such an Attendance. And in truth it would be no great advantage to them to be admitted into the *Diet,* [to give their Votes].[c] In all other things they enjoy the same Liberties and Rights with the other Princes and Free States [estates], so that they are inferiour to the Princes in nothing but Wealth [*opes*].

Divided into three Classes.

But they have no Vote in the *Diet.*

To recompence this, they have great Advantages from the Ecclesiastical *Benefices* and Cathedral Churches [chapters] in which they are *Can-*

---

a. E.p.: but that have now been brought under the dominion of princes, so that only Hamburg and Bremen, in particular, remain of their number. Hamburg, the richest city in all of Germany, is claimed by the dukes of Holstein, who assert that it is located in their territory. However, this claim has been rebuffed until now by means of contrary legal grounds [*juribus*] and by strong fortifications, with the support of Hamburg's neighbors, who have never been so mad as to allow the Danish king to control so rich a prize, which would gravely burden both upper and lower Saxony. The same reason prevents the princes along the Weser from allowing the Swedes to control Bremen.

b. Rather: , taken altogether, the

c. Rather: so that they can cast a vote or two there

36. See note 25 in this chapter.

37. In German, *Ritterhauptleute* and *Ritterräte.*

ons; and by this way many of them [very easily] become Princes of the Empire. They that obtain this Honour [rank], have learned{, by the Pope's example,}[a] to take good care of their Family and Relations; and besides, [I imagine] there is a wonderful satisfaction in the [enjoyment of great Revenues with small][b] Labour. {For they employ their Curates or Vicars to make a noise in their Churches, so that they are in no peril of spoiling their Voices by any thing but Intemperance. And as to the inconveniences of living unmarried, their Concubines, which are not wanting,[c] cure [easily remedy] them. [Those that <48> make themselves Eunuchs for the Kingdom of Heaven, are in the mean time very scarce in *Germany:* And it is almost as infamous in a Nobleman, to be continent, as not to love Dogs and Horses].}[d]

[Moreover,] I have heard some of them complain that some of the Princes have an apparent disgust at their Priviledges [openly threaten their liberty], and look upon them with an evil Eye, because living in the midst of their Territories, they enjoy such large Exemptions [freedoms]: [And others say,][e] such vast numbers of small *Royolets* [do much weaken the Empires in which they are suffered].[f] And [For] if a foreign War happen, they become an easie Prey to the Invaders [either side]: Yet for all this, these Gentlemen [knights] will not part with a certain Liberty for an uncertain Hazard or Danger; and the rest of the Princes will not [easily] suffer so considerable an Addition to be made to the Power and Riches of the [few] Princes they [the knights] live under, except some

a. Rather: by our Most Holy Father's example / Bohun's translation reduces the sarcasm and Pufendorf's constant insinuation that the popes cared only for wealth and worldly power rather than spirituality. [Ed.]

b. Rather: ability to consume in leisure a rich income that has been acquired without any

c. That is, they are remunerated [*venales*] for their services. [Ed.]

d. Rather: I have yet to see anyone who has castrated himself for the sake of the kingdom of heaven, and the gift of continence is [considered] as shameful in a nobleman [knight] as not to enjoy dogs and horses

e. Rather: On the other hand, [I have heard] others say openly that

f. Rather: contribute little to the strength of great empires

great Revolution open a way to this change, or by length of time and crafty Projects their [the latter's] Estates be wasted and consumed.[38]

The Empire is divided into ten Circles. 15. We must here, in a few words, admonish [also advise] the Reader, that this vast Body of the Empire|[, by the appointment of *Maximilian* I. in the year 1512, was divided into ten [regions or] Circles[, as they are commonly called]]|,[a] the names of which are these; *Austria,* [the four Electorates on the Rhine:] *Mentz* [*Mainz*], *Trier, Cologne,* and the Palatinate, call'd *the Lower Circle of the Rhine,* the *Upper Circle of the Rhine, Schwaben, Bavaria, Franconia,* the upper and lower *Saxony, Westphalia,* that of *Burgundy.*[39] The Kingdom of *Bohemia,* with the [adjoined] Provinces <49> of *Silesia* and *Moravia,* belong not to any of these Circles [or constitute a special circle]: Which yields us a clear proof, that it is rather united to *Germany* by a kind of League, than [a part of that Empire].[b] To which of these Circles any Place belongs, may be found [here and there] in common [reference] Books[, every where to be had][+]. This Division was made [especially] for the more easie Preservation of the Publick Peace, and the Execution of Justice against contumacious [insubordinate] States and Princes. To which end each of them [the circles] has Power to name a General [*ducem*], for the commanding their Forces, and [the appointing their *Diets,* in which the principal Prince in the Circle, for the most part, presides;][c] in which they take care for the de-

a. E.p.: was divided into ten regions or circles, as they are commonly called, by the appointment of Maximilian I in the year 1500, when six were initially designated, with four more added in the year 1512

b. Rather: fused with it into one state [*civitatem*]

c. Rather: to convene *Diets,* which are usually called by the chief prince of that circle, and

38. Pufendorf's point is that since the majority of knights resided in the Rhenish, Franconian, and Swabian circles of the empire, those princes would benefit most from a corrosion of the knights' position; and this would surely be opposed by the other princes unless social unrest leveled the playing field or the knights' privileges were lost piecemeal over time (Monzambano, *Über die Verfassung,* trans. Breßlau, 54, note 1).

39. The electorates of Mainz, Trier, Cologne, and the Palatinate jointly constituted the circle of the Lower Rhine, with the Upper Rhine, Swabia, Bavaria, Franconia, and the rest being independent circles.

fence of the Circle, and for the levying Moneys for the publick use [fiscal matters]. Yet a man may well question, whether this Division doth not tend [more to the Distraction and weakening of *Germany,* than its Preservation, the whole Body being by this means made less sensible and less regardful of the Calamities which oppress or endanger the Parts of it, and threaten (though at a distance) the Ruin of the whole].[a]

Thus much of the Parts of the [German] Empire. <50>

a. Rather: to the dismemberment of *Germany,* in that the evils afflicting one circle have less of an impact on the rest

Of the Origine of the States of the Empire, and by what degrees [stages] they arrived to that Power they now have.

1. For the attaining an accurate knowledge of the German Empire, it is absolutely necessary to enquire by what steps those that are called the States [Estates] of the Empire arrived to the Power they now possess; for without this it will not be possible to see what was the true cause that this State [the Empire] took such an irregular form.[1] Now these States are Secular Princes, Earls, Bishops, and Cities, of the Rise of each of which we will discourse briefly.

The Secular Princes of the *Empire* are either *Dukes* or *Earls.*

The Secular Princes are Dukes or Earls [Counts, *Grafen*], who have to these Titles some other added {in the *German* Tongue}, *viz.* PFALTZ-GRAVE, LANDTGRAVE, MARGGRAVE, and BURGGRAVE; for to the best of my remembrance, none of the ancient Princes, except he of *Anhalt*, has the simple Stile of a Prince [*princeps, Fürst*], without one of these Additions; yet some of them use the Title of Prince amongst their other Titles. Thus they of *Austria* are stiled Princes of *Schwaben;* the Dukes of *Pomerania* (now under the King of *Sweden*) the Princes of *Rugen* [*Rügen*]; <the Marggraves of Brandenburg Princes of Halberstadt, Minden, and Cammin;> the *Landtgrave* of *Hussia* [*Hessia*] and *Hers-field, &c.* <51>

---

1. This is the first mention of the empire's irregular (or monstrous) form; see VI.9.

2. Amongst the ancient *Germans*,[2] before they were subdued by the *Franks*, a Duke [*dux*] was a meer Military Officer; as appeareth plainly by the German word HEERZOG, who for the most part were chosen on the account of their Valour, when a War was coming upon them: In Times of Peace, those that governed them, and exercised Jurisdiction, and governed their Cities, Districts, and Villages, were for the most part chosen out of the Nobility, and were called GREVEN, or GRAVEN, which is as much as *President* [*praeses*], though the Latin word *Comes* is more often used for it; because from the time of *Constantine* the Great downward <paying no attention to the designation of previous times>, those who were employed in the Ministry or Service of the Court, in the command of the Forces dispersed in the several Provinces of the Empire, or in administring Justice and the execution of the Laws, were all stiled *Comites*. After this, when the *Franks* had subdued *Germany* [*Alemannia*], and were become Masters of all its Provinces, they, after the manner of the *Romans*, sent Dukes to govern the Provinces in it, that is, Presidents to govern them in Peace, and command their Forces in time of War: And to these they sometimes added *Comites*, for administring Justice; and some Provinces were put under *Comites* only, and had no *Dukes*; but then all these that were thus employed by them, were meer Magistrates; but in length of time, it came to pass, that some persons were made Dukes for their <52> Lives, and the Son for the most part succeeded the Father: So that having so fair an opportunity in their hands, of establishing themselves, they began [gradually to have less respect for the authority of kings and] to look on their Provinces [entrusted to them] as their Patrimony and Inheritance.[a]

Nor can a Monarch commit a greater Error than the suffering these kinds of Administrations to become hereditary, especially where the

> The old *German Dukes* military Officers, as
>
> Their *Grevens* or *Earls* were *Judges* in times of Peace.
>
> The *Dukes* and *Earls* made Officers for their Lives, and at last became hereditary Proprietors.

a. Thus, *dux* = *Herzog* = duke, *comes* = *Graf* = earl or count, *princeps* = *Fürst* = prince, and *baronus* = *Freiherr* = baron. [Ed.]

2. According to Breßlau, Pufendorf errs in referring the Frankish title of *Grafen* (earls, counts) to pre-Frankish times, when *Fürsten* (*principes*) were in charge of the various municipalities (Monzambano, *Über die Verfassung*, trans. Breßlau, 54, note 1).

Military Command is united to the Civil: And therefore I can scarce forbear laughing when I read this Custom, in some *German* Writers,[3] defended, as commendable and prudent; for it is the Honour of a Prince to reward those who have deserved well of him: But then, if a Master should manumise all his Servants at once, I suppose he might, for the future, make clean his Shooes himself: A Father may be the *fonder* of a thing, because he knows he can leave it to his Son after him; but then the more passionately he loves his Son, the greater care he ought to [will] take, that a Stranger may claim as little Right as is possible to it. Thus we usually take more care of what is our own, than of what belongs to another:

But then a good Father [*paterfamilias*] will not give his Estate[a] to his Tenant, that he may use it so much the better. There is a cheaper way of preventing the Rebellions of *Presidents,* than that of granting Provinces to them, to be administred as an Inheritance. And 'tis a very silly thing to measure the Majesty of a Prince [ruler], by the number of those in his Dominions, who can with safety despise him and his Soveraignty.
<53>

|[To say more were to no purpose; for to expose the Stupidity of these men, it will be sufficient for us to consider, that they are not ashamed to compare the *German* Lawyers with the *Italian, French,* and *Spanish* Writers; and yet the [abortive] Writings of the greatest part of them [the

a. Here, *feudum;* but e.p.: *fundum* (*Grundstück,* plot of land). Salomon insists on *fundum* (*Severinus,* ed. Salomon, 68, note 1), and Denzer silently inserts the same (*Verfassung des deutschen Reiches,* ed. Denzer, 1994, 86). Still, the original and subsequent Latin editions have *feudum,* and the earliest German translations, in 1667 and 1669, speak of *Lehen;* see Salomon, "Literaturverzeichnis," 15, nos. 20–21, and *Severinus,* ed. Salomon, 68, note 1. [Ed.]

3. Thomasius (*Severini,* ed. Thomasius, 259–60, note o) refers here to Johann Nicolaus Myler ab Ehrenbach (1610–77), whose *De statibus Imperii eorumque jure* (1640) was later expanded into *Delineatio de Principum et Statuum I[mperii] R[omani] G[ermanorum] praecipuis juribus* (1656) and widely used in the education of young princes.

former] shew, they never understood the first Principles of civil Prudence.]|[a]

3. *Charles* the Great observing the Error committed by his Ancestors, took away the greatest part of the Dukedoms, which were of too great extent; and dividing the larger Provinces into smaller parts, committed them to the care of *Counts, Comites,* or *Earls,* some of which retained the simple Name of *Counts,* and others were call'd PFALTZGRAVES, or PFALTZGRAVEN, *Comites Palatini, Count Palatins,* or *Prefects of the Court-Royal,*[4] and in that capacity administred Justice within the [Verge of the][b] Court. Others were call'd LANDTGRAVES, that is, *Presidents* set over a whole Province. Others were call'd MARGGRAVES, *Presidents* of the Marches or Borders, for repelling the Incursions of Enemies, and administring Justice to the Inhabitants. Others were called BURGGRAVES, that is, Prefects or Governours of some of the Royal Castles or Forts.

> *Charles* the Great endeavoured to redress this error.

And these Offices and Dignities were not granted by *Charles* the Great, in Perpetuity or Inheritance, but with a Power reserved to himself, to renew his Grants to the same person, or bestow them on another, as he thought fit.

But after <54> the Death of *Charles* the Great, his Posterity returned to the Errors of the former Reigns, and not only the Sons were suffered to succeed their Fathers in these Magistracies [or Governments][+], but by

> But his Posterity returned to the former ill management.

a. E.p.: Moreover, though no one who cares about preserving the character of a kingdom [i.e., the empire's] voluntarily introduces such a situation, what we have said does not mean that a state [*respublica*] where it has already become accepted is entirely to be condemned, or that an established custom which has acquired the force of public law should be violently uprooted. / This is a good example of Pufendorf's pragmatism, and of how the *editio posthuma* was tempered to reflect the new situation in Europe in the 1690s, when the emperor was allied with various Protestant states against Catholic France. [Ed.]

b. Rather: royal / A "verge" (in England) was a certain area or jurisdiction. [Ed.]

4. A *Pfaltz* (from *palatium,* itself derived from the Palatine Hill in ancient Rome, the city sector established by Romulus where Augustus and other emperors later resided) was a royal or imperial palace.

a conjunction or union of many Counties or Earldoms, or by the Will of some of his Successors, some *Dukedoms* were again formed, which contained great Extents of Lands. The *Presidents* employed by them in the Government of these Provinces, thought it a piece of Cowardice and Sloth in themselves not to take hold of these occasions and opportunities of establishing themselves and their Posterities, (as the nature of Mankind is prone to Ambition) especially when the Authority of the *French* Emperors declined, and became every day more contemptible [diminished], [and their power fragmented] by reason of their intestine Dissentions and destructive Wars with one another. And in the first

Otho Duke of *Saxony,* a King in Fact, though not in Title.

place, *Otho* Duke of *Saxony,* the Father of *Henry* the *Falconer,* having under him a large and a warlike Nation, so established himself, that he wanted nothing but the Title to make him a King: And when *Conrad* I. Emperor of *Germany,* undertook to subdue and bring under *Henry* his [Otho's] Son, he miscarried in the Attempt, and at his Death he advised the Nobility [*proceres*] to bestow the Imperial Dignity on this his prosperous Rival, thinking it the wisest course to give him what he could have taken by force, for fear he should canton himself, and disjoin his Dominions from the rest of *Germany.*[5] <55>

Other Princes raised to this Dignity by the *Emperors.*

There are yet some Princes, who owe their Dominions to the Liberality of some of the Emperors; Examples of which occurr frequently in the Histories of the *Otho*'s; and whether this is consistent with the Laws of Monarchy, I am not now at leisure to enquire. After these Beginnings or Foundations [Imperial donations], Princes encreased their Power af-

Others by Purchase, Inheritance, or Usurpation.

terwards by Purchases, [and] by Hereditary Descents, not only in the Right of Blood; but also by mutual Pacts of Succession, which the *Germans* call, *Confraternal Inheritances or Successions,* which are of the same nature with that League between the potent Houses of *Saxony, Bran-*

---

5. Otto became duke of Saxony in 880. His son, Henry (the Falconer), succeeded as duke in 912 and became king of the eastern (i.e., German) realm of the Franks in 919, after the death of Conrad I, duke of Franconia and king of the German Empire (r. 911–918). Conrad, on his deathbed, had persuaded his brother, Eberhard, to cede the crown to Henry, an action confirmed at the Diet of 919.

denburg, and *Hassia,* which is now in force: And by vertue of such a League, the Dukes of *Saxony* obtained the Earldom of *Henneberg,* and the House of *Brandenburg* the Right of *Pomerania,* {though that [latter] League was not reciprocal}⁶|[; and yet it is apparent, these Leagues are injurious to the Emperor, who has the Right of a Lord over the Dominions of the Princes [*tanquam Dominus feudi*], and ought, upon a vacancy, to dispose of the Fee.]|ᵃ Lastly, Some Estates [Domains] have been seized by force, by some of them [the Princes], when *Germany* was involved in Wars and Disturbances.

4. But then, in after times, when it appeared, that the Power which these Princes had once gotten, could not be dissolved without distracting [disturbing] all *Germany,* and perhaps not so neither, without hazarding the Ruin of him that should attempt it, it seemed better to the succeeding Kings, especially <56> after they saw they could not obtain the Empire without it, to confirm their Possession; so that from thenceforth they enjoyed their Territories as *Fees* [fiefs, *feuda*], acknowledged to depend on the Emperor, and swore Allegiance to him and the Empire.

In after times these Powers were confirmed by the Emperors.

|[From hence it is, that by what means soever the Princes got their Estates [*opes*], they now hold them as *Fees* of the Empire]|:ᵇ Yet the name of *Vassal* has not deprived these Princes of any *considerable part* of their Power and Grandeur [recognition]. For, if I grant a man any part of my

a. E.p.: . And yet since the Emperor's power over the territories of princes, which he has as feudal lord, is clearly made illusory by such agreements, in that such consolidations can be continued indefinitely, they are not valid without his ratification, nor are they easily consented to by him and by the remaining Estates at times when the state is calm.

b. E.p.: Hence it came to be that any territories thereafter bestowed on Princes by the Emperors were accepted under the designation of a fief / The e.p. version is less sweeping. [Ed.]

6. According to the Treaty of Grimnitz (1529), Pomerania should have gone to Brandenburg when its ruling house died out in 1637. Yet the Treaty of Osnabrück (1648) assigned Western Pomerania to the Swedes, leaving Brandenburg with limited control over Eastern Pomerania. Even after the Swedes were driven out in 1678, Brandenburg was forced in the Treaty of St. Germain (1679) by France, then still an ally of Sweden, to return its recent Pomeranian gains. It did not gain formal control over the region until 1720, at the end of the Nordic War.

Estate, to be holden of me as a *Fee,* though I put him thereby into a full possession, yet I [make him my Subject],[a] and I, as the Lord of the *Fee,* may prescribe what Laws or Conditions I please to the possession of what I thus grant: But then [on the other hand], he who consenteth to acknowledge what he already hath, to be a *Fee* holden of the Party thus consented to, is supposed only to own the Lord of the *Fee* as a superiour Confederate in an unequal League, and so [his own obligation gladly] to respect his Majesty and reverence his Dignity.[7]

Upon the failing of the Line of *Charles* the Great, *Germany* was perfectly Free. The Line of *Charles* the Great failing, *Germany* became perfectly free, and many of the Nobility, before that time, had acquired to themselves great Dominions. When therefore it was thought fit to give the *Regal Title* to some one Person chosen out of the Nobility, that *Germany* might not return into her ancient weak, defenceless state, by being broken into small Governments: It is not to be thought, that the Princes were willing to <57> cast away their Dominions [*opes*], or to submit them to the Absolute Dominion of another; but rather to seek a strong Protector [or Defender of their Rights] +<, and to tie themselves to a great state [*reipublicae*] through a bond that was by no means productive of the condition of a simple citizen>. Thus the State [status] of these Princes being once introduced and confirmed, it was fit that those who were afterwards exalted to that Dignity by the Emperors, in the stead of any Families that happened to be extinguished, should also be advanced to the same state of Freedom and Power with the ancient Princes.

And in the mean time, those that are well versed in Civil Prudence

a. Rather: can make him a complete subject, albeit an honorary one

7. Pufendorf's claim that the German princes had given their territories to the emperor and then received them back as fiefs (*feuda oblata*) was very controversial and, in fact, historically inaccurate. As he himself suggested in two letters to Christian Thomasius (June 9, 1688; April 9, 1692), it was more of an explanatory hypothesis than an established historical fact. See Pufendorf, *Briefwechsel,* letters 137 (p. 195) and 218 (p. 340), and Döring's note 7 on page 196. Thomasius, who had written a dissertation (*De feudis oblatis,* 1687) on the topic, also returned to it in his annotated edition; see *Severini,* ed. Thomasius, 274–77. As is evident in the passage at hand, Pufendorf's claim was vital to his characterization of the empire as an unequal confederacy rather than a genuine state ruled by sovereign authority. See VI.9.

[*scientia civilis*], or Politicks, will easily acknowledge, that this *Feudal* Obligation [tie] of the Princes to the Emperor, only made them unequal Allies or Confederates, and not Subjects, properly so called. For it is inconsistent with the Person or Notion of a Subject to exercise a Power of Life and Death over all those that are in his Dominions, or to appoint Magistrates as he thinks fit, to make Leagues, and levy Moneys to his own use, without being accountable for the same to the Royal Treasury, or [giving to it any more than he himself shall think fit].^a But then, to force an Ally by [means of] the rest of the Confederates, who offends [grossly] against the Rules of the League, is very usual in all such cases, and there are many Examples of it both in ancient and modern Story [History]. But to acknowledge the Emperor to be the sole Judge of the Cases for which a Prince may deserve to be deprived of his Dominions, as it would pull up the Foundations of the Power of *German* <58> Princes, so those who have alwaies [fiercely] opposed the Emperors that have attempted at any time to do it, have thought it a slavish and base Respect or Reverence to him, to betray their Rights so far, as to suffer him to do it.

The Princes of Germany not Subjects, but Allies to the Emperor.

5. From thenceforward, as it has ever happened in |[all Empires]|^b where the Power of the Subject has been formidable to the Soveraign, so more signally has it happened in *Germany, viz.* "That when they [the Germans] had Emperors of great Wealth, or very much Reverence, on the Score of their eminent Virtues, the Princes were most obsequiously subject to them; but when they have had weak or unactive Emperors, they [the Emperors] have had only a precarious^c Command over them [the Princes]." And those Emperors again who have endeavour'd to pluck up this so deeply rooted Power of the Princes, and to reduce *Germany* into the condition [to bring *Germany* back under the laws] of a true Mon-

Great Emperors are well obeyed, the weaker are despised.

a. Rather: to render no service to which he has not freely consented
b. E.p.: proper kingdoms [*justis regnis*]
c. Not merely insecure but also dependent on the agreement, cooperation, or pleasure of others (cf. the Latin *precor:* to ask, pray for, beg, implore). This meaning is important in view of Pufendorf's notion of effective sovereignty. See V.1–9 and *On the Law of Nature and of Nations*, VII.4. [Ed.]

archy or Kingdom, have sometimes pull'd Ruin down upon themselves, and have ever failed of their hopes, and gained nothing by it, but the disquieting themselves and others. Nor have those that endeavoured to do it by Craft made any progress, because some or other have found out the Design, and disappointed it; and if any thing were gained from the Princes at any time [in] one way, it was lost [in] another. Thus it is [well] known to all men, what ill Successes, in the last Age, attended the Attempts of *Charles* V. and[, in ours, of] *Ferdinand* II.

Yet Luxury, [(ii)] Sloth, and Prodigality have <59> wonderfully [notably] weakened some of the Princes, because they took no care to augment or keep what they had. And several of the Families are also weakened by dividing their Patrimony and Dominions amongst their Brethren and Kindred:[a] And some, without any fault of theirs, have been ruined by the Calamities of the Civil Wars.

The election of the Bishops.

6. I must in the next place speak something of the Bishops too. Now it is certain, that in the first times of Christianity the Bishops were elected and constituted by the [remaining] Clergy and the Faithful People; afterwards, about the IV. Century, when Princes embraced the Christian Religion, a Custom was taken up by them [by those with supreme authority over states] of not [easily] suffering any person to be made a Bishop without their Consent, because they very well understood, that it tended very much to the preservation of the publick Peace, to have good and peaceable men in that eminent Office.[8] The Kings of the

(ii). Luxury has impoverished some of the *Princes*.

a. That is, *cognatos*, vs. *agnatos* (in the e.p.). / The latter is more specific and refers not merely to blood relations but to those in the male line subject to the power of a *paterfamilias*. According to agnatic succession (also called Salic Law), the first-born male descendant of a line succeeds, no matter what rank; it essentially excludes female succession. See Bretone, *Geschichte des Römischen Rechts*, 74–75. [Ed.]

8. Pufendorf, *Of the Nature and Qualification of Religion*, §§6–7, pp. 18–21, and §§44–45, pp. 96–99, grants sovereigns certain rights and responsibilities toward the church as a civil institution, though not in the determination of religious doctrine as such. As heads of state, sovereigns have a right of "general inspection" over the churches in their territories and, as the chief members of a particular religion, a shared right to appoint its ministers. Proper inspection entails ensuring that clergy do not

Franks took up the same Custom [exercised the same right (*ius*)], and would suffer none to be made Bishops in their Kingdom, but such as they approved of. And the Emperors of *Germany* continued the same Right [claimed the same power (*potestas*)] till the Reign of *Henry* the Fourth: *Gregory* the Seventh began a [strange] Quarrel against this Prince on that Score, which was carried on by his Successors, against the succeeding Emperors; till at length his Son *Henry* V. weary of the Broils this Controversie had occasion'd, in the *Diet* of *Worms,* in the year 1122, renounced this <60> Imperial Priviledge [*ius*] of constituting and investing the Bishops[, which was formerly done by handing over a ring and a staff]; but yet the Emperor had still the Right [*potestas*] of delivering to [conferring on] the elected Bishop the *Regalia* and [Imperial] *Fees,* by the [ritual] delivery of a *Crosier* [*sceptrum*].⁹

Now it is not easie [difficult] to conceive what the Emperor lost by the yielding this great point; for though his power before over the Secular Princes was not great, yet as long as the Church was [priests were] subject to him, he could easily equal, or, if need was, overrule their Forces. In the Agreement between the Pope and *Henry* the Fifth, the Election of the Bishops was setled in the Clergy and People jointly, yet afterwards the *Canons* of the *Cathedral* Churches began to claim the sole power of chusing them, the Pope conniving at this their Usurpation [no doubt with the silent acquiescence of the Pope], it being more for his Interest to have this Affair in a few hands, than in many. At length things came to this: That the Confirmation of the new elected Bishop was to be sought [by cathedral chapters] from *Rome,* whereas this, as well as the Consecration before, [since this, as well as the Consecration, had earlier]

Renounced by the Emperor.

---

abuse their spiritual powers in nonspiritual ways and thereby undermine secular authorities and disrupt the state. Also see VIII.7, pp. 228–29, and note 14.

9. This refers to the famous Investiture Controversy (1075–77) between Emperor Henry IV (1050–1106) and Pope Gregory VII (1020–85). Henry V (1081–1125) forced his father to abdicate in 1105, reopened the controversy (even setting up an antipope), and secured a compromise in the so-called Concordance of Worms (1122) or *Pactum Calixtinum* (after Pope Calistus II, r. 1119–24), whereby the pope invested bishops and abbots with their spiritual rights (symbolized by ring and crozier) while the emperor gave them their secular powers.

belonged to the *Metropolitan*.[a] But then, the Examples of Men, provided beforehand with Bishopricks, by the power of the Pope, was |[very rare in *Germany*]|,[b] and I suppose the reason was, because the Chapters would scarce have submitted patiently to [acknowledged] a Bishop, so obtruded on them [(though it was practis'd frequently in other Countries)] [+] <, unless internal turmoils did not allow any opposition>.

The Bishopricks of Germany endowed by the Emperors.

7. The Bishops of *Germany* are indebted to the Liberality of the first Emperors, for all those Provinces and great Revenues <61> they now enjoy; a fervent Piety and Zeal in those times ruling in the minds of Princes, because they thought the more they gave to the Church, the more they united themselves to God. Which Opinion is much abated in our times, because many now (how truly I know not) have taken up another, contrary to it, *viz. That over [too] great Wealth, bestowed on Church men, tends rather to the extinguishing than nourishing of Piety and Religion.* [The Church-men also of those early times seem to have had the Grace of asking, without fear, whatever might seem convenient for the allaying the Hardships of their Profession].[c] Thus the Bishops and Churches obtained of these good Princes not only *Farms, Tithes*,[10] and *Rents* [*other incomes*], but also whole *Lordships, Counties* [*Earldoms*], *Dukedoms*, with all the *Regalia's* or Royalties [royal rights] annexed to them, so that they became equal in all things to the Temporal Princes. But then, in truth, they obtained the Degree of Princes but [most of them were elevated even to princely rank] in the times of the *Otho's*, and

a. The "archbishop of the mother-city" (i.e., Rome). [Ed.]

b. E.p.: more rare in *Germany* than before

c. Rather: Many Church-men seem also to have had the nerve of asking those upright men [i.e., rulers], without any hesitation, for whatever appeared capable of allaying of the harshness of their profession / That is, they took advantage of lay rulers, who hoped to mitigate the clergy's religious rigor by meeting their other demands. [Ed.]

10. The *decima* was a tithe of ten percent originally levied by kings (with the pope's permission) on the clergy during the Crusades but then expanded to other purposes (Haberkern and Wallach, *Hilfswörterbuch für Historiker*, 1:140).

those that followed;[11] and [but] they got not the *Regalia* all at once, but by little and little, some at one time, and some at another: And from thence it comes, that some of the Bishops have not yet got them all, and others have them under the restraint of certain Limitations.

There were two other things contributed very much to the acquiring all these great Riches and Honours for the Church [to their ascent to such dignities]. 1. That many of the Nobility in those times took Orders, and became Church-men; and, 2. That all the little <62> Learning those barbarous Ages had, was in the Clergy. This [early on] occasion'd the calling the Bishops to Court, to give their Advice, and the employing them as Judges and Governours in the Provinces, because these things [and the putting them in charge of those offices that] cannot be well perform'd without some Learning. [And this was the true reason why the Office of Chancellor was at first annexed to the principal Bishops *Sees*].[a]

I do also believe, that the Riches of the Church were very much improved by many Princes and Noblemen, who [voluntarily] resigned their Estates, or a part of them, to the Bishops, and took them again as *Fees* from them, that they might so oblige them to take the more care in recommending them, and their Salvation, to God in their Prayers, and as their Families afterwards were extinguished, their Estates were united to the Bishopricks. [Finally] Who knows not also what vast Additions have been since made [to the clergy's riches] by the [gifts and] Wills of Dying Men[, both nobles and plebeians], [when a Nation that is naturally afraid of Heat and Thirst, saw they must buy off the Roasting in Purgatory, by that means which they feared above all men?][b]

a. Rather: Hence the chief bishops are still distinguished by the rank of chancellor

b. Rather: since they deem the burns of Purgatory—which a nation otherwise averse to thirst and heat finds strangely fearful—as something to be avoided at any price. / Probably a reference to the sale of indulgences in Germany during the previous century, a practice famously challenged by Luther. [Ed.]

11. The Saxon line of the so-called Ottonen began with reign of Henry I (the Falconer) in 919–36 and ended with that of Henry II (the Pious) in 1002–24.

When they became very rich, they would not be subject to their Benefactors.

8. The Church-men might have been well contented with their Condition in *Germany*, though they had neither abjured Ambition nor Avarice [entirely]: But then, as they of all men are [most] desirous to have others under them, so they could least endure to see others above them, and therefore thought this [one thing] was still wanting to perfect their Happiness in this World, because they were <63> still forced to receive all they had [such fine benefices] from the Emperor, and consequently were forced to live in a [special] dependence on him. If the Reverence I owe that most Sacred Order of Men, did not restrain me, I should say, they were the worst of men, who, as the event shews, abused the Imprudent Liberality of the Emperors, to the Ruin of that [Majesty and Power that had raised and enriched, dignified and ennobled them].ª Certainly, he is not worthy of Liberty, who is not willing to own his Manumissor for his Patron [and Master] ⁺.¹² That therefore this Tribe of *Levites* [*Sacerdotum natio*] might wholly free themselves from the Subjection of [to] the *Laicks,* the *German* Bishops strenuously solicited the Pope to send abroad his *Vatican* Thunders [threats of excommunication], and raised plenty of Commotions in the Empire, to second [assist] them, by both which they at last gained their Point: For the Archbishop of *Mentz* led the way, and the rest of the Flock followed him faithfully, and would never suffer their Prince to have any rest, till he would permit them to depend on no body but the Pope.

This, as many think, brought a signal Mischief [very grave illness] on the *German* State, *viz.* The having so many of its Members [citizens] acknowledge a Foreign Head, unless we can think the Pope was so fondly [fatally] in love with *Germany,* that he desired nothing more than its Preservation, and that they at *Rome* knew better what was for the Good of *Germany,* than the very *Germans* themselves did. <64>

---

a. Rather: Imperial position

12. A reference to the ancient Roman practice—eventually banned by the *lex furia caninia* (ca. 7 A.D.)—of manumitting slaves (especially in one's will) in order to augment the gratitude and honor they were obligated to show their liberator (*Verfassung des deutschen Reiches,* trans. Dove, 139, note 11).

9. It remains now, that we say something of the *Free Cities. Germany,* till the V. Century after Christ, had nothing but Villages, without Walls, or dispersed Houses, in all that part of it which lies to the East and North of the *Rhine:* [a] Even in the IX. Century, there is only mention made [of a City or two in that part which borders on the State of *Venice*]:[b] But then there were many Cities built by the *Romans,* much more earlily [*sic*] in that part which lies on the French side of the *Rhine,* of which the *Romans* were possess'd; as also between the *Danube* and the *Alps,* which belonged then to them, but was afterwards a part of *Germany.*

Of the Free Cities.

The reason why in those ancient Times they had no Cities, was first, because the old *Germans* had no skill in Architecture; which Ignorance still appears in many places of this Country; and secondly, The *Fierceness* of the Nation, which made them averse to these kinds of Habitations [Places], as a sort of Prisons [Cloisters]; and also, thirdly, Because the Nobility placed their greatest Pleasure in Hunting, and therefore neither knew nor much valued the Conveniencies of having Cities and great Towns. Their Dyet [diet] then was very mean, their Furniture and Clothes [Equipment] cheap, and they neither knew nor regarded [valued] the Superfluous Effects of Wealth or Luxury; but after their Minds were civiliz'd and softned by Christianity, they began, by degrees, to affect the elegant way of living; the love of Riches, and a studied Luxury followed, and was brought <65> in from abroad, both which are nourished by great Cities [greatly nourished by Cities]:

Why the Germans of old had no Cities.

The Princes also having amass'd great Riches, took a Pride in building Cities, and invited the Rusticks of *Germany,* and the Inhabitants of other Nations, to settle in them, by the Grant of large Priviledges, especially after the Christian Religion had abolished [or mitigated] *Villenage* or *Slavery* [*Servitude*], and the *Liberti* or Freemen had no Lands to subsist on, they flew by Flocks to the Cities, and betook themselves

---

a. *transrhenana;* e.p.: *cisrhenana* / As before, the e.p. consistently exchanges *trans-* and *cis-* (this side, near side) because Pufendorf is then speaking as a German rather than as an Italian. See pp. 25, note a; 26, note 8; and 32, note b. [Ed.]

b. Rather: among the Venetians of a City or two

to Manufactures and [or] Trading. The Irruption of the *Hungarians* forced *Henry* the *Falconer* to build many Cities and strong Holds in *Saxony,* and he made every ninth man [*ingenuus,* free-born] be drawn out of the Country to inhabit them:

The Leagues afterwards between the Cities, for their mutual Defence and Trade, gave them great Security, and by consequence made them populous and rich. The principal of these Leagues is that made by the Cities on the *Rhine,* in the year 1255, in which some Princes desired to be included: The *Hanse* League was chiefly made on the account of *Maritime Commerce,* and grew to that height of Power, that they became terrible [formidable] to the Kings of *Sweden, England,* and *Denmark.*[13] But then, after the year 1500. it became contemptible [almost completely collapsed], because the lesser Cities, when they found the greater got all the profit, fell generally off, and deserted them. And the [other] Nations [*gentes*] upon the Ocean and *Baltick* Sea, by their example, began, about the same time also, to encourage Trade in their own Subjects [increase their commercial activities], especially <66> the [(*English*)]⁺ *Flandrians*[14] and *Hollanders.* Thus their *Monopoly* failing, their Strength fell with it.

Cities at [*sic*] subject to Kings or Emperors of Germany.

10. Though in the beginning the Cities were in a better condition than the Villages, yet they were no less subject to the King or Emperor than they, and these Princes took care to have Justice exercised in them by their *Counts* or deputed *Judges* [*royal emissaries*], as they call'd them. After this, by the enormous and imprudent Liberality of the Emperors, many of the Cities were granted to the *Bishops,* others to the *Dukes* and *Counts,* and the rest remained (as before) only subject to the Emperor. In the XII. Century they began to take more liberty, as they found they

13. The League of the Rhine was founded in 1254 (see *Verfassung des deutschen Reiches,* ed. Denzer, 1994, 101, note 5), while the Hanse in the North and Baltic Seas was formally organized around 1356.

14. An area of Belgium bordering on the North Sea, Flanders was noted in the medieval period for its textiles. It had close commercial ties with England, from which it imported wool, and which supported the struggle of its powerful counts to be independent of France. This led to the Hundred Years' War (1337–1453).

could relie upon their Riches, because the Emperors, by reason of the Intestin Wars [internal disorders], were not able then to reduce them to a due Obedience; some Princes were but just advanced to the Imperial Dignity, and so were forced also to purchase the Favour and Assistance of the great Cities, by the [voluntary] Grants of new Priviledges and Immunities, that they might employ them as a Bulwark against their Refractory Bishops and Princes; after this, by degrees they shaked off the Emperor's Advocates [and officials]. The succeeding Emperors observing also, that the Bishops employed their Wealth against them, encouraged the [their chief] Cities to oppose the Bishops [by bestowing privileges on them]. The Dukes of *Schwaben* failing [dying out], many small [insignificant] Cities in the Dukedom catched hastily at the opportunity of being made free.

[Y]et they [those cities] did not obtain <67> their Freedom all at once, but one after another, as they could gain [an opportunity and] the Favour of the Emperor; and that is one Reason that they have not all the same Priviledges [rights], and some of them want a part of the *Regalia* to this day. [Some of them bought these Priviledges of their Dukes or Bishops, and others shook them off by force, and then entred into Treaties for the purging that Iniquity].[a] For when these Princes were poor or low, their last Remedy was, to sell the richest of their Subjects their Liberty; [and others, when they saw they could no longer keep them in subjection, took what they could get from them, and were unwillingly contented with it].[b] <68>

a. Rather: Finally, some cities acquired what right over them belonged to Emperor, Dukes, or Bishops by means of sale, exchange, or some other legal title; others shook it loose by violence and later legalized the injustice of their title by means of a subsequent settlement / The first Latin edition included the emperors, though the e.p., like Bohun (who translates the first edition), omitted them. [Ed.]

b. Rather: or when they saw that they could no longer take from them what they had already seized for themselves, they deemed it advantageous to be content with the modest return they received for it

CHAPTER IV

Of the Head of the German *Empire, the Emperor; and of the Election and the Electors.*

The Emperor the Head of *Germany.*

1. Though *Germany* consisteth of so many Members, many of which are [like] great and perfect [*justarum*] States, yet it has at all times (excepting the *Interregnums* which have happened) since *Charles* the Great, been united [subjected] to one Head (which the Ancients only [simply] call'd their King, the later Ages by the more ambitious Titles of the *Roman Emperor,* and *Caesar*) and upon the sole account of this Head, it has seem'd, to the most of men, to be one single simple State: And my next business is, to shew how this Head is constituted or appointed; but then it will be worth my while, by way of Introduction, to represent this Affair from its Rise [to trace this matter somewhat further back], that it may the more clearly appear how much the present differeth from the ancient Election, and what is the true Original of the *Electoral Princes.*

The Empire of the *Romans* pretendedly given by the Pope.

As to *Charles* the Great, and his Posterity, the *Roman* Empire and the Kingdom of *France* are to be severally and distinctly considered: The first of these was collated [conferred] upon *Charles,* by the [<acclamation and> consent of] the People of *Rome,* and by the Pope, as the <69> principal Member of that Empire [City],[a] or rather, as upon one who plainly designed to make himself Emperor, and that as appeareth, in an

---

a. "Pope" and "people" are reversed in the text to match the editorial addition. [Ed.]

96

Hereditary way: So that the Crowning [of] his Successors had not the force of a new and free Election, but [only] of a Solemn Inauguration: For we read, that *Charles* the Great made *Lewis* his Son, and *Lewis* made also *Lotharius* his Son their Consorts [partners] in |[the Empire]|,[a] and yet there is no mention made of their [first] asking the Consent of the *Pope,* or of the *People* of *Rome,* on either of these occasions.

{But then, as to the ancient Kingdom of *France,* we cannot affirm, that it was either meerly elective, or meerly hereditary, but a mixture of both [mixed mode of succession]:} For we read frequently, that the Kings of *France* were constituted by the Consent and Approbation of the Nobility and whole People of *France,* but in such a manner yet, that they never chose out of the Line of the dead King, but for very great [grave] reasons;[1] {which kind of Election is (as we know) still observed in *Poland;*}[2] yet he that shall curiously observe it, shall find, *France* had more of a Successive than of an Elective Kingdom; *So that it seems to have been collated [conferred] on the first of the Race [Line], with a Condition, that he should transmit it to his Posterity, unless they appeared to the People very unworthy of it.* So that the Children [*filiis*] of the Deceased King did not so much gain a new Right to the Kingdom by this Approbation of the Nobility and People, as a Declaration, that they were not uncapable <70> of succeeding, by the Right that was at first collated [conferred] on them:[b]

The Kingdom of *France* more hereditary than elective.

Afterwards the Line of *Charles* the Great being deposed or rejected, and denied the Throne of *France* [*the Franks*], the Kingdom of *Germany,* or, as they then called it, the *East Kingdom of France,* was, by the

a. E.p.: the Imperial title
b. Rather: . . . uncapable of exercising the right acquired from that first conferral
1. See I.7.
2. The Polish branch of the Swedish Vasa dynasty ended with the abdication of John Casimir II in 1668, when the Polish nobles elected Michal Korybut Wisniowiecki (1640–73), a descendant of the original Piast dynasty, and then John III Sobieski (1629–96). The latter ruled 1674–96 and was known especially for his significant victories over the Turks in 1673 and 1683, when he rescued Vienna.

Germany given freely to Otho, and after to Conrad.

most free Consent of the Nobility, given to *Otho* the *Saxon,* who excusing himself on the account of his Age, by his Advice *Conrad* Duke of *Franconia* was by them chosen King of *Germany,* who was, as some think, of the Line of *Charles* the Great. By his Counsel also afterwards *Henry* the *Falconer,*[3] Son of *Otho* Duke of *Saxony,* was by a free Election advanced to that Kingdom [Kingship], who being contented with *Germany,* would not accept the Title of *Emperor,* though the Pope offered it to him;[4] but *Otho* the Great his Son, having subdued *Italy,* so united *Rome,* and the Lands of the Church to *Germany,* that from thenceforward he that had the Kingdom of *Germany* without any new Election, should be Emperor of *Rome,* the Crowning by the Pope being nothing but a Solemnity, though before this Ceremony the Kings of *Germany* had not usually used the Title of *Emperors.* The same form of Succession hereupon was used in *Germany,* which had been observed in the old Kingdom of *France, viz.* That the Consent of the Nobility and People did not easily depart from the Order of a Lineal Succession in the Royal Family [*ab ordine sanguinis*]: And this continued to *Henry* IV. who being young, and <71> perhaps not Governing well the Nobility thereupon, by the procurement of the *Pope,* rose up against him, and deposed him from the Kingdom, {and, for the time to come, made a Law, *That though the Son of the last King were worthy to succeed him, yet he should attain the Throne by a Free Election, and not by a Lineal Succession;* as the words of that Constitution run.}[5] And from that time on |[hereditary succession gradually ceased]|.[a]

The Empire of Rome united to the Kingdom of Germany for ever.

a. E.p.: the power [*vis*] of successive right gradually diminished, until at last it was openly replaced by elective right

3. According to Breßlau, the epithet has no historical basis (Monzambano, *Über die Verfassung,* trans. Breßlau, 65, note 2). On the Ottonen, also see I.6, note 20; III.3, note 5; and III.7, note 11.

4. Denzer (*Verfassung des deutschen Reiches,* ed. Denzer, 1994, 107, note 1) traces this incorrect claim to Otto von Freising's (d. 1158 A.D.) *Chronicle or History of Two Cities,* VI.17.

5. Hermann Conring, *De septemviris* (1644), §§20, 21, relying on Bruno, *Historia de bello Saxonico,* chapter 91 (*Verfassung des deutschen Reiches,* ed. Denzer, 1994, 107, note 2). The e.p. variation was prompted by the comment of Kulpis (*Severinus,* ed. Salomon, 79, note 3).

2. That old Approbation and Election was made by all the People <or by the leading men [*proceres*] and the selectees of the more powerful cities>, though it is not to be doubted but the Authority of the Nobility [leading men] and Princes, or [and] of the Bishops and Peers [*Nobilium*], was much [most] valued: But now, for some Ages past [several centuries], Seven chuse the Emperor in exclusion of all others; and since the Treaty of *Osnaburg*,[6] Eight of the principal Princes are to do it, who from thence are called, The *ELECTORAL PRINCES* [Electors, *Kurfürsten*]: Of these, Three are stiled *Ecclesiastical Electors, viz.* The Archbishops of *Mentz, Trier,* and *Cologne;* and Five are *Temporal* or *Secular Electors,* the King of *Bohemia,* the Dukes of *Bavaria* and *Saxony,* the Marquess of *Brandenburg,* and the Count *Palatine* of the *Rhine.*

The ancient Elections not made by any certain number of Princes exclusively.

It is not very clear how these Princes came by this Right [for][a] two Ages, *viz.* from [around] the year 1250, to the year 1500, it was a received Opinion, That *Otho* III. and Pope *Gregory* V. instituted the Seven Electors, but with this Difference, that some Authors ascribe the principal share in the Act to the Emperor, and others to the Pope, as each man was affected to them [depending on their respective sympathies].[7] {Our Countryman} *Onuphrius Panvinius* <72> was |[[to my knowledge] the first man that opposed]|[b] this Opinion in a Book, *De Comitiis imperatoriis,* of the Imperial Diets, which is since [today] approved by all the

The 7 Electors not instituted by *Otho* III.

a. Rather: . For more than
b. E.p.: among the first to oppose
6. The Treaty of Westphalia (1648) created a new (eighth) electorate for Karl Ludwig of the Palatinate, instead of restoring him to the original dignity lost by his father, Frederick V (the Winter King), in 1623, when the electorate was transferred to Maximilian I, duke of Bavaria, as a reward for his support of Emperor Ferdinand II. Two concurrent conferences led to the Peace of Westphalia (1648): The emperor and other Catholic powers negotiated with France at Münster, and with Sweden and its Protestant allies at Osnabrück. Also see notes 15, 22, and 24 in this chapter.
7. Pufendorf was acutely conscious of how national interests shape the writing of history, and his *Introduction to the History* was explicitly (see its preface) written from the viewpoints of the respective national historians.

wisest of the *German* Nation.[8] His best Argument against it, is, Because this *Ottonian* or *Gregorian* Constitution was never yet produced by any man, and no man has mentioned it from the times of *Frederick* II. to those of *Otho* III,[a] which contains 240 years; for the first that mentions the Electors was one *Martin a Polonian* [*Pole*], who lived under this *Frederick* [II., some 250 years after Otho III.],[9] and therefore his Testimony was justly liable to exception [not beyond all doubt], seeing it was not supported by any better [evidence] in an Affair which happened so long before his own times: And yet, after all, he doth not mention any such Constitution; nor doth he say, the Electors began in the time of that *Otho,* but [only] that, after his times, the *Officers of the Empire began to elect:* Which is capable of a double sence, [1] either because they were then possess'd of [they then acquired] very large Dominions [*ditiones*], who before had the principal Offices [*munia*] in the Court; or [2] because those Offices were then first collated [conferred] for ever on Princes that had very great Dominions, who, though perhaps they had a Signal Authority, as the most eminent men above all others; yet that the Election [of kings] belonged to other Princes besides these Seven, can be denied by no man who is not very ignorant of the *German* Antiquities.

Others have ascribed the appointing [of] the Seven Electors to *Frederick* II, but then there is no Record of any Law <73> to that purpose any where to be found; nor is it probable, that the rest of the Princes so early [suddenly] and so easily parted with their Right of Electing.

But yet they seem ancienter than *Frederick* II.

3. The current Opinion of the most Skilful in the *German* Affairs, is, That [already] before the times of *Frederick* II, those Seven Princes, as the great Officers of the Empire, and persons that had great Estates,

---

a. Rather (if earlier to later): the times of *Otho* III to those of *Frederick* II. / Otto III lived 980–1002, and Frederick II 1194–1250. [Ed.]

8. Onuphrius Panvinius, *De comitiis ac potestate imperatoris* (Basel, 1568; Straßburg, 1613) (*Verfassung des deutschen Reiches,* ed. Denzer, 1994, 109, note 3), and Melchior Goldast, *Politica Imperialia* (Frankfurt, 1614) (*Severinus,* ed. Salomon, 80, note 1).

9. Martinus Polonus (d. 1228/29), a Dominican from Silesia, became confessor to various popes (Hammerstein, "Kommentar," 1188).

began by degrees to overtop the rest, and to have the greatest Authority in the Elections of the Emperors<, and—as some reasonably conjecture—since they were required to be present at elections by virtue of their office, other princes used frequently to delegate their votes to them>; but after the times of this *Frederick,* the *German* Affairs being wonderfully [unusually] disordered, whilst the rest took little or no care of the Publick [business], these Seven assumed it [that electoral right] wholly to themselves. This, after it was confirm'd into a Custom by some repeated Acts, was at last passed into a Law by the solemn and publick Sanction of the Golden Bull,[10] in which the whole form of the Election, and all the Power of the Electors, is contained; and from thenceforward those Princes added to their former Titles that of *Electors,* and were ever after esteemed as persons set in an higher Station and Dignity than the rest.[11]

4.[a] Thus, though at the first these Princes seem to have assumed the power [function] of electing the Emperor, [insofar] as they were the great *Officers* of the *Empire;* yet afterwards, by the Law call'd the *Golden Bull,* those very Offices, as well as the *Electoral Dignity,* are [were] annexed to certain Dominions; so that whoever is legally possessed of them, <74> is thereby made one of the Electors.

Of the Privi-
ledges of the
Electors.

[T]he *Ecclesiastical Electors* [in the mean time][+] are made by Election or Collation [Conferral], as the other Bishops of *Germany* are; where it is to be observed, that though these Bishops, to enable them [properly] to perform the other Functions belonging to their Office, stand in need

---

a. This section is wrongly designated as §5, with the misnumeration continuing to the end of chapter 4. I have silently corrected the error hereafter. See note a for IV.3 in the original table of contents, p. 20, above. [Ed.]

10. The Golden Bull was an imperial edict (with a golden seal) issued by Charles IV in 1356 after the Imperial Diets of Nuremberg and Metz. It settled various constitutional matters for Germany, such as the number and rights of the electors, and the manner of the imperial succession; it also excluded any papal role in the electoral process and codified the semiautonomous status of the seven electors.

11. The higher rank demanded by the electors was not acknowledged by all and was still disputed as late as the Peace of Nimwegen (1678) (Monzambano, *Über die Verfassung,* trans. Breßlau, 67, note 1).

of the Pope's Confirmation, and the Pall, which they must not expect
gratis; [12] yet they are admitted without them [even before papal confir-
mation] to the Election of the Emperor, because these Secular Dignities
pass without the Character [do not depend on a religious stamp of ap-
proval]: But then, when the See is vacant, the *Chapter* has no Right to
meddle with the Election [to act in the Elector's place]: [13]

In the Secular or Temporal Electors [Electorates] the Succession pas-
seth in a lineal Paternal [*agnaticam*] Descent, [14] so that neither the Electoral Dignity, nor the Lands united to it, admit of any Division: But if
a new Elector [Electorate] is to be made, or for some Offence any one
is to be deprived of that Dignity, it is, without doubt, agreeable to the
other Laws and Customs of the Empire; for the Emperor [alone, by his
own authority,] not to dispose of the said Dignity, without the Consent
of the other States [Estates], or, at least, not without that of the Electors.
Though it is not to be denied, the last Age [and our own] saw an Example
to the contrary, against which however one or two of the Electors protested [in vain], the Emperor despising their words, because he saw his
Arms prosper [inordinately at the time]. Yet this Prince had wit enough
to bestow the Dignity [taken away] on one of the same Line and
Family, [15] which tended very much to the abating the Envy of [ill will

12. The *pallium* was a white sash worn over the shoulders and decorated with six
black crosses. Although also used to honor bishops in the Middle Ages, it was the
formal symbol of an archbishop's office and had to be purchased from the pope (with
Palliengeld) before one could exercise the powers of that role. This widely resented
financial requirement was eliminated during the thirteenth century, when it was essentially replaced by the annates. Even so, there were calls for its elimination as late
as 1769 (*Verfassung des deutschen Reiches,* ed. Denzer, 1994, III, note 5; *Verfassung des
deutschen Reiches,* trans. Dove, 139–40, note 12; Haberkern and Wallach, *Hilfswörterbuch für Historiker,* 2:467).

13. A chapter or *capitulum* comprised the diverse clergy active at a cathedral, formally under the authority of the bishop. This quasi-monastic institution became
quite complex by the Middle Ages and included secular as well as religious com-
munities, some of them restricted to nobility (Haberkern and Wallach, *Hilfswörterbuch für Historiker,* 1:156–58).

14. See p. 88, note a.

15. After Elector Johann Friedrich of Saxony (of the Ernestine line) was captured
at the battle of Mühlberg in 1547, the electorate was given to Duke Moritz of Saxony
(of the Albertine line). In the seventeenth century, Elector Frederick V of the Pa-

created by] the Fact<, in that his resort to war seemed motivated not by a longing to dominate others or seize their things, but by the demands of his office and the securing of his own prerogative>, <75> and [also] divided two most potent Families, by raising an endless Emulation between them, and made that Party that was obliged by the Grant, obnoxious to [dependent on] the Imperial Family, for the preservation of it.

[It must be added that] If any of the Electors happen to be a Minor, their Guardians supply their place [in the election of Emperors], and the Minority ceaseth when the Prince is Eighteen years of age.

5. The manner of the Election is [approximately] thus:[16] The *Elector* of *Mentz,* within one Month after he knows of the Death of the Emperor, signifies it to his *Colleagues,* and calls them to the Election that is to be made <within three months>, who meet in person, or by their Proxies: When they enter *Frankford,* each of them is allowed Two hundred Horsemen, and no more; but this thing at this day is not nicely [precisely] observed.[17] Whilst the Election is making [taking place], |[all Strangers]|[a] are commanded to depart [from the city]. They begin the Election in the Chancel [sanctuary] of the Church of St. *Bartholomew,* with the Ceremony of the Mass, then they come to the Altar, and each of them sweareth, that he will chuse a fit person to be Emperor<, without any side agreement, payment, bribery, or promise>. The Bishop of *Mentz,* as Dean of the College, gathereth their *Votes,* and first he asketh

Of the manner of the Election.

---

latinate was deposed and lost his position to Duke Maximilian of Bavaria at the *Reichstag* in Regensburg in 1623 (*Verfassung des deutschen Reiches,* ed. Denzer, 1994, 113, note 6; *Verfassung des deutschen Reiches,* trans. Dove, 140, note 14). See note 6 in this chapter.

a. E.p.: all outsiders or those whose legal residence is not in the city, beside those accompanying the Electors,

16. According to the Golden Bull, chapters 2 and 4 (*Verfassung des deutschen Reiches,* ed. Denzer, 1994, 113, note 8). The provisions are rendered more accurately in the e.p. (*Severinus,* ed. Salomon, 82, note 2).

17. The rule was violated by the election of Leopold I in 1658, and the transgression explicitly censured in a decree appended to the articles of election (*Verfassung des deutschen Reiches,* ed. Denzer, 1994, 113, note 9).

the Bishop of *Trier,* then the Bishop of *Cologne,* and so all the rest in their order, and gives his own in the last place. The majority of Votes is as good as the whole; but then, whereas there is now eight, it was never yet certainly agreed what should be done, in case the Votes should happen to be equally divided. None <76> of the Electors is excluded from the Right of nominating himself. When the Election is made, it is recorded in Writing, and confirmed with the Seals of the Electors; then they all together go to the Altar, and the Elector of *Mentz* assembles the People, and declareth to them the Name of the new elected Emperor[, out of the Writing]⁺: After this, the Empire is committed to him upon certain Conditions [*legibus*], but so, that he is forthwith bound to confirm to all and every one of the Electors, all their Rights and Priviledges.¹⁸

By the *Golden Bull, Aix la Chappelle* [*Aachen*]¹⁹ is appointed for the City where he is to be Crowned, though for the most part, ever since, the Coronation is perform'd in the same place where the Election is made, and because that City is in the Diocess of *Cologne,* that Ceremony has been commonly performed by the Elector of *Cologne;* yet the Bishop of *Mentz* alwaies puts in his Claim for it, and, if I be not deceived, of late this Controversie is thus determin'd; |[That they shall do it by Turns, whereever the Emperor is Crowned]|.ᵃ

The rest of the Ceremonies may be easily found in |[*German*]|ᵇ Writers.

The Electors have deposed an Emperor.

6. |[Perhaps it would be too hard, and too invidious [offensive], to make a Publick and Formal Law, to declare, That the *Electors* have a full Right and Power to depose the Emperor, if he deserves it, as well as to elect

a. E.p.: That the Archbishops of Cologne and Mainz shall perform it in their respective dioceses of Cologne and Mainz, and that outside of these they will alternate / This is explicitly stated in the agreement of 1657, which Pufendorf had rendered inexactly in the first edition (*Verfassung des deutschen Reiches,* ed. Denzer, 1994, 115, note 11). [Ed.]

b. E.p.: public law

18. Compare Pufendorf's *On the Law of Nature and of Nations,* VII.6.7, on limited sovereignty. Of course, the emperor actually had no sovereignty at all, strictly speaking, given the irregularities of the empire as a state.

19. See Golden Bull, chapter 29.1 (*Severinus,* ed. Salomon, 83, note 1).

him:]|[a] [Yet it is certain, they exercised this *Power* upon *Wenceslaus, Sigismond,* the Son of *Charles* <77> the Fourth being elected in his stead, in the year 1411. This Prince [Charles II], that he might gain the Empire, made the *Golden Bull,* and rewarded the Electors with great Gifts, which is very much resented by those who are not well affected to the Electors].[b] [*Henry* the Fourth was deposed by the other Princes joined with the Electors:][c] <Although, even if Wenceslaus seems himself to have given up his throne, I would not guarantee that judicial procedures [*regulas iuris*] were observed in the case of Henry the Fourth.> And in truth [it is said that] the Bishops of *Mentz* have pretty plainly and fearlesly sung this Tune, and claimed the Right of deposing the Emperors, to one or two [the other] of them, who were engaged in Designs that were not acceptable to these Prelates. <This must be ascribed to the character of the age, when the popes sought, with the aid of the German clergy, to withdraw themselves from the power of the emperors.>

a. E.p.: It is obvious that though the Electors have the right to elect the Emperor, they do not automatically [*haut statim*] by virtue of this right [*eo ipso*] have the power to strip him of this rank if he so deserves. But perhaps it would be too hard, and too invidious [offensive], to ordain this expressly through a Publick Law. / This seems to reverse the idea of the first edition by focusing the possible offense on the electors instead of the emperor, which is consistent with Pufendorf's concern to maintain the emperor's position in the struggle against France in the early 1690s. Thomasius (Monzambano, *De statu Imperii,* ed. Thomasius, 329) quotes the e.p. change in a footnote, but without comment. [Ed.]

b. Rather: Still, it is well known that they exercised this power in the case of *Wenceslaus,* son of the very *Charles* the Fourth who—according to the loud complaints of those who envy the Electors their preeminence—supposedly enacted the *Golden Bull* and placated the Electors with great largesse in order to secure the Empire for his son <at a later time> / Wenzel of Luxemburg (1361–1419), a son of Charles IV (1316–78), was deposed in 1400 for his general neglect of the imperial role. He was succeeded first by Ruprecht of the Palatinate (d. 1410), and then by his half-brother Sigismund (1368–1437). [Ed.]

c. Rather: Other princes [beside the Electors] also helped to remove *Henry* the Fourth from the throne [*imperio*]. / Henry IV (1050–1106) was forced to abdicate in 1105 by his son, Henry V (1086–1125). See III.6, note 9, p. 89. [Ed.]

The Electors have some other special Priviledges.

7. The Electors have some other Princely [special] Rights, beyond what belongs to any of the other Princes; for they are not only the greatest Officers of the Empire, but they have Right [*possint*] also, in some Cases, to [convene meetings and] exclude all the rest of the States and Princes, and to consult amongst themselves about things of the greatest importance. The Archbishop of *Mentz* is Lord Chancellor [Archchancellor] of *Germany*.[20] The Archbishop of *Trier* of *France*, and of the Kingdom of *Arles* (by which Names the most skilful [learned authors] do not understand all that Country that is now call'd *France*, but only so much of it as in the XI. Century belonged to the Kingdom of *Burgundy*, and was then united to *Germany*).[21] And the Archbishop of *Cologne* is Chancellor of *Italy*: But then, at this day, the first of these has an effectual Power, and the other two have nothing but meer empty Titles.

The King of *Bohemia* is Lord CUP-BEARER, <78> and in the highest Ceremonies and Solemnities, gives the Emperor the first Cup of Wine. The Duke of *Bavaria* is now Lord HIGH SEWER [steward], and carrieth the *Pome* or *Globe* [Imperial orb, *Reichsapfel*] before the Emperor in the Solemn Processions.[22] The Duke of *Saxony* is Lord HIGH MARSHAL, and carrieth the naked Sword before the Emperor. The Marquess [Markgraf] of *Brandenburg* is Lord HIGH CHAMBERLAIN, and gives the Emperor Water [to wash] +, and in the Solemn Procession carrieth the Scepter. The Count *Palatine of the Rhine* is Lord HIGH TREASURER, and in the Procession to the Palace, at the Coronation, scattereth the Gold and Silver Medals [Coins] amongst the People. Each of the Secular Electors

20. As chancellor (see IV.7), the archbishop of Mainz (after 1623) was also head of the Council of Electors (*Kurfürstenrat*); this gave him considerable influence at the *Reichstag* (Imperial Diet) when there was no set agenda (Monzambano, *Über die Verfassung*, trans. Breßlau, 69, note 2; *Verfassung des deutschen Reiches*, trans. Dove, 140, note 15).

21. The kingdom of Arles was formed in 933 and annexed to the Holy Roman Empire by Conrad II in 1034. It covered portions of Provence, Savoy, and Switzerland; and it ceased to exist as a separate kingdom in 1378 when Charles IV ceded it to France.

22. This function belonged to the Counts Palatine until it was lost in 1623 by the defeated Frederick V (the "Winter King"), whose electoral status was transferred by Emperor Ferdinand II to Duke Maximilian of Bavaria. See note 6 in this chapter.

has his certain known Deputy [*vicarios*] for the performance of his Function; *Limburg* beareth the Cup for the King of *Bohemia; Wal*[*d*]-*burg* is Sewer [steward] for *Bavaria; Pap*[*p*]*enheim* carrieth the Sword for *Saxony;* the Count of *Ho*[*h*]*enzolleren* is Deputy for *Brandenburg;* and *Sintzendorf* for the Count *Palatine of the Rhine.*

There are also other Priviledges belonging to the Electors, which are express'd in the *Golden Bull,* [as peculiar to them, but]ᵃ are at this day possess'd by other Princes too, two [privileges] only excepted, *viz.* 1. That there lies no Appeal[23] from their Judgment; and, 2. That in the regranting their Dependent Fees [*feuda,* feudal rights], they are [above controul; and as to the taking up their own, they do it without any Charge]:ᵇ And perhaps there may be some others. <79>

8. When there is an *Interregnum,* or want of an Emperor, the Count *Palatine of the Rhine,* and the Duke of *Saxony,* supply that Defect, and Govern as Viceroys; the first, all the Countries [parts of the Empire] on the *Rhine* and [in] *Schwaben,* and whereever the *Franconian* Laws [*ius*] and Customs take place: The second takes Care of all the Countries which are under *Saxon* Laws; but then neither of them are allowed to dispose of [bestow on anyone] the Fees of the Empire, which shall become vacant by the Death of any Prince, [and those] which are [customarily] given by the delivery of a Banner. Nor can they alienate or mortgage any of the Demeans [possessions] of the Empire; all the rest of their Acts are for the most part [customarily] confirmed by the new elected Emperor.

What is done during the Interregnum.

a. Rather: most of which

b. Rather: unencumbered [*immunes*] / That is, they are not required to render new or additional services in turn; the renewal is, as it were, automatic and on the same terms as before. [Ed.]

23. That is, to the imperial courts. The only exception to this right of no appeal (*privilegium de non appellando;* see Golden Bull, chapter 11) was in the case of a complete denial of judicial procedure (*Verfassung des deutschen Reiches,* trans. Dove, 140, note 17).

In the last Vacancy [*interregnum*], upon the Death of *Ferdinand* III.[,] the Duke of *Bavaria* disputed the Count *Palatine's Viceroyalty;*[24] to gain his Point, the Duke of *Bavaria* used great Policy [cleverness], that he might not be disappointed in his design:[a] He laid Post-Horses and Curriers [Couriers] on the Road, who gave him an account of the Death of the Emperor very early, and upon that he presently sent Letters to acquaint the Princes, and States with it, and that he had taken upon him[self] the Care of the Empire in the *Franconian* Circles; whereupon many of the Princes and States being surprized by this subtile Management [without sufficiently considering the matter], congratulated his Honour [responded with hasty congratulations] before the Death of *Ferdinand* was [barely] known to the Count *Palatine,* whose Right it was. But however, that Count did not patiently <80> suffer his Right to be thus sliely stoln from him, but declared for the future he claimed [declared to all that he would exercise] this his *Vicarian Power,* and entered a Complaint against the Duke of *Bavaria,* for thus usurping his Right: And it is very certain, the far greatest part of the Princes repented they had consented to this Attempt of the *Bavarian,* but could not then recall their Letters to him: But then, as is usual in such Encroachments, no man was willing to join with the Oppressed, and make his Quarrel his own, [though] afterwards they printed Books one against the other [against one another debating the matter].

Now, though no man could wonder that the Duke of *Bavaria* should venture upon this Practice [attempt to acquire that dignity for himself], who in the more flourishing state of the Count *Palatin's* Affairs, had pretended [already laid claim] to the *Electorate,* and now having got part

a. Rather: In this matter, the Duke of Bavaria very cleverly took care to pursue his designs with the greatest dissimulation, so that they could not be prematurely eluded.

24. Ferdinand III died in 1657, succeeded in 1658 by Leopold I. Bavaria's claim was strengthened by the fact that the (original) Palatine electorate had been transferred to it in 1623. However, the matter had been disputed already in 1612. See Ezechiel Spanheim's (anonymous) *Discours du Palatinat et de la dignité électorale contre les prétensions du Duc de Bavière* (1636) (Monzambano, *Über die Verfassung,* trans. Breßlau, 70, note 1).

of the *Palatin's* Country, had encreased his own Power, and was otherwise well assured of the Concurrence and Favour of the House of
Austria [both on the account of Kindred and Religion]⁺; yet the far
greatest part of the indifferent [impartial] Spectators thought the Count
Palatine [Palatine writers] had sufficiently shewn his Right, and demonstrated that this *Vicarian* Viceroyalty was no part [or appendage] of
the Great *Lord High Sewer's* Offices, but was [a peculiar right] perpet-
ually annexed to the *Palatinate* of the *Rhine,* [just] as the Duke of *Saxony*
has the other half of that [Vicarian] Power in the rest of *Germany,* not
as *Elector,* but as [*Count*] *Palatine* of *Saxony:* But then, as there were
many that openly favoured the *Bavarian,* [so the rest were not willing
openly to espouse <81> the opposite side, and that Prince would not
confess he had done wrong, and so]ᵃ the Controversie remains unde-
termin'd still.

9. Sometimes there is joined to the Emperor *Extra Ordinem* [*the usual*
procedure aside], a *King of the Romans,*²⁵ [at least in name,] in pretence
as his General Vicar or Deputy, who in his Absence or Sickness [In-
ability] is to Govern the State, and upon his Death, to succeed without
any new [further] Election. But then, though [necessity or] the Good of
the State has ever been pretended, as is usual in such Cases; yet the real
Cause [reason] has ever, or, at least, most usually been, That they might
with the greater ease, in their own lifetimes, preferr [convey] their Sons,
Brothers, or near Kinsmen, to the Empire [Throne], by the Influence or
Recommendationᵇ of a Regnant Emperor; foreseeing, that one that was
chosen in a Vacancy or *Interregnum,* would have harder terms [*arctior-*
ibus legibus] imposed on him by the Electors.ᶜ

Of the King
of the
Romans.

a. Rather: and the rest did not wish to criticize him openly, nor is it customary
for Princes readily to confess their own injuries [toward others],
    b. The Latin *prenso* or *prehenso* means literally to go around and press or shake
people's hands. [Ed.]
    c. Pufendorf's chapter ends here; the rest was added by Bohun. [Ed.]
    25. "King of the Romans" (*rex Romanorum*) was the title of an emperor after he
had been confirmed as such but not yet crowned by the pope. Eventually it came also
to designate the emperor's heir or successor, whose crowning as king of the Romans,
during the emperor's lifetime, virtually ensured his succession. Also see V.23.

//*Joseph* King of *Hungary,* the eldest Son of *Leopold* the present Emperor of *Germany,* who was born the 25th. of *July, 1678.* was chosen *King of the Romans* the 24th. of *January,* 1689/90. and Crowned the 26th. at *Ausburg.* This Emperor has another Son [i.e., Leopold Joseph, d. 1684] of his own Name, who was born the 12th. of *June,* 1682. who ought to have been taken notice of in the end of the former Chapter, where the Males of the House of *Austria* are set down, but it slipped my Memory till that Sheet was wrought off.\\ <82>

Of the Power of the Emperor, as it now stands limited by Treaties; and the Laws and Customs of the Empire; and the Rights of the States of Germany.

1. I have already shewn by what degrees and upon what occasions the Nobility [*proceres*] of *Germany* mounted themselves to that excessive height of Power and Wealth, as is wholly inconsistent with the Laws of a [regular] + Monarchy. Nor is it worth our wonder, that when the Election of the Emperor in aftertimes was devolved upon them, they set their Hearts upon the preserving what [power] they had gotten. By this Change in the State of Affairs the Kings (of *Germany*) lost the Power of Disposing or Governing as they thought fit, the Concerns of that Nation, and were necessitated to consult the Princes [*procerum*] in things of great moment, and transact more of their business with the States by their Authority, than by their Soveraign Power.[1] And there is no question to be made, but the Princes inserted a Clause to this purpose very early into the Coronation Oath of *Germany*, (which is usually ad-

Of the Limits set to the Imperial Power.

---

1. The distinction is between authority (*autoritas*) and sovereignty (*imperium*): the emperors could assert their authority or formal entitlement to rule, but they could not actually enforce their commands. Yet this, too, was required for a genuine obligation to exist (see Pufendorf's *On the Law of Nature and of Nations,* I.6.9 and 14; *The Whole Duty of Man,* I.2.5). The emperors' inability to sanction or enforce their will demonstrated more than anything their lack of sovereignty and the empire's "irregularity."

ministred to all Christian Princes, [in a very solemn manner,] + upon
their <83> Accession to any Crown) *viz. That the King should Promise
and Swear to Defend all the Rights of all and singular the Inhabitants* [each
and every citizen] *of* Germany, *and observe and keep all the laudable Customs in that Kingdom* [Empire] *received and used.*

But whether in process of time any particular Laws were added [to
the old] +, and comprehended in Writing, is not so manifest, because
before the times of *Charles* the Fifth, we have no Copies [examples] of
any such Capitulations or Agreements; and [those that are pretended to
be more ancient, are of no great certainty]. [a] And whereas it is said in the
Golden Bull, [*that*] *The Emperor shall presently* [*upon his election*] *confirm
all the Rights, Priviledges, and Immunities of the* Electoral Princes, *by his
Patent* [*in writing and*] *under Seal,* this seems to belong only [apply
specifically] to them, and therefore is a very different thing from the
Agreement [an article] [b] by which the Emperor is [now] + obliged to engage for the Liberty or Freedom of the whole Empire. Now, the Reason
why the Electors desired to have *Charles* the Fifth bound to them, in so
many express and tedious Articles and Covenants, was, That they considering the great Power of that Prince, his Youth, High Spirit, (testified
by his Motto [*Plus ultra*) and his other Advantages], [c] feared lest he
should imploy [the power of] his Patrimonial Estates to subdue the *German* Nation [the Germans], and took this way, to make him consider,
That he must Govern Germany *after another manner than he did his other
Dominions.* And this Custom being once taken up, has <84> been ever
since continued, though there are not the same Reasons there were at
first for it.

    a. Rather: if any are ever produced, they will not be very credible
    b. A *capitulatio* or *Kapitel* (Bohun's "capitulation," "capitular") was a short for-
mulation or "article" in a formal document or agreement. A so-called *Wahlkapitu-
lation* was a specific provision or condition, agreed to ahead of time by the one to be
elected. [Ed.]
    c. Rather: *Plus ultra* [*Still further*])

2. These Conditions [articles] have been prescribed to the Emperors by the Electors [alone], without consulting the other States of *Germany*, though they [the latter] have sometimes complained of it, and in the last Treaty of *Munster* [*Westphalia*] it was moved, *That in the next Diet* [*s*] *there might be care taken to draw up a standing form of Articles, which should be perpetual* |[[—a formulation that means, in the manner of the Germans, that the matter will be postponed forever] +. And I heard [I heard, however], when I was at *Ratisbone* [*Regensburg*], that it was then under serious Debate, and that much Paper had been spent in that Service. But the Wiser part thought the *Electors* had no reason to fear the event of this Consultation,]|a because it was the Emperor's Interest, [as well as theirs,] ꞌ that the *Electors* should still be in a better condition than the other Princes; for they being few in number, might more easily be brought to a compliance with him, than the other States, which were more numerous, and [therefore it was reasonable on the other side, that he should rather indulge them of the two].b And those Princes of the Empire who were descended of the Electoral Families were very inclinable to it too, and [thought that] the Demands of the rest might be deluded [evaded], without much difficulty. Nor doth it agree with the Manners of *Germany,* to deprive any man of what [right] he has by Force and [or] Combination,c however he came by it. They added, That though what the States <85> asked was not unreasonable, *viz.* That they might be equally secured [considered] in the Capitular with the Electors; yet that it was not possible to pen an Instrument in such manner, but that upon the change of times and things, it would be necessary [thereafter] to change and correct it. That in the former Agreements there were many things changed, added, and altered, as the necessity of the times required, and as they found the Chinks and starting Holes [gaps] their Emperors had endeavoured to escape out at. That the Electors would willingly, at the request of the Diet [remaining Orders], insert [into the

a. E.p.: . Whether this will ever be clearly formulated may be rightfully doubted,

b. Rather: which he would then have to indulge in equal measure

c. *coitionem* (partnership, association) / That is, reducing someone's special right by having him share it with others. [Ed.]

article] whatever was necessary for the preservation of [the Liberty of *Germany;* but then it was absurd, to think the Electors would not preferr their own proper Interest to that of all other men: Nor could they divest themselves of the common Inclinations of Mankind] [a] <whereby every-one loves himself most of all>.[2]

{Some others suspect there was another reason at this time, which brought the business of the Capitulars upon the Stage. The Emperor, who [otherwise] hated the thoughts of a Diet, was then necessitated to call one, by a *Turkish War,* which then threatned his Dominions; and this Affair was then set on foot, to the end he might by this means [pretext] obtain plentiful Contributions from the States of *Germany.* But then they offered Souldiers instead of Money; and this not answering the Designs of the Emperor's Ministers, they thereupon clapt up a Peace with the Turks much sooner than they otherwise intended, and then were doubtful what *Recess* [(iii)] they should <86> draw up for the Diet:[3] for the business of giving Succours against the *Turks,* which has often been the greatest part of their former *Recesses* or *Edicts,* was now wholly at an end. Yet, after all, some curious and inquisitive men [must needs know to what purpose so many men were called together from all parts of *Germany,* and sate so many years;] [b] what good came of all the *Sack* [c] they drank in the Forenoon, and the *Rhenish* and *Burgundy* [Mosel] Wine they drank after Dinner. To answer this, they put them [the legates] upon an inextricable business, that they might at their return be

---

(iii). *The* Germans *call the Law which they form up on the Debates of the Diet, in the end of it, the* Recess.

a. Rather: the latter's liberty; and, finally, that it was quite absurd to fault the Electors for preferring their own interests to those of the rest, as if they alone were bound to put aside that common human inclination,

b. Rather: might wish to know what such a great multitude of legates did for so many years, and

c. A strong and dry Spanish wine (from the French *vin sec*). [Ed.]

2. Compare *On the Law of Nature and of Nations,* II.3.14, and *Elementa jurisprudentiae universalis* [Elements of universal jurisprudence], book II, observatio 3.1, on self-love as the most basic and most powerful impulse of human beings.

3. The collective resolutions of an Imperial Diet, sent to the emperor for his final approval, were called the imperial recess, or *Reichsabschied.*

able, if need were, to swear they had not been wholly idle; and that repeating all their vain useless Brangles about the Capitular, and referring it over to the next Diet, [as a thing which could not now be determin'd,] + they might make this Story serve for a *Recess,* or parting Edict, such as it was.}

3. Whatever was the true cause of that Debate, it cannot be denied, but that the introducing the Custom of Comprehending the Laws the Emperor was to govern them by, in express Articles in Writing, was a thing of great good use. For this [it] tended altogether to the Reputation and Honour of the States, that seeing they would not [allow themselves to] be governed in the same manner as the Subjects of other Monarchs are, [their Liberties which they enjoyed might not seem meer Contumacy or Usurpation, but the effects of a Contract made with their Prince when they chose him to be their Emperor].ᵃ <87> They consulted hereby also the Safety of their Liberties, the Emperor being limited in such Bounds, as he ought not in any case to pass over, and being deprived of all reasonable cause of Complaint, that he [was not as Absolute as the rest of his Neighbour-Monarchs, whose Subjects profess themselves, on all occasions, to be their]ᵇ most Dutiful and Obedient Subjects. [The *Germans* on the other side, in the introduction of their *Capitular,* say, *Upon these terms the Emperor has undertaken the Government of the Empire, and has yielded, by way of* Compact, *the said terms to the* Electors, *in the behalf of themselves and the other States of* Germany.]ᶜ Now, if he had disliked these Conditions, he ought to [could] have refused that Dignity, or to have shewn the Electors beforehand, that there was something of Injustice or Absurdity in them, and they, without doubt, would [readily]

The usefulness of the *German* Capitular.

a. Rather: they were believed to be doing this not out of contumacy or mere usurpation, but because they had gotten the emperor to agree to such laws

b. Rather: could not treat according to the model of other monarchs, those who did him the verbal homage of calling themselves his

c. Rather: For he acknowledges at the very beginning of the Capitular that he has assumed the Empire on such and such terms [*leges*], and that he has contractually agreed to them with the Electors, acting on behalf of themselves and the remaining Orders.

in that case have corrected them. But then, when [once] the Emperor has accepted a Limited Power [*potestas*], it is utterly unreasonable [impermissible] he should endeavour to exercise a full and Regal Authority over them [the Estates]; or, [at least, it will appear much the more reasonable for them to oppose him in it];[a] for there are none of the more understanding *Germans,* who do not believe the Regal Power may be included in [contained within] certain Limits. [And I suppose, the more understanding Politicians will not deny, that there may be such a Competent Power assigned to the Head of a Confederate Body, <88> as shall be very different in Degree from that of a full and perfect Kingdom or Empire].[b, 4]

The extravagant Opinions of some Writers concerning the *Capitular.*

4. But then, when one happens to read any of the {*German*} Writers which mention [treat of] the *Capitular,* he cannot but observe their abominable Flattery, or wonderful [remarkable] Ignorance in State-Affairs, and civil Prudence [*doctrinae civilis*]. Some of them have the Impudence to assert, That the *Capitular* doth not set bounds to the Emperor's Power, but only take care that the Forces of the Empire shall not be lessened by Alienations, Mortgages, and the like. The greatest part of them do yet acknowledge, that the Imperial Power is limited by it [in certain ways], and so is not absolute, but yet it is still *Supreme;* or, as some of them love to speak, there is something thereby taken from the fulness [*plenitudini*] of his Power, but nothing from the Supremacy [*summitati*] that is the height of it:

As we shall in the next Chapter examin[e] this notion more accurately, it will be sufficient for the present to say [in passing], that they are de-

a. Rather: if he dares to act in such a way, they may [*licebit*] oppose him with impunity

b. Rather: Indeed, I think that the more discerning political writers will not deny that there is also a power belonging to the head of a body of confederates that differs in type [*specie*] from a royal or complete sovereignty [*regio et pleno imperio*]

4. See *On the Law of Nature and of Nations,* VII.3.1 and VII.6.7–8. See V.4 in this chapter for Pufendorf's important distinction between supreme and absolute sovereignty. A (regular or perfect) state is not possible without supreme sovereignty, but it may be limited by laws according to the contract of subjection. Bohun's translation lacks the necessary precision here, perhaps because of his royalist or Tory leanings.

ceived who think to take away the ground of this Controversie, by distinguishing between those Laws which oblige, as prescribed by a superiour Authority, and those whose Obligation ariseth from our own Wills, and are bound upon us by our Fidelity and the obligation of a Compact [agreement][, referring the Capitular to the latter class].ᵃ For all they can pretend to get by this distinction, is to prove, that the Emperor is not subject to the States, and not that he has a Soveraign Authority over them [properly speaking]: For to invest a Prince [someone] with such an Authority [supreme sovereignty], <89> it is not enough to shew, that he has no Superiour,ᵇ but he [one] must also shew, that all the rest [of his Subjects]⁺ are bound, without dispute, to obey all his Commands, and have no Right to appeal from him; much less will it be sufficient to shew, that he is the Highest in that State [according to his rank]. As for example: In |[our]|ᶜ Common-wealth of *Venice;* as if the Duke were not the Highest [in rank]; and yet no man dares ascribe the Soveraign Power to him: For, as in all Common-wealths [*respublica*], whether they be *Aristocracies* or *Democracies,* there may be Princes properly so called, who may be rightly stiled the Highest in their Commonwealths and yet still not be Kings. So also in all *Systems* of [co-ordinate States, which are Confederates each to other],ᵈ there may be some one more eminent person, to whom the particular Care of the whole [common affairs] is committed, and so he may rightly be called the Highest[, or the Head of]ᵉ that Body, though he has in truth no Soveraign Authority over the Confederates [allies], [nor can or ought to]ᶠ treat them as his Subjects.

But I think it were better here for the present to consider distinctly what part of the Soveraign Powers are intrusted to the Emperor; for if

a. Omitted by Bohun. / The distinction seeks to characterize the nature of the emperor's obligation, as defined by the capitular, without undermining his authority. That is, the estates do not (through the capitular) obligate the emperor as his superiors; this is captured by the second notion of obligation, which does not, however, suffice as an explanation of his supposed sovereignty over them. [Ed.]

b. As in the case of promises or agreements. [Ed.]

c. E.p.: the

d. Rather: allies [*sociorum*]

e. Rather: in

f. Rather: and cannot

a man doth not know them, he [is utterly unqualified to judge of]ᵃ the *German* Government [*respublica*]. And here it will befit us rather to follow the Order which agrees with the *Genius* of that Empire, than that which [is prescribed by *Politicians,* as more regular and exact].ᵇ <90>

The Emperor doth not appoint or punish the Magistrates in the Empire.

5. We will therefore begin with the Appointment of *Magistrates,* which in every Polity [*civitate*] is a part of the *Soveraignty.* For if they [sovereigns] are at last accountable for the mismanagement of their Ministers, it is fit [necessary] they should have a Right [*facultas*] to examin their Actions: and if they [the latter] have failed in the performance of their Duty, they must have Power to remove, or some other way to punish them. Now there is no question to be made, but the Emperor has this Power in a Sovereign Degree [undiminished], in his Hereditary Countries; |[but then, as to the rest of the Empire, it is disputed]|.ᶜ

For in the beginning the *Dukes* and *Counts* of *Germany* were Magistrates properly so called, as we have above shewn, and yet [now they have Supreme Authority within their Limits, under those Titles].ᵈ Nor will any of the Princes of *Germany* yield the Emperor the Government of the People within their Dominions, or [admit] that they [the people] are the Subjects of the Emperor, <at least in the sense that he has more right over them than they do,> though they will with great Ceremony and much Submission own themselves to be his most dutiful [humble] Subjects, and [repeatedly] testifie their great Loyalty to him. And although there may be an Hereditary [Jurisdiction in a Kingdom which shall still be a meer Magistracy];ᵉ yet then the Supreme Authority must [always] have reserved a Soveraign Power [a right] over that person that is invested with it.

a. Rather: he can render only an unsuitable and imprecise judgment about

b. Rather: exactly follows the rules of political [*civilis*] science / This is a small example of Pufendorf's tendency to offer independent analyses instead of following established patterns of scholarly commentary. [Ed.]

c. E.p.: but there is a question as to the rest of the Empire, and this chapter's disputes about the power of the Emperor all focus on the matter.

d. Rather: today they would consider that designation a severe insult

e. Rather: magistracy in a kingdom

|[We shall give some examples for the illustrating this]|.ª The Emperor may give to one the Title of a Prince or Count of the Sacred Roman Empire; but then he can give him no Right to vote in <91> the *Diet,* without the Consent of the rest of the States, (*Conf. Artic.* 44. *Capitul. Leopoldinae*).⁵ And seeing he [someone] is vainly puffed up with the Title of a Prince of the Empire, who has no Dominions to sustain the Dignity and Splendor of his Title, that he [the Emperor] may never be able to enrich these *Upstarts* [new princes], care is taken by the Thirtieth Article of the same Capitular, by which all vacant Fees [are to be united to]ᵇ the Empire, *Art.* 29. For this there is a double reason, first, That all the vacant Fees should not be swallowed up by the House of *Austria,* [nor given to men obnoxious to that Family];ᶜ and, secondly, That in time *Germany* may be able to give something to its Emperor, besides an empty Title, by which the Charges of that high Station may be born[e], that so in their Elections they may not be tied to chuse only persons of very great Estates[, but may be able, in time, to assign their Prince a Patrimony equal to the Title, and set him in a condition which is proportionable to the rest of the Princes of *Germany,* which if it had been to have been done at once, and out of their proper Dominions, would have been too much for them to have parted with].ᵈ

a. Rather: The entire matter will become clearer from the following / e.p.: Even if, in place of the Emperor's right to appoint magistrates, we focus on his right to elevate others to certain ranks and honors, we will find that it does not depend entirely on his will

b. Rather: revert back to the patrimony of

c. Rather: which, if it retained the faculty of bestowing them on others, would not forget itself or those beholden to it

d. Rather: . But [for the Emperor] to bestow on a recently created prince, from his own domains, a patrimony worthy of that title, and to elevate him to the same status as the rest of the German princes, would in my opinion exceed the measure of a sober liberality

5. The *Capitulatio* of Leopold I was issued in 1658, the first year of his reign. Like similar documents since 1519, it constituted a sort of *Herrschaftsvertrag* (contract of subjection) between the emperor and the German estates, published at the beginning of his reign. Article 44 makes admission to the diet dependent on certain territorial possessions (*Severinus,* ed. Salomon, 91, note 1).

Perhaps the Emperor might be allowed to admit [amongst them]ᵃ a foreign Prince, who is not subject to any of them [other superior]. But then, [if any of them could be contented to impair so much his condition],ᵇ what Place could he hope for in the *Diet?* He would be ashamed to sit on the lowest Bench, and except he were a <92> King, the ancient Princes of *Germany* would never give place to him.

It is probable, however, there would be less difficulty in receiving foreign Cities into the number of the free [Imperial] Cities of *Germany,* 1. Because they are not so ambitious of Precedence as Princes are, and [2.] |[*Buckhorn,* and such other [similarly splendid] Cities, would perhaps readily]|ᶜ yield them their Places for the Encrease of the *German Empire:* But then it is not likely that any such Free Cities will join with us, till one or two of our Neighbour-States are dissolved. And the Emperor cannot raise any of the [German] Cities that are [now] subject to any of the Princes [Estates], to the Priviledges and Dignity of a free Imperial City.

The Emperor cannot deprive any of the Princes of their Dignity.

6. Much less is it in the Power of the Emperor alone to take away or deprive any Prince of his Dignity, or expel any of the States out of his Dominions, though they are guilty of a great Crime against the Empire [*rempublicam*], but [even] in the most notorious Fact [case] he must obtain the Consent of the *Electors,* before he can interdict the meanest of them [the offender], *Capitul. Leopold. Artic.* 28. They thought fit to get this Bar, lest if any of the Princes had by chance offended the Emperor in his private personal Concerns, he should presently persecute him as an Enemy to the Empire. Whilst this *Capitular* was drawing [being drawn] up at *Frankford,* some of the States [prudently] desired there

a. Rather: into the order of the remaining German princes

b. Rather: even if anyone were willing [so] to worsen his condition / That is, by giving up his independent status and acknowledging the formal primacy of the emperor. [Ed.]

c. E.p.: little cities [*oppidis*] notable only because they are formally free, of the sort that abound in Swabia, might be readily persuaded to / Buchhorn, a free imperial city until 1811, is now part of Friedrichshafen (in Baden-Württemberg). Bohun's translation obscures Pufendorf's sarcasm. [Ed.]

might be a Clause [expressly] added to this 28th. Article, *That the execution of all Judgments given against any [proscribed] Prince of the Empire, [ought by Law to be committed to]*[a] *the rest of* <93> *the Members of the same Circle to which his Dominions belonged;* because if the Emperor himself undertook the execution of the Sentence, he might perhaps seize the Estates [of those proscribed] under pretence of the Charges [expenses] the Execution put him to. [And perhaps it might have become attractive to render such harsh judgments, if they worked to the judge's advantage.][b]

On the other side, |[the Emperor never concerns himself how the Princes treat their own Subjects, and whether *they [flea or fleece]*[c] their Flock is all one to him]|,[d] because one of the principal things he promiseth in his Oath, is, *That he will save to every of the States their Rights and Priviledges, and disturb none of them in the exercise thereof.* And this is one of those *Rights* in which the Princes and States of *Germany* take the greatest Pride; *That every one of them can govern their own proper Subjects, according to his own will, or to the Compacts he has made with them.* See the 3, 7, 8, & 9. *Artic. Capitul. Leopold.*

Besides, there are [only] few instances in which the Emperor can directly and immediately command the Subjects of [another Prince];[e] |[as for instance: To]|[f] give Testimony or answer an Action in a Suit depending; [and he is without any remedy from the Law in all those Citations, which he sends out in his own Name (if the Party will not appear.)][g] Yet he may reward or priviledge any of the Subjects of another

a. Rather: *should be carried out according to the received laws by*

b. Omitted by Bohun. [Ed.]

c. Rather: shear or flay

d. E.p.: although some of the Estates can be summoned before Imperial courts by their subjects for certain reasons, the Emperor has little concern about what care they have for their citizens, or how well they administer their domains

e. Rather: the Estates (*Ordinum*)

f. E.p.: indeed, many are even unwilling to concede that he can require them to

g. Rather: by means of a summons issued in his own name, against which there is no legal recourse [or: without any assistance of the law]. / There is an ambiguity in the phrase *absque omni subsidio iuris:* either those summoned (or the estates to which they are subject) cannot legally resist the summons, or (less likely), the emperor himself has no legal recourse if his summons is ignored. [Ed.]

State [the Estates], [but only] so he doth not diminish the Authority or Rights of their proper Prince [the Estates]. But then this Imperial Priviledge seldom goes further than the giving them Titles of Honour. <94>

The Emperor has no Revenues from the Empire.

7. Let us now see what Power the Emperor has over the [Estates of the Princes],[a] as to the Contributions that are to be raised for the bearing the Charges of the Government [*respublica*] in Times of Peace or War.

As far as I can understand, all the publick Revenues [outside the Emperor's domains] (a very few excepted) belong to the [respective Princes and Free Towns],[b] only the Emperor promiseth, (*Articul.* 21, 22, & 23. *Capit. Leopold.*) That he would prohibit overrating [excessively raising] the Customs, lest the Princes should thereby ruin the Trade of *Germany:* [Nor is he allowed to levy new taxes for himself in the domains of the Estates.][c] And if any thing of this nature comes into the Emperor's Treasury [from the Empire], it is not worth the mentioning, [and for the most part][d] belongs to the Officers of the *Chancery,* who reap the greatest profit [of all others,]⁺ from the renewing the Fees [(or Estates)]⁺ in the Empire. See *Artic.* 17. *Capit. Leopold.* [He can lay no new Impositions on any Merchandise, imported or exported within the Dominions of any of the States; and it was never heard in *Germany,* that the Emperor should <arbitrarily> lay any Tax upon any that lives out of his Hereditary Countries]:[e] Neither are the States obliged to any standing Charge towards the Necessities of the Government, except what is agreed for the upholding the Chamber of *Spire,* and even that very small Charge is very ill [grudgingly] paid by many of them.

In ancient times, when the Emperor went to *Rome* to demand [*petendam*] the Imperial Crown, the States of *Germany* were bound to arm and maintain Four thousand Horse and Twenty <95> Thousand Foot, to attend upon him during his Journey. But as these [Roman] Expedi-

a. Rather: possessions of the Estates
b. Rather: Estates
c. Omitted by Bohun. [Ed.]
d. Rather: or it
e. Rather: It is unheard of in Germany for the Emperor to levy direct taxes <at will>

tions have a long time been omitted, so the proportions that were then fixed [for that purpose] serve now only for the [immediate] appropor-tioning the Rates of the several Princes in all extraordinary Charges granted in the Diet: Yet there are many Complaints made against this old Proportion, because the Estates of some are, in length of time, sunk in their value, and others are as much raised above what they were.

[A *Turkish* War is ever a vast charge to *Germany*, and they never more willingly part with their Money than on that occasion; and yet even here the Emperor doth not proceed upon his own Authority].[a] All is granted and transacted in the Diet [by the Princes or their Deputies],[b] and the more easily commonly, because the [some] Princes are great Gainers by it, for they rarely pay to the Emperor's Treasury all they levy.

8. The Arbitriment of Peace and War is now also included in very narrow Bounds [*legibus*], whilst Money, the Sinew of War, is thus put out of the Emperor's Power. It is true, the *Austrian* [hereditary] Dominions will maintain a potent Army, but then, if they alone bear the charge of it, they will apparently [obviously] be very much exhausted.

Nor is he the Arbitrator of Peace and War.

//It is to be considered, our Author wrote before the recovery of *Hun-gary, Sclavonia, Serbia,* and *Bosnia,* out of the hands of the *Turks,* which are much larger than all the old Hereditary Provinces, and upon a Peace of Twenty years, will be able to raise <96> and maintain a much greater Army than the Hereditary Provinces could when they lay exposed to the Ravage and Incursions of the *Turks,* as now they will not; so that the Emperor is now three times more considerable than he was before the last War, in the extent of his Dominions, the security of his Subjects,

An Addition.

---

a. Rather: The greatest financial burden imposed on Germans has been for the war against the Turks, fear of whom has always led ordinary folk to expose both their bellies [in military service] and their wallets. But not even here has anything been exacted from the Estates [*Ordinibus*] on behalf of the Empire. / e.p.: The greatest amount of blood and money has been spent by Germans on the Turkish War; but not even here . . . / Bohun misses the contrast between ordinary people and the estates to whom they are subject. [Ed.]

b. Rather: , or through legates sent around for that purpose

and the acquiring of new Countries, to bear the Charges of defending themselves and the old too.\\ᵃ

Except therefore the States consent to the War, and promise their Assistance towards the Charges of it, the Emperor cannot promise himself any thing of help from them. As it is not their manner to be [entirely] wanting to the Emperor whenever he is invaded by another, so it is certain, if he should [spontaneously] begin a War upon any of his Neighbours, none of them would concurr with him in it, except a few of them, whose Interest unites them to the House of *Austria.* For it is, of the two, rather their Interest to hinder him from warring upon others, and that not only because all *Germany* may thereby be involved in Troubles, but also because the very Victories of the Emperor are no welcome News to the States, [as raising his Power (which perhaps is already too great) to the endangering of their Liberty].ᵇ (*Vide Art.* 13, 14, & 16, *Capit. Leopold.*)

Nor of Leagues and Alliances. The Tenth of these Articles shews, how the Emperor's Power is bounded as to Leagues and Alliances. |[A man here will not be able to forbear wondring why the Emperor is not permitted to begin a War against any Neighbour upon <97> any pretence whatsoever, or to enter into any Alliance with a Foreigner, without at least the Consent of the Electors[. And yet]ᶜ we are lately told, many [several] of the Electoral Princes had had a meeting [banded together], and drawing over to them a parcel [pack] of Thievish Souldiers [robbers], have made an Inroad upon the Elector *Palatine's* Dominions, under pretence of forcing from him some Rights which they are not well pleased he should any longer enjoy: And when they entred upon this action, they thought it was sufficient for them to give the Emperor a very superficial and insolent account of what they intended to do.⁶ There was [likewise] another Bishopᵈ of that Nation, [not far from the *Hollanders, (Munster)* took up Arms, and invaded

---

a. Bohun's insertion into the text. [Ed.]

b. Rather: since they will excessively swell his power, which they fear—perhaps justifiably—as a threat to their liberty

c. Rather: , since

d. That is, besides the archbishop of Mainz. [Ed.]

6. This refers to the so-called *Wildfangstreit.* See Pufendorf's 1667 preface, note 12.

that State, which War may involve a great part of *Germany*].ᵃ And all these bold Attempts of the Princes were entred upon whilst the *Diet* was sitting, and yet it took not the least notice of them. For it is now become a Custom for some of the Princes to League with the *Swedes* or *French*, both which Nations have for many years been the Enemies [or rivals] of the House of *Austria*]|.ᵇ

9. Let us see next what Power the Emperor has in the Affairs of Religion. |[[Because the new Politicians will needs have Temporal Princes, according to their new Divinity, intrusted in things of this nature];ᶜ whereas the *Roman Catholicks* constantly believe and profess, That it would be very prejudicial [damaging] to the Grandeur [position] and Wealth of <98> the Church [priests], to have any but [the Clergy intermeddle with the disposing of the Church-Preferments],ᵈ and therefore would [(very wisely)] ⁺ have the Laity content themselves with the Glory of enriching and defending the Church [clergy]]|.ᵉ

Nor is he the Governour of the Religion of *Germany*.

a. Rather: who singlehandedly began with his neighbors, the Dutch, a war that could easily have involved a great part of Germany / See chapter 2, note 25, on Bernhard von Galen of Münster. [Ed.]

b. E.p.: Yet there are many examples of the liberty taken by some Estates, in forming ties with outsiders, to the Empire's great detriment / Pufendorf no doubt means the Confederation of the Rhine (*Rheinbund*) of 1658, which was supported by France. Also, the Imperial Diet began to meet in permanent session at Regensburg after 1663 and was active during the events of *Wildfangstreit*. See Pufendorf's 1667 preface, p. 7, note 12. [Ed.]

c. Rather: We must treat of this here because the teachers of politics [*politici*] who adhere to the new [Protestant] theology do not hesitate to call on the civil sovereignty [*civile Imperium*] to share that power

d. Rather: the latter claim the right [*facultatem*] of disposing over sacred things

e. Bohun's substitutions (e.g., "church" for "priests" and "clergy") do not maintain the precision of Pufendorf's (Protestant) critique, which saw an important role for the laity in the furtherance of church affairs, even in theological debates, and which was in fact more a political challenge to priestcraft than a secular attack on religion as such. [Ed.] / e.p.: For the reform of sacred affairs throughout much of Germany has also led writers on public law [*ius publicum*, *Staatsrecht*] to inquire about this matter. According to the old theology committed to the teachings of Rome, the care of sacred matters belongs solely to the Roman Pontiff, and the highest civil rulers are left with nothing but the protection and material support of the clergy, and the occasional distribution of certain offices and sacred benefices. However, the

An account of
Martin Luther
and the Refor-
mation.

When therefore there were no other Rites received in *Germany,* but those of the Church of *Rome,* the few Disciples of *John Huss* in *Bohemia* excepted, and the *Jews,* who [are every where tolerated.]ᵃ *Martin Luther*[, beyond all men's expectations, sorely weakened the Papal Authority in that Nation],ᵇ and taking the advantage of a small Brangle, of no great moment at first, drew off a considerable part of the Empire [Germany] {from their Obedience to the See of *Rome*}. |[If I may be allowed to speak the truth, this inconsiderable Spark was blown up to this dreadful Fire, by]|ᶜ the folly of them who at first opposed *Luther,* and the inconsiderate rashness and haste of *Leo* X. For some contemptible [*miselli*] Monks [were] contending one with another, one Party of which was very zealous for Religion, and the other Party no less concern'd for their Profit{; and at first both of them had the Papal Power in great esteem, as Sacred}. Now it was certainly here the part of a prudent Judge, to shew himself equal and indifferent to both the contending Parties, or presently to have silenced both of them, lest his Commodities [(his Indulgences)] ⁺ should become cheap, and suspected by the People: At least, he ought not so manifestly to have espoused the [Quarrel of his <99> Factors],ᵈ for fear this highest Priest [shepherd] might be suspected to be more fond of getting Money, than preserving the Souls of those under his care; or lastly, to prevent being suspected to be better pleased with [the price of Mens Sins (paid to him) than with the most Innocent and Holy Life].ᵉ The more indevout sort of men were not to be [should not have been] tempted neither by this Affair, to suspect, that the Priests

---

more recent [Protestant] doctrine grants far more power to the supreme [civil] rulers and has thereby provided an occasion for much disruption [*magnae rerum conversioni*] throughout Germany. We must give a brief account of this, in accord with the focus [*captu*] of our work

    a. Rather: were tolerated here and there,

    b. Rather: unexpectedly inflicted a great loss upon the papacy

    c. E.p.: First place among the causes of that affair is rightfully assigned to divine providence; but among those that led men to that point, beside a disposition already prone to such a change, blame belongs mainly to

    d. Rather: side of the indulgence sellers

    e. Rather: sins that are paid for than prevented

were very like Physicians and Chirurgeons, who reap too much Benefit from the Diseases and Wounds of Men, to be heartily sorry for them:

So that [But] if it was foolish and sacrilegious to give Sentence against the Indulgences, to the damage of the Church, it had been prudent to sweeten a man of too warm a temper with Presents, Preferments, and Promises, that he might not light the Laity into the way of shaking off the Church's [priests'] Yoke; and when so many have by Ambition and Gifts aspired to the highest Dignities in the Church of *Rome,* I think, for my share, it would have been worth the while to have wrapped this Monk in Purple,[a] to prevent his doing her so great a mischief: For when *Martin Luther* saw he could have no Justice done him [at the Pope's Tribunal],[b] he began to court the Grace and good Opinion of the Laity, and soon after, he positively refused to submit to the Judgment of the *Pope,* because he [the latter] had [openly] made the Quarrel his own, by entring into it: And that he might not want a Patron, he began to teach, That the Care of the Church belonged <100> to Secular Princes, and those who had the like Authority. And they again reflecting, That the great Revenues their Ancestors had given to pious uses, were spent in [nourishing the] Sloth and Luxury [of the clergy], [quickly embraced the opportunity of turning these lazy fat Cattel to Grass].[c]

This [teaching] was greedily followed by many, partly because [most of] what *Luther* said seemed true, and partly because they found they could considerably improve their Revenues [therefrom]. There was then a [spreading] Rumour also, that the *Italians* imposed upon [were taking advantage of] the old *German* Honesty and Simplicity, and that they spent the Money they had torn from them on the account of their Sins, in Gaming, Luxury, and filling the insatiable Avarice of [the Pope's Officers and Creatures].[d] They called to mind a Saying of Pope

What is said of the design of enriching themselves by the Revenues of the Church, is to be understood as spoken in the Person and Name of a

a. That is, to have made him [Luther] a bishop or a cardinal. [Ed.]

b. Rather: before a tribunal of priests

c. Rather: thought it right to deprive these lazy flocks of their fodder

d. Rather: papal nephews / That is, the pope's relatives and even his own illegitimate children. [Ed.]

Roman Catho-
lick; for all the
Protestant
Princes have
ever denied
they had any
such design,
and it is not at
all probable at
first they
could have any
such.

Martin V.[7] which in truth was very worthy of a Spiritual Pastor, *viz.*
That he could wish himself [*vowed to become*] *a Stork, provided the* Germans *were turned into Frogs.* Hereupon they began to bemoan themselves to one another, and say, *We who of old so valiantly repell'd the*
victorious Arms of the Romans, *are by an unwarlike sort of men, under*
pretence of Religion, reduced almost to a necessity of eating Hay [*with our*
Beasts][+]. I cannot tell how much the [restoring Learning in this part
of the World might contribute to this Revolution, which was thereupon received with][a] great Applause. However, < 101 > we may well and
safely affirm, That Men of Learning are not easily perswaded to believe
what is (or seems) contrary to Reason.

Many of the
German
Princes
deserted the
See of *Rome.*

10. The effect of this Controversie was, that a great part of the ancient
Rites, and all those Doctrines which seem'd superfluous to these new
Teachers, were laid aside by a considerable part of the *Germans;* and at
the same time many of the Clergy were deprived of their Church-Lands.
Thereupon many Suits were commenc'd in the Chamber of *Spire,*[b] by
the Clergy, against those that had deprived them of their Possessions;
and [that Court was also very willing to have restored all to the outed
Clergy, but then][c] the PROTESTANTS {(as they are call'd)} refused in this
matter to acknowledge the Jurisdiction of that Court: "For though (said
they) the Laws in all Cases [above all] command, that they which have
been dispossess'd, should be restored to what they once had; yet, in this
Case that was now depending, it was fit and reasonable, that a lawful
general Council, or some other publick Convention, [(that is a National
Council of *Germany*)][+] should first consider and determin, whether the
outed Clergy did profess and teach the true Religion. For if this was not
first well proved, (as they [themselves] believed it could not) it was

---

a. Rather: restored cultivation of letters at that time contributed to the reception
of that new doctrine [*disciplina;* i.e., Protestantism] with such

b. That is, the Imperial Chamber Court (*Reichskammergericht*) at Speyer; see §20
in this chapter. [Ed.]

c. Rather: since that Court also seemed more inclined toward the outed Clergy,

7. Martin V was pope from 1417 to 1431 and belonged to the Roman Colonna
family, which had already produced twenty-seven cardinals.

[in vain, and to no good purpose, for them]ᵃ to expect the enjoyment of those Revenues which had been given by their Ancestors, for the maintenance of <102> the true Worship of God."

Now, because they were quickly sensible, that Reasons and Protestations alone would not secure them, the greatest part of these Protestant States and Princes joined in a League at *Smalcald,* to repell any Force or Violence which might be offered to any of them, because they had embraced the Reformed Religion: At length it came to a War, which proved very unfortunate to the *Protestants,* and the Elector of *Saxony,* and the *Landtgrave* of *Hess,* [the two principal persons of their Party,] ⁺ were both taken Prisoners, and their Religion seem'd to be in a desperate and hopeless condition; but then *Maurice* the [next] ⁺ Duke of *Saxony* restored [it to its former Power, by his Arms, and the *R. Catholicks* were forced to come to a Treaty at *Passaw,* for the securing all Parties] ᵇ{; the terms of which may easily be found in any of the *German* Historians of that time}.⁸

After this, in the *Diet* of *Ausburg,* in the year 1555, the *Protestants* obtained the securing their Religion by a Law passed there in favour of it, [by which Law they had sufficient Security given them, that they should live in Peace, and]ᶜ that neither of the Parties should hurt or invade the other on the account of their different Religions, nor compel [any man by force to abjure that Religion which he professed].ᵈ If any Church-

The Decree of Ausburg for the Liberty of Religion.

a. Rather: shameless for the latter
b. Rather: their power by his arms, and the Treaty of Passau was entered into
c. Rather: called the religious peace [of Augsburg], whose main stipulations were
d. Rather: one another to abjure it
8. Formed by a number of Protestant princes in 1531 at Smalkalden (in Hesse-Nassau) after Charles V refused to accept the so-called *Confessio Augustana* (formulated by Luther and Melanchton) at the Diet of Augsburg (1530), the league was finally defeated in 1547 after some defections from its ranks and the capture of Landgrave Philip of Hesse and Elector Johann Friedrich of Saxony. In 1552, Moritz of Saxony entered into the Treaty of Passau with Ferdinand I of Austria, an agreement that paved the way for the so-called Peace of Augsburg (1555). This treaty officially acknowledged Protestantism (i.e., Lutheranism) in the empire through the principle of *cuius regio eius religio,* whereby individual princes could dictate the official religion of their own domains while eschewing interference in those of others.

Lands had been seized by any of the Secular Princes [Orders], which did not belong to any other immediate [State or Prince of *Germany*],[a] it should be left to the <103> present Possessor, against whom no [Suit should be commenced in][b] the Chamber of *Spire* [on that account], if the Clergy were not in possession of the same at the time of the Treaty of *Passaw,* or after it: That the Ecclesiastical Jurisdiction should not [no longer] be exercised against those who professed the *Protestant Religion* [*Augustanae Confessionis*]; and that they should manage their Religious Affairs as they thought fit: That no Prince should allure the Subjects of another Prince to his Religion, nor undertake the Defence of them, on the pretence of Religion, against their own Prince. But then those Subjects of either side, that were not pleased with the Religion or Ceremonies of his own Prince, might sell their Estates, and go where they pleased. And lastly, if this Difference of Religion cannot be composed by fair and lawful [*licita*] means, this Peace shall nevertheless be perpetual.

The Liberty of the Clergy more fiercely disputed. 11. In the mean time there was a sharp Contest [dispute], Whether the Catholick Clergy should have liberty to embrace the Protestant Religion, and also possess [retain] notwithstanding their Dignities and Church Revenues [holdings]; which was urged with the greatest vehemence by the Protestants, who said, That the contrary Practice was a [great] reproach to their Religion, if [they should consent, that][+] those that entred into it should be deprived of their Honours and Estates: That the way that leads to the Purer Religion [doctrine] was by this shut against many: That they had no intention to turn the Church-Preferments [holdings] to Secular uses, or to take <104> away the Freedom of Elections from the [cathedral] Chapters. But then, because it was [quite] apparent, that this exposed the *Roman Catholick* Religion, in *Germany,* to the utmost danger, the Catholick States opposed it with equal obsti-

---

a. Rather: Estate / That is, those directly (immediately) subject to the emperor, rather than through intervening (mediate) powers or authorities; see chapter 2, note 3. [Ed.]

b. Rather: verdict [*ius*] should be rendered by

nacy, and *Ferdinand* the Emperor favouring that Party, they got this Clause added to the Law; *If any Clergyman becomes a Protestant, he shall forfeit his Church Preferments* [*beneficia*], *but without any loss or diminution of his Honour* [esteem].[9] And although, at that time and [often] after, especially in the Case of the Archbishop of *Cologne,* who became a Protestant,[10] the Protestants complained very much of this Clause, and protested against [maintained that they were not bound by] it[, yet they could not get it repealed] +. <Yet it was confirmed as such in the Treaty of Westphalia.>[11]

12. But this Peace [of Augsburg] was not able to take away all the Seeds of Discord, which sprung from this Diversity of Religion. For they that embraced the Protestant Religion, divided it into Parties and Factions, because the greatest part of them stook [stuck] simply to the Words of the first *Augustane Confession,* whilst some others thought some Doctrines ought to be more nicely [exactly] exprest. And although wise men thought this was not a Controversie that was worth the entring into a Civil War for, yet their minds on both sides were very much exasperated by the Intemperance of the Preachers, and the Frauds [intrigues] of the *Roman Catholicks,* who expected to make great use of these Dissentions

The Differences in Religion cause great disquiet in *Germany.*

9. This refers to the so-called ecclesiastical reservation (*reservatum ecclesiasticum*), a clause in the Peace of Augsburg (1555) by which Protestant officeholders were allowed to retain the lands then under their control (which would not have to be returned to Catholics), but which required that if a Catholic became Protestant thereafter, any Church lands under his control would go to a Catholic appointed in his place.

10. The reference is to Gebhard Truchseß von Waldburg, Catholic archbishop and elector of Cologne, who was excommunicated, deposed, and replaced by Gregory XIII in 1583 for publicly converting to Protestantism (Calvinism) and marrying a countess. These actions violated not only the *reservatum ecclesiasticum* but also the Golden Bull, and they generated hostilities that lasted until 1589.

11. Article V.15 of the Treaty of Westphalia not only reaffirmed the *reservatum ecclesiasticum* for Catholics but also granted it to Protestants in turn. Moreover, it established January 1, 1624, as the "normal year"—i.e., the point at which the distribution of ecclesiastical possessions would be taken as normative, in the sense that any revisions would not look back to conditions before that date. See V.12, p. 133, in this chapter.

amongst their Enemies, as a means to overcome them in the end. And whereas [since] all those that profess'd neither the *Roman Catholick* <105> nor the *Augustane Confession,* were excluded from the benefit of the aforesaid Peace, the *Roman Catholicks* hereupon craftily endeavoured to perswade those who simply stuck to the *Augustane Confession,* to disown all those that had refined upon it, as not at all belonging to their Party. Though the strict Protestants often declared publickly, that they would not disown those that differed from them in some points that were of less moment, but that they also ought to enjoy the Benefit of the Peace; yet the over-great Zeal of the Priests divided them so far, that they began to separate [each from the other, and not to consult so frequently together as they had done before]:ª Nay, after this, when one of the Parties was oppressed by the Popish Party [Catholics], the other would unconcernedly [quietly] look on whilst they perished or [even] lend Assistance to their Enemies.

Afterwards other occasions of Discontent arose, and last of all, a Fire was kindled in *Bohemia,* which in a short time involved all *Germany* in a War: Here Fortune at first smiled upon the Emperor, and prospered his Affairs beyond his hopes, so that in a short time his Armies subdued and brought under the greatest part of *Germany;* and [finally] in the year 1629, he presumed to publish an Edict, That [all the Clergy should be put in possession of all the Church-Revenues, which had been taken from them by the |[Laity]|,ᵇ since the Treaty of *Passaw*].ᶜ The secret Design of this Edict was, to bespeak [procure] the Assistance <106> of the Clergy and [other] Catholick States, and to perswade them, that all his Designs tended to the resettling [reestablishing] that Religion, and not to the oppressing the Liberties and Rights of the *German* States and Princes: But then, if they had either [sate still, or helped him to subdue the Protestants; nay, if they had not hindered the reduction of them, it

a. Rather: their respective interests and consult less frequently about what they had in common

b. E.p.: Protestants

c. Rather: ecclesiastical goods seized by the |[laity]| after the Treaty of Passau should be restored / Ferdinand II issued the Edict of Restitution in 1629. [Ed.]

would have been very easie for the Emperor (thus flush'd with Victory, and arm'd with Power) to have model'd them at his pleasure].ᵃ

How this Project came to fail, is too well known to be represented here: And at last, in the Treaty of *Osnaburg* (or OSNABRUCK) in *Westphalia*, in the year 1648, by the V. Article, there was a large Provision made for the Security and Peace of Religion, the Treaty of *Passaw*, and the Recess of *Au*[*g*]*sburg*, being both confirmed, and an express Declaration inserted, that it extended equally to the *Lutherans*, and to the ‖[*Calvinists*]‖,ᵇ as they call them now. It was added also, That all Changes that had been made since the First of *January*, 1624 in [the State, under pretence of favouring the Church],ᶜ should be put [back] in the same state [condition] they were then; and that all those Revenues [sacred holdings] which were then possess'd by *Roman Catholicks*, but were since taken from them by the *Protestants*, should be restored back again to them; and the like should be done by the *Roman Catholicks*, to the *Protestants* [, that all the immediate States]ᵈ which the *Protestants* possess'd at that time; should be their own for ever.

   The Right of changing Re-<107>ligion, which before seem'd to be left free to all the States, was for the future so restrained, that the Subjects of the Catholick Princes, who were of the *Augustane Confession*, and in the year 1624, had the Free Exercise of their Religion, were still to retain it. And they that had been in the mean time disturbed, were to be [should have it] restored. Those who had not enjoyed their Liberty in the said year, should have Liberty of Conscience, but should only [exercise their Religion in their own private Families, or the Neighbour places]:ᵉ But

The Peace of Religion resettled in Germ[any].

---

   a. Rather: assisted or at least not opposed him, he would have subdued the Protestants, after which it would have been easy as well to bend the rest [of the Estates] to his will

   b. Rather: Reformed, or *Calvinists* / E.p.: Reformed

   c. Rather: Ecclesiastical affairs, and by reference to them in political affairs / See note 11 in this chapter. [Ed.]

   d. Rather: . Mediate sacred holdings [*bona sacra*] / On mediate and immediate, see chapter 2, note 3. [Ed.]

   e. Rather: conduct their worship [*cultum*] in the privacy of their own homes, or nearby [*vicinis locis*] / That is, not in public. [Ed.]

if their Lords should command them to be gone [emigrate], they should have liberty to sell their Estates, or manage them by their Deputies [*Ministros*]: And the Emperor himself, in some things, indulged his own Protestant Subjects, for the sakes of the [Protestant] Princes. It was also agreed, that if any Prince should hereafter think fit to change his Religion, it should be no prejudice to him;[a] and that he might have Priests in his Court of his own Opinion [religion]. But then, that he should not force his Subjects to his Religion, but should leave that he found in [their] possession, but so, that it might [also] be lawful for his Subjects, if they would [voluntarily] take up the Religion professed by their Prince.

It is also to be noted here, that this Liberty of Religion was settled by way of Compact or Agreement made between Equals, and [that] the Emperor himself is [joined with] one of the Parties; so that neither he nor any other of the Catholick States, though they should happen to be the more nume-<108>rous Party, ought to alter any thing of it:

And it is also manifest, that the Condition of the Protestant Princes is better [here] than that of the Roman Catholicks, because the latter are subject to the Pope; whereas the former govern their Affairs of Religion in their own Right, and as they think fit. {Now [That is], if any share of the Government of Religion [*cura sacrorum*] belongs, by the Laws [according to the Doctrines] of Christian Religion, to the Civil Magistrate [at all]:[12] It is plain, [at least, that] the Authority of the Churchmen will thereby be [was thereby] reduced into a very narrow compass.} *Add. Artic.* 1. *&* 19. *Capit. Leopold.*

The Legislative Power not in the Emperor.

13. We proceed now to the Legislative Power. That it may appear to whom this belongs, we must consider by what Laws *Germany* is governed, and how they were introduced. Here the learned *Hermannus Con-*

a. That is, he could do so with impunity. [Ed.]
12. This qualification was removed in the e.p., in accord with Pufendorf's position in *Of the Nature and Qualification of Religion.* See III.6, note 8, p. 88.

ringius has led the way in his learned Book, *De Origine Juris Germanici,* whom I shall very near wholly follow.[13]

This [celebrated] Author takes great pains to confute the commonly-received Opinion, That the *Roman* or *Civil Law* was in the year 1130, by the Command of *Lotharius* the *Saxon,* [then Emperor of *Germany,*]⁺ received both in the Schools and Courts of Justice: Whereas he shews, that to the XIII. Century, the Courts of *Germany* did not so much proceed upon any written Laws, as upon ancient received Customs, and upon Equity and good Conscience; and the Judges for popular [civil] actions were not chosen on the account of any eminent Learning, but rather [for being] ancient men, < 109 > well esteemed for *Prudence, Piety,* and *Justice,* the far greatest part of the People [laity] being then not able to write or read. In the XIII. Century the Canon Law, by slow degrees, began to creep into *Germany,* and not only that began to be studied [derived from it], which concerns Church-Affairs, but the Processes of Civil Affairs were [also] regulated or formed by it, though many stuck stifly to their own ancient Customs. About the same time these *Old Customs* were also put in Writing, amongst which the Laws of *Lubeck* are most esteemed, and those of *Magdeburg,* which in the *German* Tongue is call'd *Weichbild;* the *Mirror* of the *Saxon* and *Schwaben* Law,[a] and the *Feudale Saxonicum & Suevicum;* and these were very near all the Laws used in *Germany,* in the XIII. and XIV. Centuries.

The Canon Law first introduced.

The ancient German Customs after this set down in Writing.

In the XV. Century, the *Civil* or *Roman Law,* and with it the *Jus Feudale Longobardicum,* began also by degrees to creep in [come into use], the Skilful in these Laws being often advanced to the Honour of being Counsellors to the Princes, who [they] took all opportunities to recommend their own Profession to the good Opinions of Men: And it began thereupon to be taught in all the Universities of *Germany,* and that after |[the manner of *Italy,* which gave them the example]|.[b] After

The Civil Law introduced in the XV. Century.

---

a. The so-called *Sachsenspiegel* and *Schwabenspiegel.* [Ed.]

b. E.p.: the example of the Italian schools, it seems, attendance at which Germans then thought something to boast about

13. Conring's work was published in 1643. See Pufendorf's 1667 preface, p. 6, note 11, on Conring.

this, when men that had studied it, were call'd to the Bar, it began by little and little to be received into the Courts [*forum*]: And in the year 1495, *Maximilian* I. appointed [ordained] the *Civil Law* to be admitted and used in the Chamber of *Spire,* but *saving* <110> *all the Ancient* [*received*] *Customs, and the Local Statutes of all places.* So that the Law now

That at present in use is a mixture of Canon and Civil Laws, and the old Customs.

used in *Germany* is a *Mixture* of *Civil* [*Roman*] *Law, Canon Law, Ancient Customs, and the Statutes of the several Provinces and Cities, which are very contrary one to the other.* And in all Courts this is observed, That if there be any Provincial Statute or municipal Law extant, [concerning the Case depending, that takes Place in the first place];[a] but if there be none, then they have recourse to the *Roman* or *Civil Law,* as far as it is commonly received.

Particular Laws made by the several States.

The States of *Germany* [the Empire] in the mean time are allowed to make Laws concerning Civil Causes, in their respective Provinces [domains], which may [even] differ [(if they think fit)][+] from the Common and Usual Law; [and that they shall][b] enact Statutes for their own use, without ever consulting the Emperor, so [long as] they contain nothing in them prejudicial to the [other States of *Germany*].[c] [And although][d] many of them have desired the Emperor to confirm their Provincial Statutes<, to lend them greater authority, or to give proof of their respect toward him >. And they can also make particular Laws concerning Criminal Cases. Nor is the *Caroline Constitution*[14] in all points every where observed. The States have also a Power to pardon Offenders: But if any thing [new statute] is to be introduced that shall bind all, it cannot be

The general Laws in the Diet.

settled but in a Diet, and by the Consent of all; and when it is so passed, it obligeth the Emperor as much as any of the other States. *Vide Artic. 2. Capit. Leopold.* <111>

a. Rather: that takes precedence
b. Rather: just as they may
c. Rather: condition [*statui*] of the Empire as a whole
d. Rather: Still,

14. The *Constitutio Criminalis Carolina* was the penal law of the empire, introduced by Charles V at the Diet of 1530 and ratified at Regensburg in 1532.

14. The Jurisdiction [judicial process] of *Germany* has been very differently managed in different times, as is accurately set forth by *Conringius*
in his Tract *De Germanici Imperii Judiciis,* from whom I shall transcribe
the principal Heads, to save my own labour.[15]

And I will begin with the Times of *Charles* the Great. When any of
the Royal Family had any Controversie, either one with another, or with
any other [outsider], it was determined in the Council of the Nobility
and People, as were also those Cases of the Nobility, that were of great
concernment [importance]. The smaller Controversies the Nobility had,
were determin'd by the King, or those he sent [emissaries], (for so they
were then called, who are now call'd Commissioners, Visitors, or [ex-
traordinary] Delegates). For the ending the Contests of others, there
were settled in the [individual] Hundreds[a] and Districts certain Judges
called GRAVES [*graviones,* counts], who had to assist them, and sit with
them, others called SCABINS [or assessors],[b] chosen out of the Nobility,
or the better sort of the People [*honesta plebe*], and these heard and determined all Civil and Criminal Cases. The *Graves,* by reason of the
greatness of their Hundreds, had certain *Deputies* in every Village, or,
as they call them SCULTESIO's, (like our *constables*)[c] from whom yet
there lay an Appeal to the *Grave.*

The Priests also punished the Vicious Lives of Christian Men [Chris-
tians] by Canonical Censures. The Bishops exercised a Jurisdiction over
the Clergy and the Monks: And the Bishop was also accountable to his
Metropolitan, or a Synod [called <112> by him][+], though afterward Appeals to the Pope [Roman Pontiff] began to be made, on the account
of the Authority of that See<, at the beginning, it seems, usually by

a. A "hundred," according to the *Oxford English Dictionary,* was a subdivision of
a county or shire with its own court; Bohun uses it to translate *pagus:* a village or
county district. [Ed.]

b. *Assessores* "sat with" or advised the counts or *graviones; scabini* [*Schöffe*] were
lay judges who worked together with another lay judge and a professional judge. [Ed.]

c. A *scultetus* (in German, *Schultheiß*), was the equivalent of a sheriff. The phrase
in parentheses is Bohun's clarification. [Ed.]

15. The reference is to Conring's *De Imperii Germanici republica: Acroamata sex
historico-politica, seu discursus novi historico-politici de Imperii Germanici civibus, ur-
bibus, duribus & comitibus, electoribus, episcopis & judiciis* (Ebroduni [Yverdon], 1655).

mutual agreement [of the contending parties]>. Yea, the Cases of many Laymen were promiscuously [generally] referred to the Bishops, [upon an opinion of their]ᵃ Sanctity and Integrity:

But then the Judgment of [about] the Church-Revenues was not in the Clergy, but in the *Advocates* or *Vicedames* [*vicedominos*], which were particularly appointed by the Kings. And so the persons of the Clergy were subject to the Judgment of the Clergy, and their Revenues [goods] were subject to the *Advocates* Judgments, who were Laymen. From these fixed settled Judges they appealed to the King's Messengers, who at certain times travelled over the Provinces [(like our itinerant Judges of Assize)]⁺ and from them to the King's Palace,ᵇ in which Appeals the King himself, or the Count *Palatine*, gave Judgment; which last was also appointed to determine the Causes which arose in the Court. But then they hardly admitted an Appeal, but where the *Grave* or *Messengers* refused to administer Justice:

And all Cases were determined by a short and very plain Process, and in a few Sessions or Hearings. So that in all this [judicial] form there was nothing wanting [to criticize], but an Appeal for the Clergy to the Pope, who {though an holy person,} was [then considered as one out]⁺ of the Bounds of *Germany* [(and so not to be taken notice of)]⁺. <113>

The old forms changed in after times. 15. In all these things, in process and length of time, almost every thing was changed. After the *Golden Bull*, the Electors [took cognizance of]ᶜ all the Royal Cases. And the Pope assumed to himself so great Power [on that account, that he made no scruple to excommunicate the Emperors, and declare, that their Subjects were free from the Obligations of their Allegiance to them; and he boldly said,]ᵈ the Emperor was his Vassal, and the Empire a *Fee* which belonged to his See.

---

a. Rather: on account of their reputation for

b. *Palatium, Pfalz,* or Palatinate—used generally (etymologically) here and not just in regard to the Palatinate on the Rhine; see III.3, note 4, p. 83. [Ed.]

c. Rather: retained for themselves alone almost

d. Rather: over them [linguistically, the only available referent is the electors (Ed.)] that he did not hesitate to excommunicate them and to pronounce their subjects free from their obedience to them; moreover, he boasted that

As to the Princes' Suits or Cases, [this was ever observed from the very beginning of the *French* Monarchy],[a] that they were never determin'd by the Judgment of the King alone, but were alwaies decided in a *Convention* of the Nobility, upon a simple and short Process, according to Equity and good Conscience [*aequo et bono*]. And even [in the first Ages of the *German* Empire, if any of][b] the Emperors assumed a Power singly [by themselves] to judge of the |[*Fees*]|[c] belonging to any of the Princes [Estates], the more couragious of them alwaies protested against it: Yea, if all the [other] Testimonies we have were lost, the very form of the whole Empire, [or its Constitution,] + does sufficiently prove, that things of that consequence which these Suits are of, ought not [(by it)] + to be left to the single Judgment of the Emperor<, or, at least, that the Electors must first be consulted>: And therefore they are notoriously [manifestly] guilty of palpable Flattery, who [pretend, that this Judgment of the Cases of the Princes of the Empire, which the *Germans* call DAS FÜR-STENRECHT, is a meer <114> Pretence].[d]

But [then, it was long after these times that these inferiour Princes took upon them to judge arbitrarily of the Cases of their own Vassals, which was done only by some Families, and imitated by the Free Imperial Cities, as to their Subjects. The *Germans* call these Counts in their Language AUSTREGA's, and it is probable they began about the times of *Frederick*][e] and the great *Interregnum*. [Those][f] that trusted more to their Power or Force than to the Justice of their Cause, would commit

a. Rather: the old custom remained

b. Rather: if, especially during the previous century,

c. E.p.: persons and the Fees

d. Rather: dare to call the judgment of the princes, or what the Germans term DAS FÜRSTENRECHT, a mere fiction

e. Rather: later on most princely families, who were imitated by the free cities, established arbitration tribunals [*judicia arbitraria*] for themselves, which the Germans call *Austraegas* [*Austrägalgerichte, Austragsgerichte*]; their origin probably dates to the final years of *Frederick I* Frederick II ruled 1212–50. The time between the extinction of the Staufers and the start of the Hapsburg dynasty (with Rudolf von Hapsburg) was known as the Interregnum (1256–73). See Bohun's addition in §19, p. 143, of this chapter. [Ed.]

f. Rather: Very often, too, those

the Trial of it to the Sword. It is also a late Practice, which has been taken up by [some of our later] + Emperors and Princes, to referr the Cases depending to their Ministers [and profess'd Lawyers],ᵃ rather than to give themselves the trouble of hearing them. But then this became necessary, when instead of a few plain Country [ancestral] Customs, we had [there were] introduced the Intricate, Papal [Canon], and Civil [Roman] Laws, which it would have been the utmost punishment to have put the Princes to the trouble of learning.

The Innovations brought in by the Churchmen.

16. As to the *Churchmen,* they innovated in these particulars: By degrees they drew all the Personal Cases of the Bishops to the Pope's Tribunal, utterly destroying [*neglecta*] thereby all the Authority of *Metropolitans* and *Synods;* and they took from the Laity all Right of judging in any Case [a Clergy-man].ᵇ This is by the *Protestants* returned to the ancient method; but by the *Roman Catholicks* still retained, though *Charles* V, and some other Princes since, have to the great <115> vexation of the Pope, [and without consulting him,] ordered some things pertaining to Religion and [punished some Clergy-men for great Offences too].ᶜ

In the times also of *Frederick* II, and those that followed, [the Bishops and Clergy]ᵈ assumed to themselves the free Administration or Management of their own Church-estates, and shook off their *Advocates* or *Vicedams;*ᵉ yet still the Ecclesiastical States [Estates] are subject to the Empire, by reason of their *Fees* and other *Regalia's*, of which they may be deprived, if they act any thing insolently against [seriously violate] the Publick Peace and the Laws of the Empire.

The Monks, as to their Persons, were, in the times of *Charles* the Great, subject to the Jurisdiction of the Bishops, from whom some ancient Monasteries were [later] exempted, and were put immediately under the Pope. The new Orders which have arisen since the XIII. Cen-

a. Rather: with legal expertise
b. Rather: the persons [vs. the goods] of the clergy
c. Rather: laid hands on the persons of the clergy
d. Rather: most clergy
e. See §14, p. 138, of this chapter. [Ed.]

tury,[16] are [only subject to their]^a Provincials and Generals, and only acknowledge the Pope's Jurisdiction as their Supreme Ordinary [judge]<, apparently to restrict the authority of the bishops>. The Administration of the Lands of the Abbies were at first committed [mostly] to *Advocates,* from which dependance, in length of time, some Houses were exempted, but the greatest part have still remained in the same state they were at first; and some few of them are free from all publick Taxes and Charges.

17. The Secular Cases of the meaner People [*plebeiorum*] were heard [already] in the times of *Charles* the Great, either in the Secular Courts, or by the Bishop in his Consistory; which later <116> way has since been much extended beyond what it was at first. These [plebeians] were first (as to the Secular Courts) to make their Complaints to the *Scabins,* which in ancient times were appointed in all the Hundreds (*Pagi*) and Villages; from him [scabin] they might appeal to the *Graves* or *Comites,* (*Earls* or *Sheriffs*) whose Jurisdiction was after[wards] usurped by many *Dukes* and *Bishops.* From the *Counts* or *Graves* they had an Appeal to the *Itinerary Messengers,* (or Judges) sent into the Provinces by the King, and from them to the King himself, who in his Court made a final Determination of all Cases:

But in the XV. Century, when Appeals became very frequent, by reason of [the bringing in the tedious Forms, and the Iniquity of the Rabble];^b for the more commodious determining [of] these, it was resolved, to erect a [certain]^c fixed Tribunal or Court, which was at last settled at *Spire* [Speyer]. The reason of this was not because the Imperial Court was too ambulatory or unsettled,^d but because the vast quantity of these Cases might most conveniently be determined in a place set apart for that end.

Secular Cases, how managed.

The Chamber of *Spire* erected for Appeals.

a. Rather: subject to their own
b. Rather: wide-ranging proceedings and pettifogging lawyers
c. Rather: more comprehensive [*amplissimo*],
d. Because of the emperor's travels. [Ed.]
16. Including the Dominicans and Franciscans (founded in the early thirteenth century) and the Jesuits (founded after the Reformation).

Since removed
to *Wetzlar.*

//The *French,* in the year 1688, having seized *Spire,* the *Diet,* in the year 1689, agreed this Court should be settled, for the future, at *Westlar* (WETZLAR) a City of *Hassia* [Hessen], seven *German* Miles from *Frankford,* to the North, and about fifteen from *Cologne* to the S.E. which being approved by the Emperor, Commissioners are appointed to adjust all things for the opening this Court there; <117> and it is very probable it will never be returned back to *Spire,* that City being too much exposed to the Insults of the *French,* who, when they please, can seize the Records of this Court, to the inestimable damage of the Empire. And besides, the *French* had before burnt and destroyed the whole Town of *Spire,* not leaving any thing standing in it that Fire and Gunpowder could fetch down.\\

The present
form of
Process.

18. The modern way of Trials now received in *Germany,* is thus: When any private person commenceth a Suit against another of the same quality [*cum privato*], he in the first instance goes to the *Praetor* [(*Scabin*)]ᵃ of the City or Village in which he lives, except the Defendant be [some way priviledged above the *Scabin*].ᵇ [There]ᶜ is in all the Principalities which I have been acquainted with, some superiour Court, which is common to the whole Province, {which they call the Palace or Provincial Court,} and to this Superiour Court there lies an Appeal from the *Scabin:* But then the most part of the Free Cities have only one Court, from which there is no Appeal.

In Civil Cases
there is no
Appeal from
the Electors,
Emperor and
King of
Sweden.

The Chamber of *Spire,* and the Emperor's *Palace-Court,* are common to the whole Empire. But then some of the Princes [Estates] have a Priviledge [right] which restrains their Subjects from appealing to either of these Courts, [and] of this number are the Electors: Yet there are some, who question whether this Priviledge belongs to the Ecclesiastical Electors, [though] only because they do not exercise it. <118>

    The House of *Austria,* and the King of *Sweden,* enjoy the same Ex-

---

a. Added by Bohun. / The *praetor* was the chief judicial officer. [Ed.]
b. Rather: equipped with a privilege
c. Rather: Moreover, there

emption[, the latter] for all his *German* Territories. (*Westphaliæ Art. cap.* 10. *sect.* 12.) This last Prince has erected a Court at *Wismar,* for the determining all those Appeals which before belonged <to the Princes of those provinces, and otherwise> to the Chambers of *Spire* and *Vienna.* (*Add. Capitul. Leopold. Artic.* 28, & 27.) But then all the Princes [Estates] of the Empire are equal in this, [so far as I know,] that there [lies no Appeal],[a] except the thing in dispute exceed such a [a certain] value, which yet in some places is more, and in others less. In Criminal Cases, [however,] not only the Princes [Estates] of the Empire, but many [some] of the Burroughs or Corporate Towns, and many of the Nobility, exercise a Soveraign Jurisdiction without any Appeal.

In Criminal Cases there lies no Appeal.

19. But then, if there be any Controversie between the States or Princes, the greatest part of them, in the first instance, have their resort to the *Austraega's* or *Arbitrators:*[17] Of these some are [appointed in a peculiar Convention][b] of the States, and others depend upon the common disposition of the [public] Laws. The first Institution [origin] of this Judicature is very obscure; but their Opinion seems most probable, who date its Rise about the times of *Frederick* II, and ascribe it to that long *Interregnum*[, as already mentioned]. //This *Interregnum* began in the year 1198, when *Philip* Brother of *Henry* VI. was chosen by one Faction, and *Otho* Duke of *Saxony* Son of *Henry* the Lyon, and *Maud* of *England* by another; from henceforth there was nothing but War and Misery; till in the year 1212, <119> *Frederick* II. Son of *Henry* VI. was, after many other, chosen, who yet could not obtain the peaceable Possession till the year 1219. so that it lasted about 21 years. But to return.\\ It is certain, *Maximilian* the First was not the Author of this Court, [as some wish him to be,] though he gave it a new form, which is extant in the *Ordination of the Chamber* in 1495, made at *Worms.* Of the various forms of *Austraega's* there mention'd, there are [only][c] two now in use; as, 1.

How the Controversies of the States or Princes are determined.

a. Rather: is no appeal from them [to Speyer or Vienna]
b. Rather: constituted by special agreement
c. Rather: most frequently
17. See §15 and note e, p. 139, of this chapter.

The Defendant names Three Princes [or other Estates] a of the Empire, out of which the Plaintiff chuseth one: Or, 2. They obtain by consent of the Emperor one or more Commissioners: But then there are some Cases which ought not to be brought before the *Austraga,* but immediately before the Chambers of *Spire* or *Vienna;* which [cases] may be found [in many very common Books]. b

Now, there are these Inconveniences alwaies attending [the Judgments given by] + the *Austraega*'s; 1. That there lies an Appeal to the Chambers [of Speyer and Vienna], so that very few Controversies are [finally] determined by them. 2. That great Sums of Money [are spent in treating and sweetening the Emperor's Commissioners]. c 3. [There is a Sequestration of a years continuance of the Profits of the thing in dispute, which time is allowed to the *Austraga*'s, to give in their Award; because it is thought an indecent thing to determine a Suit of moment in less time in *Germany*]. d <120>

The highest Courts in *Germany* are the Chambers of *Spire* and *Vienna.*
20. The highest Court in *Germany* is the Chamber which was lately fixed at *Spire,* which was instituted [by the *Diet* of *Germany,* under] e *Maximilian* I. in 1495. (And after many Removes, fixed at *Spire,* in the year 1530, by the *Diet* of *Ausburg,* under *Charles* V. where it remained till this year 1689.) f Now, though this Court useth the Name of the Emperor only [alone] in all its Processes [decrees and verdicts], yet [they are correct who assert] it doth not depend on the Emperor only, but acts in the behalf, and by the Authority of [all] the States of *Germany:* The Emperor names the *President,* who must be a *Prince* of the Empire, or, at

a. This distinction makes clear that Bohun's frequent use of "Princes" for "Estates" is a reductive simplification. [Ed.]

b. Rather: here and there in the common handbooks

c. Rather: are required for the tasks of stroking and properly maintaining the commissioners of the arbitrating princes

d. Rather: The judgment of the Austragas must be rendered within half a year or a year, though it would be a miracle in Germany for a lawsuit of any importance to be settled within that time frame / The enumeration is Bohun's. [Ed.]

e. Rather: with the consent of the Estates by

f. The parentheses are Bohun's, who reveals here the date of his translation. [Ed.]

least, a *Count* or *Baron*. By the Treaty of *Osnabruck* it was agreed, that under this prime President[, who is called judge of the Chamber,] there should be four other inferiour Presidents [vice-presidents] to be nominated by the Emperor, and [at least]ᵃ fifty Assessors (Judges or Companions with them) Twenty six of which should be of the Roman Catholick Religion,[18] and Twenty four of the Protestant, to take from the later all just cause of complaint, that their Cases were not [as] favourably heard and determined: Yet ||[at this day there is rarely half this number]|,ᵇ the [majority of the] Princes that should nominate and pay them, being very slow in both respects, they being much offended with the Imperious Commands of this Court, though they rarely go further than words.

He that is desirous to know the exact form of their Proceedings, must read the [entire] Order of the Chamber, inserted into the *Recess* of the *Diet*, in 1495. It is a common <121> Proverb, That the Suits at *Spire* are drawing on, but never die, (*Spirant non expirant*).ᶜ This is owing to the litigious forms and delays or perplexities in the Processes, and the number of the Cases depending [pending] before too small a number of Judges to dispatch them. But yet, after all, the great[est] Reason is, the Difficulty of executing the Sentence; for the Princes that [have great Estates]ᵈ do very little regard what the Judges at *Spire* say: And they again have so much wit, that they will not hazard the small remainder of their Authority, by giving Judgment [(how justly soever)]⁺ against a Prince of that Power, [so] that he will despise both them and their Sentence. But then, in this Court (as in others) if they catch a small Fly, they will be sure to hamper him. In the year 1654, in a Diet, there were many Rules or Provisions made for the supplying the Defects of this Chamber: There lies no Appeal from it, but if any man is aggrieved, he may desire

---

a. Rather: a total of

b. E.p.: that number has never been completely attained

c. The Latin (*lites Spirae dicuntur spirare, sed nunquam expirare*) plays on the words *Spirae* (Speyer), *spirare* (to breathe, live on), and *expirare* (expire, cease, die). [Ed.]

d. Rather: are confident in their own power

18. Twenty-six, because the emperor appointed two of them (Monzambano, *Über die Verfassung*, trans. Breßlau, 90, note 2).

[request] a Revision, which yet, to my knowledge, [was never sought, or never granted].[a]

The Chamber of *Vienna* when first instituted. 21. There is also in the Emperor's Palace another Court, which pretends to the same Authority with that of *Spire* (which is above call'd for distinction the Chamber of *Vienna*)[b] [. They both say, that][c] a Suit begun at *Spire* cannot be withdrawn and removed to *Vienna,* [and so on the contrary].[d] *Ferdinand* [I.] the Emperor, in the year 1549,[19] first opened this [court], and published the Rules or Laws by which it was to proceed: *Maxi*-<122>*milian* II. encreased them; but *Mathias,* in the year 1614, [completely] renewed it; and *Ferdinand* III. changed some of the Rules in the *Diet* [of Regensburg] in the year 1654. (See the *Treaty of Peace, Art. 5. Sect.* 20. *Artic.* 41, 42, 43. *Capitul. Leopold.*) This Court [up to now] depends solely on the Emperor, though |[the Judges of it are [also] bound to the Archbishop of *Mentz,* as *Lord High Chancellor* of *Germany* [*the Empire*] by an Oath]|.[e]

It is not hard to guess what was the true reason why the Emperors instituted this Court<, or why they renovated and solemnly enhanced it>; to which purpose it will be fit to consider, that these Princes observing, that all Appeals <and other important cases> being tried and determined at *Spire,* and that place frequented on the account of Justice, the Court at *Vienna* was in the mean time neglected, to the [great dishonour and][+] dissatisfaction of the Family of *Austria:* For the flying to them for Relief, is the greatest of the Glories of a Prince [of rulers]; and their Majesty is then most resplendant, when it gives men their Due, and repells their Injuries: Besides, he that has the Management [interpretation] of the Oracles of Justice, can [best secure his own Interest,

---

a. Rather: remains quietly sunk in a deep sleep
b. The parenthetical information is Bohun's clarification. [Ed.]
c. Rather: , so that
d. Rather: nor the reverse
e. E.p.: the Archbishop of Mainz, as Chancellor of the Empire, claims the right to hear appeals
19. Ferdinand I reorganized the Aulic Council (*Reichshofrat*) in 1559.

and take care that nothing shall be done contrary to it].ᵃ <As is well known, Cardinal Cleselius said often that there was no need for the Emperor to wage war against the Protestants, as it sufficed for him to rule against them in judicial proceedings.>²⁰

Now, the Chamber of *Spire*[, since it] depended on the whole Body of the Empire, [and was also seated at a great distance from *Vienna,* and that beyond the *Rhine,* and therefore seemed to take but little notice of the *Danube* (that is *Vienna.*)]ᵇ The form of the Law Proceedings being also changed, it was now become very difficult to adjust and end the Controversies of the Dependent <123> States in the *Diet* [at the *Diets*], as had been formerly practis'd. Now, if the Emperor could by degrees insensibly draw them to himself only, in conjunction with the Claims of private men, he |[should thereby gain a great Step toward the [gradual] acquiring a Soveraign Authority [*potestatem Regiam*] over the States]|.ᶜ Nor were there wanting plausible Reasons for the opening this Court; for, Why should he be obliged to administer equal Justice to all, [as he had promised in the Capitular,] if all might pass by him, and direct their Addresses to *Spire?* This Chamber of *Vienna* [aulic court] pretended also not to be tied to the slow methods of Process used at *Spire;* and men were pleased with the expectation of a quick dispatch of their Cases [in those instances where they merited a favorable judgment]. For the Court of *Spire* is so hampered, that tho' the Case is never so plain, and the Judges are never so willing to do speedy Justice, yet they must omit none of their appointed Forms.

[Some others, that pretend to a deeper inspection, say there is a private

a. Rather: easily ensure that that goddess does not deliver any replies contrary to his own advantage

b. Rather: was in its counsels removed from [the influence of] the Imperial court [*aula*], and being located on the Rhine it apparently cared little about which way the Danube flowed.

c. E.p.: would impose on the Estates a great necessity to acknowledge his authority [*majestatem colendi*]

20. The Austrian Melchior Klesl (Cleselius), 1552–1630, held many positions, including chancellor of the University of Vienna, privy counselor, and cardinal (1615).

[privy] Council at *Vienna*],[a] in which the greatest Affairs of the Empire are considered: Now when any great Case has been ventilated and debated in this [aulic] Court, if the Judges find it has any State-Interest in it, they give the Emperor an account of it, with their Thoughts of it, and thereupon it is again debated in that private Council, in which the State-Interest of the Case is more considered than the Justice [*juris*] of it. As for the Instance; Whether it is for the Emperor's Interest, that this or that Judgment should be given; and [how][b] and which way the execution <124> shall [conveniently] be made: So that if any Scruple of that nature ariseth, [the Judges have private Orders to suspend or delay the Judgment].[c] {I presume, the Judges of this Court would also take it very ill [to be suspected of Bribery];[d] and yet there are many that think it is their Interest to clear themselves [(if they can)][+] of this Suspicion, which might be done by shewing to the contending Parties, to which of them the Case depending is committed.}

The Form of executing the Judgments of these Courts.

22. As to the form of Execution [of sentences] in both these High Courts, it is thus: First, They enjoin the Party that is vanquished [condemned] to submit to the Sentence they have given against him, upon pain [threat] of forfeiting a certain quantity of Marks of pure Gold, to be paid in part to the Exchequer of the Empire, and in part to the Person [party] suing. If he doth not obey the Sentence upon notice of this, [within the time limited,][+] then the Sum is encreased; but if he still persist, and despise their Threats, he is put under the BANN, or proscribed,[e] and the Sentence is ordered to be put in execution by Force and Arms, till the Party submit. If the Party cast is a Subject of any of the States, the execution of the Sentence is committed to that State or

a. Rather: One penetrates still more deeply into the nature of this Court if one considers that there is a yet more secret or secluded [*sanctius*] Council at the Emperor's court

b. Rather: whether

c. Rather: the announcement of the verdict is postponed

d. Rather: if the various parties tried to gain favor by bribing them

e. That is, placed outside the law and its protection, as if returned to the state of nature, with anyone helping him being subject to similar penalties. [Ed.]

Prince whose Subject he is. If the Party condemned is a Prince, or Member of the *Diet* [one of the Estates], then the General [prefect] of the Circle, or some or other of the Members also of that Circle to which he belongs, are commanded to execute it: But if the Party is so powerful, that the Circle is not <125> able to force him to submit, two or three of the next Circles are commanded to join with them: But this rarely happens, that there are any such Executions to be made; and when there is, it is more for the Interest of *Germany,* and for the securing the Liberties of the several States to compose their Controversies of this [such] great moment by Arbitrators[, than by Suits and Military Executions thereupon] +.

23. If any thing ariseth which may affect the whole Body of the Empire [*reipublicae*], the Emperor cannot determine of it as he pleaseth himself, but [ought to propose it in the *Diet,* and it is by the States to be there] a ordered as they shall by common Consent agree [*consensu*]. (*Vid. Capitul. Leopold. Artic. 39. sub sin.*) Now, because all these Affairs have been very exactly collected [treated] by |[*German* Writers]|,b it will be sufficient for us to set down here some of the principal Heads of them.

The greater Cases ought to be determin'd in the Diet.

1.c The Emperor has the sole Powerd of assembling the *Diet,* but so, that he is bound, by his Letters or Envoys, to require the Consent of the *Electors,* and also to adjust with them [even] the Time and Place. (*Capitul. Leopold. Art.* 17.) The *Electors* also may admonish [advise] the Emperor, when they think it is for the Interest of *Germany* there should be a *Diet.* But then, because the holding a *Diet* is a thing of very great Charge [expense] to the *States,* it is expresly said [in the last mentioned article of Leopold's Capitular], That the Emperor shall not burthen them with the holding unnecessary Diets. [(*Capitul. Leopold. D. E.*)] +
During the vacancy [an interregnum], <126> the *Vicars* of the Empire

a. Rather: such a matter must be placed before the Diet, or a gathering of all the Estates, and

b. E.p.: many

c. The Latin original does not enumerate. Bohun begins to do so but does not continue. [Ed.]

d. That is, the emperor alone, or, only the emperor. [Ed.]

[(the Duke of *Saxony,* and the Count *Palatine* of the *Rhine*)] + shall assemble [call] the *Diet,* and in [his absence],[a] the King of the *Romans,* if there be one. The calling [*indictio*] of it shall not be by any [public and] General Proclamation, but by written or printed Letters, to be delivered personally to each of the States [(or Members)] + which shall be penn'd in a kind inviting Stile, and not in an imperious commanding Form like a Citation [summons]. The Indiction shall be six months before the Meeting, that the States may have sufficient time to consider what is there to be treated of.

In ancient times the Diet was held every year. 24. In ancient times there was a *Diet* held every year, and it continued but one Month, as is supposed by the *German Antiquaries.* At this day it is not agreed [firmly established] how often or how long it shall sit, but that is governed by the present Necessities of the publick Affairs{, or at least it ought to be so: Yet they [some] have adjudged it expedient for the preserving the Liberties of the States, that there should be frequent [regular] *Diets,* as for instance, once in three years at the farthest;[21] [and] that when they are [held], necessary care should be taken to expedite the Affairs depending [pending], which now move too slowly, and occasion vast expence [both of Time and Money] +, which might be saved. There are some that [are jealous],[b] that these affected Delays and Charges are [a State-Mystery, by which the Emperor hopes],[c] in time, to tire out the States, and make them abhor *Diets,* which were otherwise [deemed] the most effectual means to <127> secure [the *German*][d] Liberty}.

The *Golden Bull* has ordained, That the first *Diet* [(of every Emperor's Reign)] + should be at *Norimberg,* <unless legitimate obstacles intervene,> {which yet is not scrupulously observed now}. For in these

a. Rather: the absence of an Emperor / On the King of the Romans, see IV.9, pp. 109–10, and note 25. [Ed.]
b. Rather: suspect, however
c. Rather: to the Emperor's advantage, in that he hopes thereby
d. Rather: their
21. See Pufendorf's 1667 preface, p. 5, note 9.

Capitulars there is [only care taken]ᵃ that it shall be held in a convenient place, within the Empire, as shall be agreed with [by] the *Electors:* Of [For] a long time some one of the Free Imperial Cities has been appointed for that purpose, the reason of which is not so much in the dark; and, I suppose, the Princes would scarce meet, if the Emperor should appoint *Vienna*[, for instance].

25. All the [Members of the States]ᵇ are, without exception, to be called to the Diet; and amongst the Ecclesiasticks, [even] those that are not yet confirmed by the Pope{, and before they have obtained their Palls,²² and in the vacancy of any See, the Chapter is to be called}. And whereas the Protestant Possessors of Bishopricks, before the Treaty of *Westphalia,* were not [called or] admitted to the Diet, they in it obtained the Assignment of a peculiar [special] Place<, which is now held by the Bishop of Lübeck alone>²³ As to those Secular Princes that are minors, their Guardians appear for them; and they that are of full age, are to be admitted before they have asked or obtained their Investiture. This is true, though in the Diet of *Ratisbonne* [Regensburg], in the year 1608. *John Frederick* Duke of *Wartemburg* [*Wurtemberg*] was excepted against [opposed] on that account. If in any Family the Right of *Primogeniture* prevails, and is received, only the Eldest is called. Those that have divided their Inheritance, are called [by Families in <128> general, but they have all but one voice: But those that have obtained the Investiture of their Share or Portion from the Emperor, are personally called].ᶜ

They that are called to the *Diet,* must appear in person; or if this is

All the Members are to be summoned to the Diet.

a. Rather: mention only

b. Rather: Estates of the Empire

c. Rather: as individuals, if they have been specially invested with their portion. Those who possess their domains jointly [*indivisim*] are all called, but they have only one vote together / See II.1. [Ed.]

22. See IV.4 and note 12, p. 102.

23. Protestant principate-bishoprics were gradually secularized after the Peace of Westphalia. Thus, when the prince-bishop of Magdeburg died in 1680 (and the city went to Brandenburg), Lübeck alone retained this status (the principate of Osnabrück alternated between Protestant and Catholic bishops). See II.6, note 19, p. 64; and II.11, note 27, p. 71.

inconvenient, by their Legates [(or *Proxies*)]⁺ sufficiently instructed [empowered]: Those that neglect to appear, are nevertheless [concluded by the majority of those that do appear].ᵃ By a peculiar Priviledge the King of *Bohemia* is not bound to appear in the Diet, if it is not held at *Norimberg* or *Bamberg.* The House of *Austria,* and the [Duke of *Burgundy*],ᵇ are at Liberty to appear or not, as they please. {It is not worth our while to sum up the vain useless Rites and Ceremonies [of the Diet].}

The things to be debated are proposed by the Emperor or his Commissioner.

26. The things that are to be debated and settled in the Diet, are proposed by the Emperor, or his Commissioner[s], then they proceed to the Debate; where the first Question is, Whether they shall proceed in the order the things are proposed, to consider and determin[e] them; or, whether they shall postpone some of them undecided, and pass forward to the rest of the things proposed? Here the States [pretend]ᶜ they are not religiously bound to observe the Method [Order] of the Proposals; but the Imperial Party [(who can easily foresee what the States drive at) have ever stifly pretended, the Method of the Proposals is to be followed; that the Emperor's Concerns have ever been wont to lead the Van, and those of the States to follow in <129> the next place].ᵈ If therefore the States [will do their own Business],ᵉ they must of necessity gratifie the Emperor [first]. But then it has been observed, that when he has gained his own point, he is seldom much concerned for those things that the States would have.

When they come to debate, they are divided into three Colledges [(Houses or Chambers)]⁺ the ELECTORS, the PRINCES, and the FREE

a. Rather: bound by that which the majority has decided
b. Rather: Estates of the Burgundian circle
c. Rather: have often maintained that
d. Rather: , for reasons easily detected by those with finer noses, have always resisted this. That is, the Emperor's concerns have always taken first place, while matters benefiting the Empire as a whole [*Reipublicae universae*] have been forced to stand behind them / e.p.: . . . as some have interpreted the matter, have always resisted this, because the Emperor's . . . / Bohun's rendition of the parenthetical matter makes the estates the object of suspicion, while it is really the imperial party whose underlying intentions are being exposed. This is consistent with the tempered e.p. version. [Ed.]
e. Rather: wish to deliberate about these at all

CITIES, which Division is thought to have been first made in the year 1589,[a] in the Diet at *Frankford:* In the first of these the Bishop of *Mentz* is the [so-called] Director (*Speaker*); in the second, the House of *Austria* and the Bishop of *Saltzburg* by turns; and in the third, that [free] City in which the Diet is held: The Princes vote man by man{, the Counts and Bishops [minor Prelates] by *Benches*}: The greater part obligeth the lesser, except in the Affairs of Religion, [and those] in which the States are not considered as one Body, but as Parties, in opposition each to other. Whether the same thing ought to be admitted in the matter of Taxes, or granting Money, is a Question not yet decided. (See the Treaty of *Westphalia, Art.* 5. *n.* 19.) I should think this might easily be expedited by a Distinction, *viz.* Whether the Grant tends to the Safety and Security of the whole Body of [*Germany*],[b] or is only granted and designed for the Benefit [or special use] of the Emperor? No good [*German*][c] would decline contributing to the first; and as to the latter, it is fit every one should be left to his own <130> liberty, to determin[e] as he shall think fit.

Their way of Proceeding [deliberating] is this: What is approved by the College of *Electors,* is communicated to the College of *Princes;* this latter returns to the former their Sentiments of it (which [procedure] is called a *Reference* [or *Conference*])[d] and so it is transacted *pro* and *con* between these two till they agree. Then they two join, and communicate their agreed Resolves to the third College or Cities, and if they consent too, then the unanimous Resolves of the [whole Bodies of the State],[e] are communicated to the Emperor, or his Commissioner[s], and when he has approved of it, that Affair is settled: If the three Colleges cannot agree, their differing Votes are proposed to the Emperor, who in a friendly way, as an Arbitrator, and not in a commanding way, as a Master or Prince, endeavoureth to reconcile them. In like manner, if his Judgment is not the same with that of the States, it is friendly and fairly

---

a. Rather: 1489 [*Severinus,* ed. Salomon, 112, note 2]
b. Rather: the Empire [*Reipublicae*]
c. Rather: citizen
d. Rather: and *Coreference* [*correferre*]
e. Rather: Estates

argued between them, till he is of their mind, or they of his. [After this],[a] at the breaking up (*Recess*) of the States,[b] there is a Solemn [Form, containing the things][c] agreed between the Emperor and the States, in the manner of a Contract.

As to the College of Cities, it is to be observed, that though in the Treaty of Peace [of Westphalia] (*Art. 8. sect. 4.*) the [a] deciding Vote is assigned to it, whereas before[, the] others contended, that they were only to be admitted to the Debates (to offer their Reasons)[,] yet even now [they <131> communicate nothing to this Member of the States, but what is agreed by the two other Colleges].[d] But then neither can those two Colleges [exact Obedience, or force this third to comply with them against their wills, as a major part];[e] but where the third College disagreeth from the other two, the thing in dispute is referr'd to the Emperor, till [a way is found to adjust it].[f] And what cannot at last be agreed, is wont to be referred to another Diet. What is [thus] agreed by the whole Diet, is by the Bishop of *Mentz,* who is Director of the first College, and in a sort, of the whole Diet, drawn and reduced into the form of a *Recess,* [Edict, Decree, or Law, and then it is again considered by the States];[g] and after they have all subscribed and sealed it, then it is published.

The Emperor has yet some Prerogatives above any other Prince.

27. By all this which I have said, it will easily [sufficiently] appear how much of [the chief parts of] the Soveraign Power is left to the Emperor. Yet there are some Prerogatives [rights] which belong only to the Emperor in *Germany.* [These include] 1. the Right of the *First Prayers* [*Requests*], by force of which, the Elected Emperor has a Right to [present one person to a Benefice in every of the Ecclesiastical Chapters or Col-

a. Rather: Therefore,
b. The *Reichsabschied,* or imperial recess. [Ed.]
c. Rather: formula stating: These things have been
d. Rather: the two superior colleges do not communicate with it until they have agreed with one another
e. Rather: impose their decrees as commands or, as the major party [majority], force these upon them against their will
f. Rather: here as well concord is attained
g. Rather: checked once more

leges].ᵃ {The Emperor has less reason to be ashamed of this Restriction [right], than the Clergy, who [though] owing almost all their Wealth to the Liberality and Bounty of the first Emperors, have [been so ungrateful as to restrain]ᵇ the Successors of their Benefactors to the Collation [conferral] of [a single Benefice],ᶜ and <132> that too to be conferr'd [only] by way of [an] Entreaty, that shall not be denied.} 2. He gives all sorts and degrees of Honours or Titles: (Yet, see *Art.* 43, & 44. *Capitul. Leopold.*) 3. [He only gives and collates the Investitures of the Princes Fees, and all others that pass by the Delivery of a *Banner*].ᵈ 4. He constituteth Universities [*scholas publicas sive Academias*]. 5. And he only can give leave to build [found] a City. And there are some other [rights] too of less moment.

28. And from hence it is [also] easie to collect how little is wanting to make every of the States Independant Soveraigns. For they, or at least the greatest part of them, have the [intire]⁺ Power of Life and Death over their respective Subjects. They can enact Laws[, even ones] that are contrary to the common Laws [Right, *iuri*] of *Germany,* in their own States. They have an [intire]⁺ Liberty as to Religion.ᵉ They levy Taxes. They make Leagues one with another, and with Foreigners, so [long as] they be not against the Emperor and the Empire, (See the *Treaty of Peace, Art.* 8. *sect.* 2. *Capitul. Leopold. chap.* 6, *&* 8.) which Right is denied [the Imperial and Free Cities]ᶠ expressly. (*Art.* 9. *Capitul. Leopold.*) They defend themselves with Force and Arms, and [revenge their own wrongs,

The Priviledges of the Princes and free States.

a. Rather: recommend one person to an ecclesiastical benefice in any [*quolibet*] clerical college he chooses

b. Rather: restricted

c. Rather: only one Benefice in each college [*singulis Collegiis*]

d. Rather: He alone bestows investitures and confers princely fiefs, including those customarily symbolized by a banner / That is, *Fürstenlehen* and *Fahnenlehen,* the latter conferred by the manual bestowal of a banner subsequently displayed to indicate the recipient's newly acquired status. [Ed.]

e. Insert sentence omitted by Bohun: They take all revenues from their own domains for themselves. [Ed.]

f. Rather: to non-immediate citizens of the Empire / See II.1, note 3, p. 50. [Ed.]

especially if they have to do with Strangers].ᵃ They build Forts and
strong Holds in their Dominions{. They mint Moneys,} and do all other
things necessary to the Government of [their People].ᵇ (*Add. Artic.* 33,
34. *Capitul. Leopold. Treaty of Peace,* <133> *Art.* 8. *n.* 2.) The [5. *Art.
Capitul. Leopold.* belongs only to the Electors].ᶜ And all these things they
do in their *own* Names and Rights, and not as the Ministers of [*loco*]
the Emperor.

   <Some think that these rights do not amount to sovereignty properly
speaking, but only to a kind of regional superiority, as they say, a grade
of power that is inferior and subordinate to the former. Still, the weight
of that superiority is so great that it far exceeds the status of a civil subject, and it leaves no place for monarchical power [*majestati*] over those
endowed with it, especially when their strength far exceeds the measure
of any private individual.> Nor doth it affect their Power so much as
express the way of having or coming by it, that they acknowledge their
Dominions to be Fees holden of the Emperor and Empire. For seeing
they transmit them as an Inheritance to their Children [by right], the
Investiture is rather to be considered as a solemn Rite, than as a real and
true Collation [Conferral] or Gift, <however it was originally acquired,>
seeing it cannot be denied to any that desireth [requests] it within the
time prescribed by the Law. <And although a Fee may be said to involve
dependency, and an obligation arising from benefits received, not all
things so denominated immediately reduce their possessor to the level
of a citizen and subject. So, too, the fact that someone's power is restricted by Imperial laws or said to depend on the Empire and universal
dominion, in that he constitutes a member of that great Republic or
body, does not at all mean that he can therefore be said to have assumed
the bearing of a civil subject.>

   Their Oath of Allegiance[, which they make to the Emperor,]⁺ is
understood with a saving of their Rights and Priviledges; and |[even
those that are acknowledged to be Equals each to other, are yet frequently

---

   a. Rather: violently revenge the injuries done them, especially against outsiders
   b. Rather: a state [*civitatis*]
   c. Rather: special dignity of the Electors is treated by 5. *Art. Capitul. Leopold.*

mutually bound one to the other]|[a] by Oaths. <And, in fact, the rights of the Estates are not to be measured by their Oath, but their Oath must be interpreted according to their rights.> Nor doth their appearing in the Diet, at their own Charges, [constitute such a burden, or] prove that they are Subjects; for that is common to all the Assemblies of Allies or Confederates. Nor doth their contributing to the Necessities of the Empire prove their Subjection for the same reason. < For though, in a regular system of allies, the majority cannot obligate a dissenting minority through sheer command, as it were, in a state [*republica*], however, and an irregular civil body,[b] it is possible for the majority to obligate the minority, albeit not by commanding them [*pro imperio*] but on the basis of a pact [*ex pacto*].>

And lastly, That which seems the hardest of all, *viz.* That any of these States [of the Empire] may be sued in the Supreme Tribunals[, or Courts, or Chambers of the Empire] [+]; and if they be convicted of any great Offence against the Empire, that they may be proscribed, and deprived of their Dominions; [for even this is common to all][c] Confederacies [*societatum*]. And there <134> is an Example of it in Ancient History, in the League of the *Amphyctyones* and [that of the] *Achaeans, amongst the Greeks:* And in our own times, the Confederate or United Provinces thus forced *Groningen,* and bridled it for some time with a Citadel.[24] But then the States of *Germany* are very well secured [the

a. Rather: it is well known that allies, too, are mutually bound / e.p.: it is well known that allies and others, who are by no means to be numbered among subjects, are bound

b. Like the empire. [Ed.]

c. Rather: is not contrary to the nature of

24. During the third of the so-called Sacred Wars involving Delphi (355–346 B.C.), the Amphictionic Confederacy of northern Greece (with the support of Thebes and Macedon) disciplined Phocis, a noncompliant member state; the Achaean Confederacy of southern Greece existed for some three centuries and was finally abolished by the Romans in 146 B.C. On these and other ancient confederacies, and their relation to the regular/irregular distinction, see Pufendorf's dissertation, *De rebus gestis Philippi Amyntae filio* (Heidelberg, 1664), which anticipated many ideas in the present work and led people to suspect Pufendorf as its pseudonymous author (Monzambano). The United Netherlands built a citadel within Groningen's walls in 1600.

enjoyment of these vast Liberties. (*Capit. Leopold. Art.* 28.)]ᵃ But then, if any one of a Confederate or United [Equal] Society should insolently and injuriously [obstinately] insult upon another Confederate, [without pretending to claim any Superiority, the rest of the *Confederates* would have reason and right to curb the Exorbitant Member, and force him to do them Justice].ᵇ <For here the finding of fault is imposed on an offender not as a command from above [*ex imperio*], but as something freely consented to by him and somehow mutually agreed to. And the penalty is imposed not as on a subject convicted of violating a civil law, but as an act of war against the violator of a treaty. However, all these things are more easily explained when the discussion is not about some regular system of allies but about some irregular body, which has some things in common with a state [*civitate*] and some with a system [of states].> <135>

a. Rather: by *Capit. Leopold. Art.* 28.
b. Rather: he may be restrained by the rest

Of the Form of the German Empire.[1]

1. |[As the Health of Natural Bodies, and the Strength and Ability of Artificial Composures results from the Harmony of their Parts and their Connexion or Union with one another; so also *Moral Bodies* or *Societies* are to be esteemed strong or weak, as the Parts of which they are composed, are found well or ill formed and united together, and consequently as the intire form or whole of them are elegantly or irregularly and disorderly [monstrously] formed and united]|.[a] It will appear sufficiently in what has been already said, that [the Government, State, or Empire of *Germany* hath something of Irregularity in it],[b] which will not suffer us to bring it under any of the simple [or regular]⁺ forms of Government, as they are usually described by the Masters of Politicks<, as anyone can see who has compared that state with kingdoms and aristocracies that are generally acknowledged as such>:

a. Rather: Insofar as the health and aptitude [*habilitas*] of natural bodies, and those of artificial ones, results from an appropriate harmony and connection among their parts; so also . . . / e.p.: Insofar as there are three kinds of bodies: natural, moral, and artificial, each of which is composed of different parts, so, depending on whether these parts are properly arranged and fitted to one another, or disposed in an orderly fashion, or not, those bodies are deemed healthy or regular, or the opposite. / See *On the Law of Nature and of Nations,* I.1, on moral entities; and VII.5, as well as Pufendorf, *De rebus gestis Philippi Amyntae filio* (Heidelberg, 1664), §3, on regular and irregular forms of the state. Note, also, that the e.p. does not use the controversial term *monstrosum* in connection with irregularity. [Ed.]

b. Rather: the German state [*Germanorum Republica*] contains [*latitare*] something

1. This chapter of the work evoked the most response and immediately generated numerous criticisms and refutations.

We must therefore the more accurately enquire what its true form is, |[because the far greatest part of the *German* Writers have made gross and foolish Mistakes]|,[a] through their Ignorance in Politicks, and |[senceless transcribing one another without any Prudence or Consideration, by which they have multiplied their Books]|.[b] <136> I must therefore here bespeak [beg] the Pardon of my Reader, if by the subject of my enquiry I am forced to use more School-Subtilties or Distinctions than will please those [that love not that sort of Learning],[c] because without them it is not possible to make a true Representation of, or pass a solid Judgment on the present State of *Germany.* The Truth is, a few words would satisfie all wise men, if the Follies of some [other] men that have had the good fortune to be approved [by many], had not made it at once necessary and troublesome to confute and expose them.

All the Hereditary States are Monarchies.

2. |[As to the several parts [or Estates] of this Empire, separately taken or considered, there is no difficulty]|.[d] For all the Secular Principalities which go by Inheritance, the Ecclesiastick, which pass by Election, and the Earldoms, they are all administred and governed like Monarchies, but with this difference however, that in some places the Princes are absolute, <except where they are bound by the common laws of the Empire,> and in others they are limited by certain Pacts, or Agreement with their Provincial States [or Orders, as they are called]<, and by their [the latter's] privileges>. Amongst the free Imperial Cities, some are under

The Free Cities are Commonwealths.

an Aristocratical Regiment, the principal management of Affairs being in their Senates, into which their Principal Citizens are elected [*adoptantur*] by the Suffrage or Voices of the Senate [Senators themselves];

a. E.p.: the more carelessly the topic has been treated by most writers

b. Rather: because most among them refer to the careless compilation of others' opinions as a "new book" / e.p.: their practice of following without examination what others have handed down / See Pufendorf's 1667 preface, pp. 3–4. [Ed.]

c. Rather: with [more] discerning ears

d. E.p.: Now, nothing prevents us from inquiring into the different forms of the Empire's individual parts, or the Orders [*Ordines*], when separately considered, for even if they cannot be regarded as perfect states [*civitatibus*], they are far from provinces strictly speaking, and their princes far from [mere] governors of provinces and here the Senate [is no way subject to the People; nor]^a bound to give any account to them of their Administration of the Publick Affairs. In other places [the *Populace* is uppermost, and the *Form* democratical],^b <137> and here the Senate is filled by the choice [vote] of the [Tribes or Companies],^c and they have also a Power to call the Senate to account.

3. But then {the *German*} Writers are by no means agreed what Form belongs to the whole Body of the *German Empire,* which is an infallible sign of an irregular Form, |[and no less also of the Ignorance of these]|^d Authors, who [with small Abilities and little Learning, have pretended too hastily to write of what they did not understand].^e

The Form of the whole Body is neither of these, but an irregular System.

Yet I do not remember I ever saw one Author that did say, it was a *Democrasie.* Yet some [have had so little wit as]^f to say, none were parts [citizens] of this State, but those that had a Right to vote in the Diet; in this, without doubt, blindly following *Aristotle,* who defines a Citizen to be *one that has a Right to deliberate and vote in the Commonwealth Affairs.* Now, if we could grant this, then it [the German Empire] would [undoubtedly] be a *Democrasie,* [because all its Parts are composed of the States only],^g who have every one of them a Right to debate and vote in the Diet, and the Emperor [is the Prince or Head of the State].^h But he that should extend that [Aristotelian] Definition further than the [popular Cities of *Greece,* for whom only it was made],ⁱ would certainly be guilty of very great Absurdities: For, who [can think that Freemen

a. Rather: can in no way be reduced to order by the people; and is not

b. Rather: a democracy is in effect

c. Rather: masses [*tribuum*] / In ancient Rome, the whole body of citizens apart from senators and knights (*equites*). [Ed.]

d. E.p.: one differing greatly from the well-worn principles of ordinary political science, or of the ignorance of many

e. Rather: , have rushed to comment on public law [*jure publico*] with little or no knowledge of civil affairs

f. Rather: wish

g. Rather: whose only citizens are the Estates

h. Rather: would be *princeps* in the proper sense / There is a play on the meaning of *princeps* as "prince" and—what is relevant here—as "chief" or first citizen. [Ed.]

i. Rather: citizens dwelling in the Greek democracies

(and Gentlemen too) who have great Estates and Families of their own, and live in Kingdoms or Commonwealths, are not to be accounted Members [iv] of <138> their Government],[a] though they are admitted to no share of the Government? or, Who in a Kingdom can think the King the only Member [citizen], or in an *Aristocracy* would esteem none such but the Senators?

Many pretend the Empire is an Aristocrasie. 4. The greatest part of those who pretend to exquisite [astute] Knowledge in Politicks, and a great love of the *German* Liberty, pretend it is [meer][b] *Aristocrasie;* these maintain their said Opinion by these following Arguments.

(1.)[c] There is no reason (say they) that any man should be removed from this Opinion by the outside appearance of things which seem to represent to us a Monarchy, *viz.* The proud Flourishes of great Titles, and the usual Forms of Address; much of which is owing to the *Genius* of the *German* Tongue, which abounds in [such vain, insignificant, luxuriant Expressions],[d] and [the rest proceed from the ancient form of Government, (which was indeed Monarchical) though the present is nothing less].[e] For they in truth are in possession of the Supreme Authority, who [have the right to] dispatch the greatest Affairs of the State as they themselves think fit, by what Title soever they are call'd.

(2.) That it is not at all contrary to the nature of an *Aristocrasie,* to have an Head a little higher than the rest, who may be the Director of their Councils, and the President of their Senate, and on that Score be of greater Authority than the rest.

(iv). Cives.
a. Rather: will deny the name of citizens to free men [*liberis hominibus*] and patriarchs [*patribus familias*] living in a kingdom or aristocracy,
b. Rather: a true and simple
c. Parentheses added to distinguish internal numeration from section numbers. [Ed.]
d. Rather: empty expressions of honor
e. Rather: some are left over from the ancient form of government [*republica*], from which the contemporary [*moderna*] form differs greatly

(3.) That the form of any State ought to be distinguished from the manner of its Administration;[2] which <139> distinction is to be thus explicated: That it sometimes happeneth, that one State [*respublica*] imitates the manner of Administration proper to, or very like, that of another Form of Government [state], or [which at least may have][a] some signs of it. Thus, if a King [that is a real Monarch,][+] thinks fit to consult [an assembly of] his People, or a Senate of them, the first of these will seem to have something of a Democrasie, and the latter of an Aristocrasie, and yet, after all, the Form is a real Monarchy, and nothing else; [for][b] these Conventions of the People or Senate are nothing but an Assembly of Counsellors, and the King has no necessary dependance on them. And on the contrary, in a *Democrasie* or *Aristocrasie,* the principal Magistrate or [Prince of the Senate],[c] who has the [Office of consulting][d] the Senate or Assembly in all publick Affairs, of executing the Laws, and enforcing their Decrees, and in whose Name the publick Acts and Decrees are made; will indeed be a lively Figure [*simulacrum*] of a Monarch, but yet still the Supreme Authority will nevertheless still reside in the People or [Senate].[e]

There are some indeed who oppose this distinction chiefly on this ground; Because the *Form* is the beginning or first mover of Operations [principle of actions], [and they][f] must of necessity follow the nature of their efficient Cause. Now [(say they)][+] the Form of a State is as it were the Fountain from whence all the Operations pertaining to the Administration of that State flow, and therefore it is impossible the Form should <140> differ from the Administration. To this others reply, That we ought to distinguish in these Cases between what one doth in his own Name or Right, and what he doth in anothers. In the first of these

a. Rather: that it has at least

b. Rather: if, in fact,

c. Rather: *princeps,* properly speaking / See §3 and note h, p. 161, in this chapter. [Ed.]

d. Rather: sole or chief right to direct [*referendi*]

e. Rather: council of aristocrats [*concilium Optimatium*]

f. Rather: they [i.e., actions, operations]

2. Pufendorf made this distinction in *On the Law of Nature and of Nations,* VII.5.1.

there can be no difference between the Form [of a state] and the Manner of [its] Administration; in the latter it is not impossible for [a man to seem to be what he really is not]:[a]

The thing [in short][b] is thus; *The different Forms of States* [*or Governments*] + *result or spring from the different Subject, to whom the Supreme Power is committed or annexed, as it is a single Person, or a Council* [*or Senate, consisting of a few men, or of all the People*];[c] *but then, what Ministers are employed by them that have that* [*supreme*] *Power in the executing of it, is nothing to the purpose, or all one.*[d] I might say also, that Axiom on which the Argument resteth, is only true in natural Agents, but cannot rightly be applied (as it is here) to free Agents, who can govern their Actions as they please themselves.[3]

The *German* Empire is no Aristocrasie. 5. But then, {though these things may thus with Subtilty enough be disputed in the Schools, yet} no wise man will thereby be perswaded to think the *German* Empire is an *Aristocrasie,* especially if he has any competent degree of Civil or Politick Experience and Knowledge, because the Essence of an *Aristocrasie* lies in the committing the Supreme Authority to a fixed [standing] and perpetual Senate [or Council] +, which has a Right to deliberate, consult on, and determine all the publick Concerns and Affairs <141> of that State, committing only the daily and [emergent][e] Affairs to some Magistrates, who are to execute the same, and are bound to give an account of their Actions to that Senate: But then there is no such Senate in *Germany.* For the Chambers of *Spire* and *Vienna* do only judge of |[Appeals]|;[f] and the *Diet* is not holden as a

a. Rather: the administration to have a different appearance
b. Rather: , however, / Pufendorf is not summarizing but presenting an opposing view. [Ed.]
c. Rather: consisting of all or few
d. Bohun's italics. [Ed.]
e. Rather: particular [*singularium*]
f. E.p.: cases and judicial matters
3. This paragraph is a good example of Pufendorf's distinction between natural and moral entities and also of the stated need to use scholastic (Aristotelian) concepts in the analysis. See *On the Law of Nature and of Nations,* I.1, on the distinction between natural and moral entities.

settled [standing] and perpetual Senate, which has the Sovereign Authority, and is to direct all the publick Affairs of a State, ought to be; but has ever been call'd [only] upon [particular and emergent][a] Causes.

|[There are some so weak [simple-minded], as to conclude the *German* Empire is infallibly an *Aristocrasie,* only because in the Diet [*comitia*] things pass by a majority of Votes]|;[b] for[, as is well known,] in many Kingdoms there are Parliaments or Assemblies [*comitia*] of the States, which are of the same nature with the Diets of *Germany,* and in them too the [majority of Voices prevails],[c] |[and yet they are Monarchies and not Aristocrasies; as for example, *England, Sweden,* and *Scotland*]|.[d] What is more usual, [as well,] than for [a System of States, which are united only by a strict League and Combination, to hold their Assemblies, Diets, or Parliaments? And thus][e] have all of them |[as much Power over the Members of their States, as]|[f] the Diet[s] of *Germany* have over the States [of the Empire], that compose it<, especially if we look more at the effect of that power than at its character>. The Society [associations] of the *Amphyctyones* and *Achaeans* in old times, and [the Diets of the *Cantons* in *Switzerland,* and the *Grisons,*[4] and the Assem-

a. Rather: special [*peculiares*]

b. E.p.: Indeed, even if the Diet, which has lasted so many years since 1663, were to continue in perpetuity, which seems useful for Germany, it will by no means have the character of an Aristocratic senate / Even after 1663, the permanence of the diet (*Reichstag*) was merely *de facto,* not *de jure,* since it could have been ended at any time by common agreement (Monzambano, *Über die Verfassung,* trans. Breßlau, 101, note 3). [Ed.]

c. Rather: votes are counted

d. Rather: the kingdoms of *England, Sweden,* and *Scotland* being a sufficient example of this. / e.p.: but the right to call them into session lies with the King, and the Estates themselves do not have the right to determine how often, and about what, they convene

e. Rather: allies firmly united by a treaty into a systematic structure, as it were, to have frequent gatherings or Diets, which

f. Rather: as much Power over the allies as / e.p.: a greater or lesser power, as stipulated by the rules of the particular association [*societas*], sometimes not much less than that which

4. Grisons, or Graubünden, is the largest canton of Switzerland; Bohun apparently uses the name for Swiss cantons in general.

blies of the United Provinces, in their States-General at the *Hague*],[a] in latter times, are <142> [full and clear] [+] Instances of this.

And[, furthermore,] true Aristocrasies have all of them this in common, *viz.* That no one [in the Senate] [+] is superiour to the whole Senate; and [they all of them are bound as much to obey the Decree of the major part of the Senate, as any other Subject; and the Senate has a Power of Life and Death over all the Members of it, which is by no means true of the Diet of *Germany*][b]<, and he who denies it knows nothing of Germany or any other states [*respublicas*]>: And in an Aristocrasie the Senators [*optimates*] have their private Estates [*patrimonium*], which commonly are [much] greater than [those of the private Subjects],[c] yet [not only the publick Revenues, but] [+] the private Estates of the Senators are as much subject to the Laws and Decrees of the [whole] Senate, as the [Estates of private men]:[d] But in *Germany,* if you remove out of the Computation that which belongs to the [several Members of the State],[e] there will be nothing left [for the Diet or Body to dispose of]:[f] |[And it would be a great abatement of the *German Liberty* to assert the Diet there has the same Authority over the Estates of its Members, that the [whole] Senate of the most Serene Republick of *Venice* has over those of its Senators]|.[g]

As to that famous Speech[h] of *Albert* Archbishop of *Mentz,* when the Electors were considering whether they should elect *Charles* V. or *Francis*

a. Rather: of Switzerland and the Belgian federation / On the Amphyctionic and Achaean Leagues, see V.28, note 24, p. 157. [Ed.]

b. Rather: that individual senators are no less fully bound than other citizens to obey the senate as a whole, which exercises a right of life and death over them and the latter alike, something quite far removed from the liberty of the German Estates

c. Rather: the fortunes of the remaining citizens

d. Rather: other goods contained in the state [*civitas*] beside them

e. Rather: individual Estates

f. Rather: that belongs to the whole

g. Rather: And one is bound to have trouble if he dares to assert in their presence that the joint Estates have the same power over the goods of individuals, that the whole Senate . . . / e.p.: And one is bound to be mocked if he dares to assert that the joint . . . individuals, that a Senate has in any true aristocracy [for *democratia* (Ed.)]

h. In 1519. [Ed.]

I. *That the* [*Government of* France *was too Monarchical*],[a] *and that the Princes of* Germany *did rather incline to an Aristocrasie, which they ought carefully to preserve.* This may easily be thus answered: |[There is no reason <143> to suppose that Prelate had any exact knowledge of Politicks]|,[b] and the sence of what he said is true [clear], though he has ill expressed himself, *viz.* "That if the *German* Princes were desirous to continue in the same condition they then were, they were to avoid the Empire or Government of a King of *France,* whose great design it ever was, to reduce the [Nobility][c] of their own Kingdom under the Laws of an Absolute [exact] Monarchy, and would, without all doubt, endeavour to do the same thing [in *Germany*]."[d]

6. It remains now, that we consider whether it [the German state] may be taken into the List or Number of Monarchies or Kingdoms. Of these there are two sorts, the *Absolute* and the *Limited.* In the first, the whole Soveraign Power is in the hands of the Monarch, (by what Title soever he is call'd) and he governs all the publick Affairs [as he himself pleaseth].[e] But in the latter the King is bound up by certain Laws in the exercise of the Soveraign Power. All those that have not exactly considered the Difference between these two *Species* of Monarchies, [have committed great Errors, whilst, because the Emperor has not an *Absolute Soveraignty,* they falsly conclude, that he has not a *Limited* neither].[f]

Now, he that can think the Emperor is an *Absolute Monarch,* [is wonderful silly],[g] and the Arguments that are brought for it, deserve rather

The German Empire no Regular Monarchy.

a. Rather: latter inclined toward monarchy
b. E.p.: It would be pedantic to require of such a Prelate that he scrupulously form his ordinary speech according the rules of exact philosophy
c. Rather: leading men [*procerum*]
d. Rather: to the German princes
e. Rather: according to his own judgment / "Judgment" implies less arbitrariness than "pleaseth." [Ed.]
f. Rather: are greatly deluded in believing that the considerations whereby the Emperor is denied an absolute power do not leave him even a limited one
g. Rather: must have been born a ram [*vervecum, Hammel*] in his native country [*patria*] / This graphic expression, suggesting stubborn dullness or stupidity, was meant to insult, and was so perceived by Pufendorf's critics. [Ed.]

to be *hissed* at than answered seriously. It is full [just] as absurd to fetch
an Argument to prove <144> the *German* Emperor *absolute,* from the
Visions of *Daniel,*[5] as from the Books of the *Civil* [*Roman*] *Law.* That
the Emperor has no Superiour but God, and the Sword gives him no
more Absolute Authority over the Princes of *Germany,* than it gives to
the State of *Holland*[a] over the other Six, who may as truly say this as
he. |[As to the empty Titles, (as for example, that he is by all the States
and Princes stiled their most merciful Lord, and that in the conclusion
of their Letters [and elsewhere] they promise much in the Matter of
Loyalty and Obedience to him) the *Genius* of the Age, [and] the Stile
of the [Times][b] are responsable for them, and [there is no more to be
expected from them than from][c] other Expressions of Honour and Respect, in which the most unwilling to act is the most forward to promise
what he never means to perform. That Plenitude and Perfection of
Power which the Secretaries and Clerks [typically] ascribe to the Emperor, in their Letters and [the dedicatory prefaces that adorn] Decrees,
is a meer Jargon of insignificant words.]|[d] The States do indeed swear
Allegiance to the Emperor, but with a saving of their own Liberties and
Rights. And I have already sufficiently shewn what Power is thereby re-

a. Perhaps a reference to Holland's special role among the Dutch provinces, or
simply used as an example for any province. [Ed.]

b. Rather: Court [*curia*]

c. Rather: they have no more effect than

d. E.p.: The titles, formulas, and courtly style, with which secretaries typically
embellish letters and the dedicatory prefaces [*carmina*] of decrees, far exceed the effect [*vim*] of the matter itself.

5. Daniel 7:2–3 refers to four great beasts emerging from the sea, an image later
interpreted as the Babylonian, Median/Persian, Greek, and Roman Empires.
Seventeenth-century divine right theorists like Dietrich (Theodor) Reinking(k)
(1590–1664) used the passage to argue for a supposed transfer of sovereignty (*translatio
imperii*) from the Roman to the German Empire. The latter claim was also known
as the "Lotharian Legend" because of the associated assertion that Emperor Lothar
III had introduced Roman law into Germany in 1135. By challenging this theory in
his *De origine iuris Germanici* (1643) (i.e., by showing that Roman law had been gradually introduced into Germany through jurists beginning in the fifteenth century),
Conring not only undermined imperial claims but also deprived them, through the
link with Daniel, of their eschatological or religious dimension.

served and secured to them [him]. But to use any more words in so plain a case, [were not only needless but foolish].[a]

7. The Opinion of those who have ascribed to the Emperor a Supreme Regal Power, but limited and restrained within the Bounds of certain Laws, has seemed <145> the most probable of all other[s] to the greatest part of men. And you shall also frequently hear this Opinion defended and stoutly maintained in the Schools of *Germany:* [So far as we know,] the first that appeared openly against this Opinion was a nameless Author, under the feigned Title of *Hippolithus a Lapide,*[6] [in the heat of the *Imperial* and *Swedish* War].[b] This Writer saith many things of unquestionable veracity, which no modest man can deny; but then it is no less apparent, his implacable Hatred to the House of *Austria* has in other things mis-led and deceived him. {The prohibiting the reading of this Book was the only thing that gave it Reputation [*pretium*], and made Learned men [inquisitive after it; so that it was read with unusual Application and Care]:[c] Yet however, I should [would] never have mention'd it, but that I find many still [so fond of it, that they still think it an invaluable Treasure],[d] and that all those that have pretended to answer it, have rather trifled with the Subject, or basely flattered the Emperor, than destroyed his [Lapide's] Reasons.}

This Author [has well and clearly proved, that the Emperor has not a Supreme and Regal Authority over the Princes and States of *Ger-*

> That it is no Limited Monarch[y].

> *Hippolithus a Lapide* considered and confuted.

---

a. Rather: would be tiresome [*putidum*]

b. Rather: at the peak of the war between the Emperor and the Swedes

c. Rather: eager to read it

d. Rather: , who think it has some value

6. This was the pseudonym of Bogislaw Philipp Chemnitz (1605–78), whose *Dissertatio de ratione status in imperio nostro Romano-Germanico* (Freystadt, 1640, 1647), was aggressively anti-Hapsburg. The son of a Rostock professor, Chemnitz entered the service of Sweden under Gustavus Adolphus. After serving in the army, he was appointed Swedish state historian (the post assumed by Pufendorf in 1678) by Oxenstierna in 1644, and ennobled by Queen Christina in 1648 (*Verfassung des deutschen Reiches,* ed. Denzer, 1994, 191, note 6; *Verfassung des deutschen Reiches,* trans. Dove, 143, note 35). This rest of this section interacts silently with Chemnitz's work.

many];[a] but then is strangely [quite] absurd, when he makes the Emperor subject to the States, and [gives him nothing but the naked Dignity of a subordinate Magistrate, that wears a great many proud Titles precariously bestowed upon him];[b] as if whereever the Monarchy is not Absolute, it must presently <146> degenerate into an *Aristocrasie,* and a Prince must presently [necessarily] acknowledge all those to be his Superiors whom he could not command and govern as he pleased. He that observes this one Mistake, will be able [by it to unravel and disbowel all his weak Arguments]:[c] And yet, besides this, he mingles [in] many other silly [useless] Fallacies, of which I shall mention [only] some few to expose his Folly.

To prove that the Soveraign Majesty is [alwaies][+] in the Princes [Estates], he alledgeth [somewhere], That it is [also] in them when the Imperial Throne is vacant. But who knows not that? In all other Kingdoms, during the *Interregnum,* the Soveraign Power returns into the hands of the People, or of their Representatives the States, which yet they can retain no longer, than till they have made a new King:[7] Nor doth a man presently make every one his Master [superior], to whom he willingly gives an account of his Actions: It is one thing to give an account to a Superiour, who can punish me if [I have not performed my Duty to his satisfaction],[d] and quite another thing to do it to one who expects it according to an Agreement [pact] to that purpose made between us; and it is yet [less, when I do it to preserve my own Reputation, and without any other Motive or Reason].[e] Thus Kings, when they begin a War, endeavour to satisfie all the World in the Justice of their Cause [by means

a. Rather: correctly reduces the Emperor's supreme and regal power in favor of the Estates

b. Rather: leaves him [only] the dignity of a bare magistrate, and that as a favor because of his many proud titles

c. Rather: to disable most of his arguments [*rationes*] with little difficulty

d. Rather: that account is not satisfactory

e. Rather: something else, when I fear another's estimation [of me]

7. Pufendorf considers that the state does not dissolve into a precivil condition during an interregnum, because he makes the distinction between the contract of association and the contract of submission, which are conflated by Hobbes. See *On the Law of Nature and of Nations,* VII.2.7–12.

of public manifestos].[8] Thus one Companion or Partner [ally] gives the other, and a Guardian gives the Pupil when he comes <147> to Age an account of his Administration [activities]. Nor is he [immediately] anothers Master and Superiour, who can remove him from his Office [position]; for [that a man may by Compact and Agreement be preferred to the management of their common Concerns],[a] so that neither of these may have any [direct and true Authority or Soveraignty][b] over the other, and so when he doth not please the other Party, and for that cause is deposed or turn'd out of his Administration [office], it [has no other effect or cause][c] than the breaking off the Bargain made with him [someone], because he has not performed his part of the Contract, and satisfied the Conditions [*legibus*] of the Covenant. And yet perhaps a man might [deservedly] doubt whether all that was done in the Cases of *Henry* IV. and *Adolph* of *Nassaw,*[9] were legally and regularly done{, but that it is notorious [well known] the [most] Reverend Bishops of those Ages were the principal Agents in those Affairs}.

What he so largely [extensively] argues [from the Power of the *Diet*][d] are true, as to the matter of Fact, but nothing to his purpose for which he alledgeth them. For though the Emperor can in truth do nothing against the Consent of the States, yet I think it is as true, that no man ever heard the States pretended to do any thing without the Consent of the Emperor. [To be sure,] the Electors, in their *Capitular,* do prescribe to the Emperor what he shall, and what he shall not do; [however,] not by force of any Authority [*imperii*] they have[, or pretend to have] + over

a. Rather: a number of people may put someone in charge of their common affairs by means of a pact

b. Rather: Sovereignty, properly speaking,

c. Rather: is no different

d. Rather: about the Diets

8. Pufendorf wrote some of these himself, particularly his *Discussio quorundam scriptorum Brandeburgicorum* (1675), which defended Sweden's unprovoked attack on Brandenburg, in 1674, in terms of its treaty obligations to France during the Dutch War (1672–78). This work is contained in Pufendorf, *Kleine Vorträge und Schriften,* 281–336.

9. Henry IV was deposed in 1105 (see IV.6 and note c on p. 105; and III.6, note 9, on p. 89) and Adolf of Nassau (1250–98) in 1298.

him, but by way of Contract: So that if the Emperor <148> should pretend to enjoin any thing contrary to his Covenants [agreements] with them, they may safely and lawfully [*impune*] not obey him in those Instances: But then, this springs from the [common] nature of all Contracts [pacts], and not from any Authority [*potestas*] the Electors have over the Emperor.

That is more probable yet [that]^a he alledgeth from Ancient Custom and the *Golden Bull, viz.* That if the Emperor should happen to be [legally] complained of, in certain particulars, he shall be bound to answer the Complaint before the Count *Palatine* of the *Rhine*. And it is well known, that the *Three Spiritual Electors* cited [summoned] *Albert* I. Emperor,[10] before *Rudolph* Count *Palatine* to plead his Cause and defend himself; but then, [when they had so great a Criminal to contest with, they relied more on their Swords and Armies, than on their Counsel or Judge].^b But then, since the Date of the *Golden Bull,* there is not one Example to be found of any such [Suit commenc'd against the Emperor],^c that I have read of. The Rise [origin] of that Authority which the Count *Palatine* has, did, without doubt, spring from his Office, which in ancient time, as [*Mayor* of the Palace],^d he exercised in the King's Court: For[, here,] as he exercised a real Jurisdiction over the other Courtiers, so if any thing was demanded of the King, which was doubted of, it was wont to be referr'd to the Examination of the Count *Palatine,* to [by] whose Sentence the King stood, not because he owned [acknowledged] the Count [(who was his Servant and Subject)]⁺ for his Superior, <149> but because when he once knew the Petitioner had [a] Right to what he asked, [it was beneath a King to do him wrong]:^e As we have known many Princes in *Germany,* and elsewhere, who when

a. Rather: , what
b. Rather: military might [*arma*] smiled more upon so great a criminal than upon the accusors and the judge / That is, he was too strong to be held accountable. [Ed.]
c. Rather: judicial proceeding enacted before the Count Palatine
d. Rather: head of the household [*maior domus*]
e. Rather: he could not but fulfill his own obligation
10. Albert I (1255–1308), eldest son of Rudolph of Hapsburg, became emperor after the deposition of Adolf of Nassau (in 1298).

they doubted of any Debt demanded of them, <or in other matters where others have made a rights claim against them,> have answered the Claim in their own Courts. And yet it is not [by any means] to be supposed that these Courts [have any Authority over their Princes, or could force them to pay those Debts],[a] if the Reverence they [bear to Justice, the Publick, and their own Private Conscience, and the desire they naturally have to preserve a good Reputation in the World, did not much more powerfully move them to pay them, than the Authority of these Courts, which are managed by their Subjects and Servants].[b] And I believe the States [of *Germany* think they][+] are happy enough in this Priviledge, That the Emperor can exact nothing of them against their wills; and that the Wisest of them would disclaim the Invidious Liberty of [commanding][c] their own Emperor [besides].

8. Doubtless the Emperor would with great facility compound [settle] the Dispute with our *Hippolitus,* [and obtain his Leave to continue a Prince still,][+] and not be reduced by him to the mean condition of a Subject: But they [are not so easily baffled, who allow the Emperor to be a Soveraign, but Limited King, and ascribe unto the States great Liberties, but tempered too by Laws],[d] and so place *Germany* in the List of Limited Monarchies. {For, as for those who <150> prate of mixed forms of Government, they can never disintangle themselves [from the Objections brought against them][+], for that not only all kinds of mixture can produce nothing at last but [a monstrous deformed Government],[e] but it is also certain none of the Notions of that kind will at all fit *Germany,* in which the whole Supreme Power is not undividedly in the

The Arguments of those that pretend it is a Limited Monarchy, answered.

a. Rather: can compel those princes, or punish them
b. Rather: have for right [*juris*], conscience, and public esteem did not move them to pay the debt
c. Rather: being able to command
d. Rather: have a weightier case, who think it possible under some compromise to attribute both monarchical authority to the Emperor and liberty to the Estates
e. Rather: some monster of a state [*monstrum aliquod civitatis*] / The doctrine of *respublica mixta* is already criticized in *De rebus gestis Philippi Amyntae filio* (Heidelberg, 1664), §15, where Pufendorf says that it tends to create a new concept for every abnormality, even nonessential ones. [Ed.]

hands of many [several], nor are the Parts of it divided between divers Persons or Colleges here.}ᵃ

But to return to our former [Limited] Monarchists, They pretend [explain] that [the *Capitulars* made with the Emperors when they are chosen],ᵇ are not at all inconsistent with the nature of a Limited Monarchy; as for instance: That he is bound to administer the Government [state] according to the Fundamental Laws, and to require [seek] the Consent of the States [in their Diet,]⁺ for those things that are of the greatest moment: That he cannot enact new Laws without their Consent, nor change any thing in the matters of Religion, nor make War or Peace, or enter Leagues, without the Approbation of [his Subjects]:ᶜ That he must determine their [his subjects'] Controversies [only] in certain known Courts[, and by Stated Laws and Methods]⁺. [And whereas the Princes and]ᵈ States swear Fidelity both to the *Empire* and the *Emperor,* this they think may be thus explained: That they [the Estates] will obey the Emperor as far as he shall employ their Assistance and Treasures [goods] to the Publick Good, and as far as is expressed in the Laws [of the kingdom]; and that [as to <151> the rest of the States, they will live like good Neighbours and true Fellow-Subjects].ᵉ

Two Arguments against This.
But still at last there are two things that will not suffer us to reckon *Germany* amongst the *Limited Monarchies:* First, In [every Limited]ᶠ Kingdom, though the King is bound up by some certain Laws in the management of its Government, yet after all, he so far excells all his Subjects [citizens], that none of them dares presume to compare his Liberty or his Rights with the Power [authority] of his Prince [king]; and therefore

a. Mixture theorists are distinguished here from limited monarchy theorists. The e.p. places a revised version of these remarks about mixed states [*rerumpublicarum*] at the very end of this section, on p. 176. [Ed.]

b. Rather: the things prescribed to the Emperor by the Capitulars

c. Rather: the Estates

d. Rather: The fact that the

e. Rather: they will conduct themselves as agreeable and loyal fellow citizens toward the remaining members of the Empire

f. Rather: a true

all the Nobility [leading men] depend on the Will of the King, and are responsable to him for their Actions. Now, that it is otherwise in *Germany*, is known to all the World. For none of the *German* Princes or States will acknowledg, that the Dominions which are under them are more the Emperor's than they are theirs, or that they are bound in the Administration [governance] of them to have [respect more to the Service of the Emperor, or the People, than to their own Personal Profit and Advantage].ᵃ But on the contrary, every one of them is so far [a Soveraign, that he makes War upon his Neighbours at home or abroad, and entereth into Leagues with his Neighbours or Foreigners],ᵇ without ever consulting the Emperor; [and every one of them that]ᶜ can trust to his own Forces, or those of his Allies{, [that is, he] looks upon the Reverence he owes to the Emperor, as a meer empty piece of Pageantry}.

To conclude [Next], every King, how Limited soever he may otherwise be, must still have sufficient <152> Power left to command all the Forces of his whole Kingdom, and direct them as he thinks fit, so that the last Resort may be to him; and the said Forces [must] be united in him as their Head, for the procuring the Common Good, so [in such a way] that they may seem all of them [jointly] to be, as it were, [animated and] ⁺ governed by one Soul.¹¹ Now he that can see or find this in *Germany*, must be [wonderfully quick-sighted].ᵈ For there he that is call'd their King [head], has no Revenues from the Empire, <at least regular oncs,> but is forced to live by his own Juice [resources], there being no common Treasure; nor are there any common [military] Forces, but every Prince and State disposeth of the Forces [men] and Revenues in his own Territories, as he or they think fit, and only contributes to the Publick some small matter [amount], and that after tedious Delays, and much humble Attendance and Courtship for it. All which things have

a. Rather: more regard for the Emperor's advantage than for their own

b. Rather: focused on his own concerns, that he does not hesitate to make war on, or treaties with other Estates or outsiders,

c. Rather: if he

d. Rather: a lynx / Famed as a sharp-sighted animal since antiquity. [Ed.]

11. On the sovereign's relation to the state as a sort of ensoulment, see *On the Law of Nature and of Nations*, VII.4.12 and VII.5.13.

been [fully and clearly proved]ᵃ in the Chapter before this, and are found evidently true in the [Actions of these Princes].ᵇ

< Finally, quite a few authors class Germany among mixed states, but no matter how much they twist and turn, they can in no way extricate themselves [from the problems this presents]. What Aristotle, the author of that doctrine about mixtures, has transmitted about the mixing or respective balancing of aristocratic and democratic forms of state, does not apply to Germany, as anyone with the leisure to examine Aristotle himself will acknowledge. Nor do any of the kinds of mixture discussed by more recent authors, since the entire sovereignty does not belong undividedly to several parties, nor are its parts distributed among different persons or colleges. Those, however, who assert that Germany comprises a mixture of monarchy and aristocracy because the more powerful rights of sovereignty [*maiestatis*] are shared with the Estates, err in supposing that the Estates of the Empire have the character of a true aristocratic senate, which the thing itself shows to be otherwise. >

That it is an irregular System of Sovereign States.

9. There is now nothing left for us to say, but that *Germany* is an Irregular Body{, and like some mis-shapen Monster},ᶜ if[, at least,] it be measured by the common Rules of Politicks and Civil Prudence<, and that nothing similar to it, in my opinion, exists anywhere else on the whole globe>. [So that in]ᵈ length of time, by the Lazy easiness [negligent indulgence] of the Emperors, the Ambition of the Princes, and the Turbulence [importunity] of the Clergy or Churchmen, <as well as factions among the Estates and the civil wars springing therefrom,> from a Regular Kingdom it [has] sunk and degenerated [to that degree],ᵉ that it is not now so much as a *Limited Kingdom,* (tho' <153> the outward Shews and Appearances would seem to insinuate so much) nor[, exactly,] is it a *Body* or *System* of [many Soveraign States and Princes],ᶠ knit and united in

a. Rather: described at length / In V, above. [Ed.]
b. Rather: actual course of affairs
c. *monstro simile* / The most controversial expression in the whole work. [Ed.]
d. Rather: In
e. Rather: into such a badly ordered form
f. Rather: several states

a League, but something [(without a Name)]⁺ that fluctates between these two. This Irregularity [in its Constitution [makeup] affords the matter of an inextricable and incurable Disease, and many internal Convulsions, whilst the Emperor is alwaies labouring to reduce it to the condition of a Regular Empire, Kingdom, or Monarchy; and the States on the other side are restlesly acquiring to themselves a full and perfect Liberty].ᵃ But then, as it is the nature of all Degenerations [of states], [when they have deviated far from their original condition,] that they go forward in their Degeneracy and Corruption with great Facility, [(it being a down-hill motion) but]ᵇ they can hardly, and with much difficulty, be reduced to the[ir] pristine or ancient state [form]. For, as a Stone laid on the edge of a Precipice or Downfall, is with the smallest Thrust thrown [all the way] down to the bottom, but it is not to be replaced again at the top without great and almost insuperable difficulty: So now *Germany*, without great Commotions, and the utmost Confusion of all things, can never be reformed or reduced to the Laws of a Just [perfect] and Regular Kingdom, but it tends naturally [of itself] to the state [condition] of a *Confederate System.*

Nay, if you take away the mutual [Bond or Tie]ᶜ between the Emperor and the States, [(I suppose he means their Oaths)]⁺ *Germany* would then truly be a [body or] *System of States [allies]*, united in an unequal League, because <154> those that are called the *States,* are still bound to [promote and] reverence the [Imperial Majesty, as their Head]ᵈ<, not only as someone decked out with the symbols of royalty, but also as one who exceeds the rest in authority and a certain prerogative

a. Rather: affords a perpetual occasion for deadly disease and internal convulsions, with the Emperor on one side struggling to bring the Empire back under the laws of a kingdom, and the Estates on the other striving for a full liberty / e.p.: . . . the Estates on the other eagerly seeking to preserve their acquired liberty / In the first edition, the estates are seeking to increase their liberty; in the more Hapsburg-friendly e.p., they are trying only to maintain the liberty they already have. [Ed.]

b. Rather: as if spontaneously seeking the other extreme,

c. Rather: struggle / Making Bohun's clarificatory parenthesis unnecessary. [Ed.]

d. Rather: Emperor [*Caesarem*]

of power>. [For a *Free State,* we may take for our Example of this,]ᵃ the League between the *Romans* and the *Latin People,* before the latter were reduced [by the former] into the condition of meer I[*Subjects.* So [also] the Generalship of *Agamemnon,* in the Warlike Expedition of the *Greeks* against the *Trojans,* was [of the same nature]:ᵇ [And]ᶜ it commonly comes to pass, in length of time, that he that is the Superiour in these Leagues, if he has much the advantage of his Allies in point of Power, by degrees he sinks them into the condition of meer Subjects, and so treats them.

Thus the best account [designation] we can possibly give of the Present State of *Germany,* is to say, *That it comes very near a System of* [*many Soveraign*]ᵈ *States, in which one Prince or General* [*leader*] *of the League excells the rest of the Confederates, and is cloathed with the* [*Ornaments of a Soveraign Prince*];ᵉ *but then this Body is attack'd by furious Diseases;* of which I shall treat in the next Chapter.]|ᶠ <155>

a. Rather: As an example of an association [*societas*] of free states [*civitatum*], we may take
b. Rather: based on a military alliance
c. Rather: Although
d. Rather: several
e. Rather: symbols of royalty
f. E.p.: *Subjects* or, finally, endowed with Roman citizenship.
And that irregularity will be readily acknowledged by anyone who has compared Germany's structure and received mode of governance with the structure and administration of kingdoms, aristocracies, and systems [of states] that everyone admits and acknowledges as such. Add to this what I have said about the matter in the special treatise *De republica irregulari* [Frankfurt, 1669] and in *De jure naturae et gentium* [Lund, 1672, lib. VII. cap. 5, §14 ff.]. / See p. xiv, note 15, in the introduction. [Ed.]

✂ CHAPTER VII ✂

Of the Strength and Diseases of the German Empire.

1. The Forces of any State may be considered as they are in themselves, or [as by reason of the elegant Structure of its Form or Constitution they may be used].ᵃ Forces considered in themselves, consist in *Men* and *Things*.

As to the first of these, *Men, Germany* has no reason to complain that it wants numbers of them, or they Wit or Ingenuity. There is so great a multitude of the principal Nobility, and they too are in such splendid circumstances, that there is scarcely the like to be found elsewhere in all the World. The Gentry or Inferiour Nobility are neither for want of Ground, or by their over-great number compell'd to condescend [descend] to the exercise of mean and sordid Arts (Trades). Perhaps yet there are more of them employed in Learning [letters] than is convenient, though [amongst the many Graduates there are not many eminent Scholars].ᵇ Of Merchants, Tradesmen, and Mechanicks there is a great plenty: But then in many places there is now <156> a want of Husbandmen, considering the largeness of the Country. This is owing partly to the Thirty years War, by which *Germany* was most miserably desolated; and partly because the Countrymen [rustics] are of that Temper,

The Subjects of Humane Force.

Husbandmen most wanted.

---

    a. Rather: according to the employment they can easily have in an ordered form of state
    b. Rather: there are few Apollos to be found amongst the many laurel-bearers

that as soon as they arrive at any considerable Estate, they put out their Children [sons] to *Trades,* as thinking those that live in the Cities much more happy than themselves.

Though I can scarce think that any Man [had so much leisure as to take an exact account]ᵃ of the Cities and Burroughs [villages] of *Germany,* yet I believe no man would be suspected [of boasting] by one that knew that Country [*regionis*], if he should say, that an Army of Two Hundred Thousand Men might be levied, by taking out of every City five men [soldiers], and out of every Burrough-Town one, or two at most. For a Specimen of this, there are some Authors that say, That in the Ten Circles there are 1957 Cities, Towns, and Castles, besides the Kingdom of *Bohemia,* in which, according to Hagec,¹ in the Reign of *Ferdinand* I.² there were 102 Cities, and 308 Towns, and 258 considerable Castles, 171 Monasteries, and of Villages 30363. {In *Silesia* [there are]ᵇ 411 Cities, 863 Towns, and 51112 Villages. In *Moravia* there are 100 Cities, 410 [lesser] Towns, 30360 Villages.} And before the Protestants destroyed [so many of] them, there were 11024 [Monasteries, Priories, Abbies, and Nunneries].ᶜ Thus *Ferdinand* II.³ is, by his Zeal for the [Church of *Rome*],ᵈ said to have brought [back] into her Communion One [hundred thousand]ᵉ men<, though that number was greatly augmented by the crude adulation of priests>.

This Nation⁴ [is not only thus wonderfully Populous, <157> but]⁺ from all times of which any memory has been preserved, it has been ever

A vast Army may be easily levyed.

---

a. Rather: has taken a count
b. Rather: they count
c. Rather: abbeys and monasteries [*Coenobiorum*]
d. Rather: Catholic Church
e. Rather: ten million
1. Wenceslaus Hagecius, *Böhmische Chronica . . . Jetzt aus Böhmischer in die Deutsche Sprache . . . tranßferiret . . . Durch Johannem Sandel* (Prague, 1596).
2. Ferdinand I (1503–64) was emperor from 1556.
3. Ferdinand II (1578–1637) was emperor from 1619.
4. The following account anticipates Pufendorf's *Introduction to the History,* in which he describes the respective strengths and weaknesses of the main European states in the context of an explicit reason-of-state analysis.

famous for War, and greedy of Military Glory [eager for military service],
spending freely, for [a little] + Money, its Blood in [all the Nations] a of
Europe. As they are not over-hot in their Passions, so they are very constant, [and have Souls] b very capable of Discipline and Instruction. Nor
is this Nation less [to be admired and commended for their Mechanick
Arts and Ingenious Manufactures]: c And which [crowns all, and tends
wonderfully to the Security and Welfare of Societies], d they are not at
all inclined to promote Changes in their Governments, and [can with
Patience and Submission endure the most Rigid Government]. e

// I cannot forbear saying, the English Nation has all the German Virtues,
which they brought over with them, but these last; for no Government will
long please us, being too much addicted to hope for better days in other Pub-
lick Circumstances: And we are certainly the Nation in the whole World
that can the worst bear an overloose remiss Government, or a rigid severe
one, especially if not regulated exactly by Laws.

2. Amongst [the things in which the Strength of a Nation consisteth,
the first that is to be considered is, the *Country*] f it self: As to the extent
of it, that may easily be known, by travelling from CASSUBEN upon the
Baltick Sea, in the further *Pomerania,* to MONTPELGART, upon the
River *Alain,* 33 Miles from *Basil* to the *West;* or from [the furthest parts
of] + *Holstein, N.W.* to the <158> farthest part of *Carniola, S.E.* or from
Liege in the *W.* to the utmost *Eastern* Border of *Silesia.* g In this vast-
extended Region, if you except the top of the *Alps,* there are very few
places which produce nothing useful to [cultivation of] the Life of Man;

The Inhabi-
tants as war-
like as
numerous.

Steddy and
constant in
their
Humours.

The Temper
of the *English*
different.

In the point of
Strength the
Country first
to be consid-
ered.

---

a. Rather: almost all
b. Rather: courageous, and
c. Rather: skilled in all types of manual arts
d. Rather: contributes much to the stability of states
e. Rather: patiently endure any rule [*imperii*] that is not too strict
f. Rather: things, the first place [in importance] belongs to the region
g. Bohun adds some geographical details in each case. Cassuben was settled by the
Kassuben (Kaschuben, Pomeranians) and was wedged between Danzig and eastern
Pomerania, on the Baltic Sea; Mümpelgard is today's Montbéliard; and Carniola
(Krain) was an Austrian hereditary possession located in Slovenia. [Ed.]

but there are every where that Plenty of Necessaries, that it [life] wants
nothing from abroad, but what may promote Luxury and Superfluous
Pleasures.

The Mines, and some Rivers, afford a little Gold, and all its [Ger-
many's] Precious Stones are of small value: But then there is some Silver,
and great plenty of Copper, Tin, Lead, Iron, Quicksilver, and other Metals [minerals] of less price, digged out of the Earth in very many places.
The Fountains afford as much Salt as the Country needeth, though in
all the Countries [places] bordering on the Sea, and the Navigable Rivers,
they generally use Salt brought from *France, Portugal,* and *Holland.*
They have great Plenty of *Corn* and *Fruits* of all sorts, *Wood,* [*Cloathing,*
both *Linen* and *Woollen*];ᵃ as also *Horses, great Cattel* and *small,*ᵇ and
Wild Beasts. And they want not those Liquors that will make them
drunk. So that in the whole, *Germany* may be esteemed a Wealthy Region, because it not only produceth those Metals of which Money is
minted, but all other things too, which are required to the Support [*ne-
cessitatem*] or Pleasure of Humane Life, in that plenty, that it can serve
all its own Inhabitants, and afford great quantities to be transported to
Foreign Nations,

And those that are imported from abroad [elsewhere], are either <159>
[much less in value],ᶜ or such things as the *Germans* might conveniently
live without, if they knew how to suppress their Luxury, or lay by their
Laziness and Folly. As for example: How easie were it for them to be well
content with their own *Wine* and *Beer?* Or if they are not sufficient to
make them drunk enough, they might quicken the operation thereof
with the hellish steamsᵈ of BRANDY, and in the mean time never know
or regard the *Spanish* and *French* Wines. How easie were it for the *Germans* to cloath themselves with their own Cloth, made of their own
Wools, and leave the *Spanish, English,* and *Hollanders* to wear theirs too?
Or if they are taken with the beauty and fineness of them, then they

a. Rather: whatever is needed to make clothing
b. That is, smaller domesticated animals, such as are herded in flocks. [Ed.]
c. Rather: less in quantity than those exported
d. Referring to the "burning" sensation in the throat. [Ed.]

ought to have encouraged their own Workmen to [mend the Manufacture].ᵃ Nor would it be any Grievance to the *Germans* to want [lack] the *Italian* Silks: Or if they must needs be well and finely clad, the parts about the *Rhine* [could] produce sufficient quantities of *Mulberry Trees;* [and so they might have Silk too, if the Inhabitants could once perswade themselves to mind]ᵇ something besides their Vineyards: Thus having *Mulberries* and *Silkworms,* they might (if they pleased) learn [from us]ᶜ the Art of making *Silks.* |[And though it may perhaps be reasonable to impute the *Germans* affecting the *French* Fashions to the simplicity of this Nation [*gentis*], as believing it becomes them much more than their own: Yet it [cannot be denied, but it is a piece of intolerable Folly to fetch <160> their Stuffs, which are not fit for us];ᵈ nay, the very Name of *French* Goods enhaunceth the value and esteem [among them] of what would otherwise be slighted]|:ᵉ The [*Frenchmens*]ᶠ varying so often the [Figures and Forms of their Stuffs],ᵍ is not an Argument of their Levity [superficiality] and Inconstancy, [as some think,]⁺ but a very crafty Design, for by this means they prevent the *German* Workmen from ever imitating them.

Though in truth the greatest part of the Artificers of *Germany* [are so dull-witted as to] think it a Sin to vary from the received method they have once setled in their Trades; [nor can they possibly perswade themselves, that there is any thing in the new Inventions which is good, or to

a. Rather: to cultivate that art better

b. Rather: if those people could shake off their sluggishness and bring themselves to devote some care to the cultivation of

c. E.p.: from the Italians

d. Rather: is gross foolishness to obtain from the French even fabrics that are often thin or inappropriate

e. E.p.: Indeed, it is a considerable foolishness [on the part of Germans] that they seek from France not only the styles that change almost monthly, but often also fabrics that are thin and inappropriate, believing that nothing is elegant unless it expresses the current French standard / Pufendorf's younger friend, Christian Thomasius, wrote a *Diskurs von der Nachahmung der Franzosen* (Discourse on imitating the French) in 1687. [Ed.]

f. Rather: French artisans'

g. Rather: types of cloth and fabric

be imitated],[a] because forsooth it was not known to their Grandsires. *Lastly,* If *Germany* could possibly [command and rule][b] its own Luxury, much less *Sugar* and *Spices,* which with other things of that nature are brought from the *East* and *West Indies,* would then serve [it].[c]

Germany well stored with what will carry on a Trade.

3. Nor doth *Germany* want the means of drawing to it self the Riches of other Countries by Commerce: To that purpose it is required, that the Situation of a Country be convenient for the passage of its Inhabitants to other Nations, and also the reception of Strangers amongst them; and lastly, that the Inhabitants may have something to spare, which they may export into Foreign Nations<, beside their skill>.[d] Now all those Cities are very conveniently seated for a Trade, which stand upon the *Ocean* [North Sea] and the <161> *Baltick Sea,* and the Inland Towns which stand upon great and navigable Rivers [only somewhat less so], on the account of the [cheapness of Carriage]:[e] [for all][+] Merchandise which is carried by a Land-Carriage, affords little profit[, by reason of the charge][+]. The Goods which are exported out of *Germany*

Their Commedities.

are these that follow. *Iron,* wrought and unwrought, *Lead, Quick silver, Wine, Beer, Brandy, Corn, Wool, Course* [*woollen*] *Cloth,* and several sorts of [*Cloth*],[f] *Linens, Horses, Sheep, &c.*

Yet she wants Money, and the Reasons why.

And yet I cannot deny, but after all, there appears a far greater plenty of Money in [other Countries],[g] than in *Germany;* and there seems to be many reasons for it: For, (1.)[h] What wonder is it, that a Country [region] should appear exhausted, {at least in part,}[i] which |[has endured a War of Thirty years continuance, and has in all that time been exposed to

a. Rather: and they believe that they should not produce anything more refined
b. Rather: bridle
c. Rather: its uses
d. That is, by emigrating and working abroad. [Ed.]
e. Rather: burdensome tolls
f. Rather: woollen fabric
g. Rather: some other regions of Europe
h. The enumeration was inserted by Bohun. Parentheses are added by the editor to distinguish Bohun's item numbers from Pufendorf's section numbers. [Ed.]
i. Bohun omits this phrase, which Pufendorf then removed from the e.p. [Ed.]

the Ravage of its own and]|[a] foreign Souldiers<, and endured severe attacks thereafter>. (2.) There are other Countries [regions of Europe] which are placed much better for a Trade [with outsiders] than *Germany*, because there are [very few, in comparison of the *German* Cities, which stand well for it];[b] when as on the contrary, the Sea favoureth much more *England, Italy, Spain, Portugal, France,* and the *Netherlands*. (3.) There are [other Countries which have Countries subject to them that are no parts of them, and so represent the Wealth of many Nations in a small room crowded together].[c] This is the case of *Spain, Portugal, England,* and *Holland;* but *Germany* has no Dominions without its own Bounds [to enrich it][+]. (4.) The Beauty <162> and Greatness of the capital Cities in [some] other Countries [kingdoms], in which the Wealth of a whole Nation is sometimes contracted, strikes the Eyes, and excites the Wonder of a Stranger. Thus many ignorant [inexperienced] People judge of the Riches of *France* by *Paris; by London* and *Lisbonne* they judge of *England* and *Portugal;* but in so vast a Country as *Germany,* the Riches, which are so very much dispersed, must necessarily seem less than indeed they are. (5.) Much of the Money of *Germany* is by the Folly of its Natives carried into foreign Countries, for Commodities they might either have [produced] at home, or easily be without.[5]

(6.) I know not whether I ought not to add, That the Travels of the *German* Youth into Foreign Countries, spends much of their Money, which is drawn over into those parts; [for though perhaps it is not amiss][d] to have the *German* |[Rusticity and Dulness]|[e] allayed and tempered by

a. E.p.: was exposed for thirty years to the ravages of

b. Rather: only a few German cities that enjoy an advantageous position along the ocean

c. Rather: regions, besides, which have subject to themselves other lands [*terras*] whose entire wealth is [thereby] pressed together, as it were, and presented to a single gaze

d. Rather: though perhaps it is not useless

e. E.p.: character [*ingenium*]

5. Breßlau ("Einleitung," 11, note 3) takes this sentence as evidence that Pufendorf subscribed to mercantilism, an early modern economic system that emphasized exports and the accumulation of precious metals and monetary reserves.

[the Conversation of]ᵃ Foreigners. Yet I think on the other side they deserve Scorn or Pity, who bring [home] out of *Italy* [no other Improvements, but a Sett of Sins,]ᵇ unknown before in their native Country, together with some new and unheard-of forms of Swearing[, and Blaspheming God]⁺. Nor doth *France* for the most part return those that travel in it with any better Accomplishments than that of [a sordid Luxury],ᶜ and an exact experimental knowledge [review] of the various degrees and kinds of the Venereal Mange: Yet there are some [who had not the patience to <163> earn the Title of a *Doctor* at home, by many years Study and Applications, but having taken a great turn in *Italy,* or *France,* are ever after counted wonderfully learned: And a Foreigner too may purchase the Title of *Doctor* much cheaper in *Italy* than in *Germany,* and with less Breach of his Modesty; and this and their Ignorance is all they bring home with them, though in truth for their Honour it may be said, There are a great many *German* Doctors as errant Blockheads as they].ᵈ

The Strength of Germany compared with its Neighbours. 4. But then, seeing no man can properly and truly be said to be strong or weak, till he is compared with others, let us in the next place compare the Forces of *Germany* with its neighbour Nations. *Germany* bordereth to the *South-East* upon the *Ottoman* Empire in *Stiria, Hungary* and *Croatia,* these two, [though not parts of *Germany,*]⁺ being [like] its Ram-

a. Rather: interaction with
b. Rather: only some pleasurable vices
c. Rather: knowing how to stuff themselves / A reference to vulgar, gluttonous eating. [Ed.]
d. Rather: whom it pays to have visited Italy and France, because they find it tedious to aspire to empty scholastic titles in their fatherland by so many detours [cf. "jumping through hoops" (Ed.)]. For it is possible in Italy to bring home a doctoral title, and one's ignorance [i.e., the title is worthless (Ed.)], with less shame and expense, even though plenty such Mercuries are also hewn out of rough wood among the Germans. / Bohun's translation does not reflect Pufendorf's contempt for German academia. The latter declined to earn a doctorate at Leipzig in 1658 and left for Swedish service with only the *Magister* (master of arts) title. Mercury was the Roman Hermes, associated with commerce, border crossings, and deceit. [Ed.]

perts[, whose preservation is greatly in its interest]. Now, tho' the *Turks*, First, with the *Turks*. from their large Dominions, can raise [much more Money and Men],[a] yet there is no great reason for the *Germans* to fear them. For [he can only assault a corner of this Empire],[b] where it terminates in a sharp Angle like a Wedg, and that at a great distance from the Heart or Regal City of *Turkey;* so that they never make an *Hungarian* War, but at a vast Charge and Expence. Nor are the *Turkish* Souldiers<, except for the janissaries [*praetorianum militem*],> to be compared with the *German,* when they are well exercised, [for Strength or Hardiness][+]; and therefore the *Asian* Forces are with great difficulty <164> brought hither, where they cannot bear the [unaccustomed] coldness and sharpness of the Air. And whilst all their Forces are thus drawn to the Extremity of the *Turkish* Empire, the opposite parts [are left naked and defenceless to the Inroads of the *Persians,* who seldom fail to take these favourable Opportunities].[c] And then, because *Servia, Bulgaria,* and that part of *Hungary* which is possessed by the *Turks,* is not sufficient to maintain those great Armies [they must employ against the *Germans*][+], the rest of their Provisions, and all their Ammunition, must be brought by a Land-Carriage, with vast Labour and Expence; for, to the great Good of *Germany,* the *Danube*[, and all the other considerable Rivers,][+] run towards the *East.* So that *Germany* has very rarely employed above a fourth part of her A fourth part of the *German* Forces equal to the *Turks*. Forces against the *Turks,* and those too much [mostly] weakened by the Cowardice and [or] Discord of their Commanders [leaders], and the want of Money and good Discipline; and yet, after all, the *Germans* have oftner beat the *Turks,* than the *Turks* have the *Germans.*

Yet the very Name of the *Turks* is become terrible to the common People [of *Germany*][+], both on the score of their barbarous and outragious Customs and Manners, heightned by the Artifice of |[the *Austrian* Family, which by that means [fright] the more easily drain their

a. Rather: a far heavier amount of gold, and perhaps inundate battlefields with greater masses of men

b. Rather: the Turk grazes Germany with only a small and distant edge of his empire

c. Rather: bordering on Persia tend to rise up [*intumescere*]

Purses]|;[a] as also by the [zealous Preachments of the Friars, who find
their profit in these Terrors, which they raise in the minds of their Hear-

An Addition. ers:][b] //And also on the account <165> of the dreadful Devastations they
have made whenever they have broke in upon that Nation, by wasting
all they could over-run with Fire and Sword, and carrying the Inhabitants into Slavery: But within the last Seven years,[6] the *Germans* have
had so continual a Torrent of Victory attending upon their Arms, that
now the *Turks* are become contemptible to the *Germans,* and by the
Blessing of God in a few years, might have been driven over the *Helles-
pont* into *Asia,* from whence they first came, if the *French* King, who
began the present War, by his Arts, had not, to prevent their utter ruine,
in the year 1688, began as destructive a War on the other side of the
German Empire, which will in all probability force the Emperor to sit
down *contented* with *Hungary, Transylvania, Wallachia, Servia,* and *Bosnia,* and leave the *Turks* in the Possession of *Bulgaria, Thrace,* and *Mac-
edonia,* and a part of *Albania* and *Dalmatia,* but much-sunk in Courage,
Reputation, Strength, and Wealth, so that he is never likely to recover
his Loss again.\\

Germany com-   5. ITALY is very much inferiour to *Germany,* both as to Men and Wealth,
pared with   and being divided into many small [impuissant States],[c] is not in a con-
Italy,   dition to offer any Violence to [its neighbour Nations];[d] so that the *Italians* are very well pleased, if [the Emperor will but sit down with the

a. E.p.: those who by means of such fright have made the Germans more willing
to hand over their money
b. Rather: bellowing of priests, and their itch to prophesy doom. For it is in the
latter's interest to have the minds of the common people agitated by dread.
c. Rather: pieces
d. Rather: others
6. Hostilities began in 1683, when Vienna repulsed a large Turkish attack with the
help of the empire and Jan Sobieski, king of Poland (see IV.1, note 2, p. 97); and
they continued for sixteen years until 1697, finally ending with the Treaty of Karlowitz (1699), by which the Turks ceded most of their former European possessions.
French incursions along the Rhine did much to prolong the war, while William III's
deposition (in 1688) of England's James II, a French ally, worked in the empire's favor.
    The textual reference to the "last seven years" (i.e., since 1683) clearly places the
first (anonymous) publication of Bohun's translation in 1690.

loss of his ancient Pretences to their Country];ᵃ especially now that [the Pope's Thunderbolts, <166> which heretofore were very dreadful, are now for want of the former Zeal, become weak and contemptible].ᵇ

<There is no neighbor more pleasant than SWITZERLAND, which follows the principles [*lex*] of merely protecting its own property, without striving after anything that belongs to others, and of being useful instead of harmful.>ᶜ

Nor is POLAND in a condition to compare her self in any respect with Germany. And seeing the Interest of the *Polish State* is, rather to defend what they have, than to [make any Conquests upon]ᵈ their Neighbours, and that the Necessity [condition] of the *German* Affairs must needs teach them [the Germans] the selfsame modesty: there can hardly be supposed any [Case in which the *German* Princes can be tempted to make a War upon *Poland,* except any of the Emperors]ᵉ should intermeddle with their private internal Quarrels and Civil Wars<, or the Poles are bought by French gold and dare to fall upon Germany from the rear>.

And Poland.

The DANES were never yet in a condition [strong enough] to subdue [even] their neighbour HAMBURGERS, <whose cession to the Danes is not at all in the interest of either of the Saxonics>; much less are they able to attack the Forces of all *Germany,* |[who tremble at every motion of the *Swedes*]|.ᶠ

With the Danes.

a. Rather: only the Emperor does not seek to renew his ancient right to Italy

b. Rather: fear of the Pope's bans, which heretofore were very dreadful to the Emperors, has completely faded because of the impiety [e.p.: culture] of the age

c. According to Salomon and Breßlau, this insertion already appeared in several editions prior to the e.p. (*Severinus,* ed. Salomon, 134; Monzambano, *Über die Verfassung,* trans. Breßlau, 113, note 3). [Ed.]

d. Rather: covet what belongs to

e. Rather: occasion for war between those two nations, unless perhaps a German prince

f. Rather: seeing that they tremble . . . / e.p.: and if they tried to create a disturbance at the instigation of others, they would be easily restrained by setting the Swedes, who are always hostile toward them, upon their rear

With *England.* The *Germans* are nothing concerned to see the *English* Masters of her own Ocean, and, [just] as it were folly in the *English* to attempt the subduing [of] the Continent, so the *Germans* have no Naval Forces that [can dispute their Soveraignty of the Ocean, or ought at all to be compared with the *English* Royal Navies].[a]

With the   The UNITED STATES OF HOLLAND have neither Will nor Power to
Hollanders. attempt any thing against the Empire of *Germany,* for these Water-Rats [*aquatiles animantes*] are altogether unfit for Land-service; and although they have Money in abundance, yet it is not [for the Security of][b] their own Liberty, to maintain |[too great a Land-Army]|:[c] <167> {So that they are well pleased, if the *Germans* will but suffer them to enjoy the Forts and Cities they have taken and garrison'd to defend themselves [their borders] from the *Spaniards* [, though belonging to the Empire][+].}
An Addition. //These Towns belonged to the Dukedoms of *Cleves* and *Juliers,* and to the Archbishoprick of *Cologne,* and were all taken by the *French,* in the year 1672, and in the Treaty of *Nimmegen* restored all to their proper Owners, except *Maestriect,* which yet belongs rather to the *Spaniards* than the *German* Empire, which having happened since our Author wrote, was here to be taken notice of.\\[7]

With *Spain.* The SPANIARDS have no Territories which border upon *Germany,* which are [in any respect] worthy to be compared with it; and *Spain* it self is so very remote, and her Forces so exhausted, that she is not able to reconquer the small Kingdom of *Portugal.* Even *Charles* V. when *Spain* was in the height of all its Glory and Power, though Master of it and all the *Austrian* Dominions, and Emperor of *Germany* too, [yet after all, he was not able to oppress][d] the rest of *Germany.*

a. Rather: can have any significance when compared with those of England
b. Rather: conducive to
c. E.p.: a Land-Army greater than suffices for their defense
d. Rather: sought in vain to subdue
7. Maestricht was under Spanish control until 1632, when it was retaken by the States General. Louis XIV overran it in 1672 but relinquished it again in 1679 according to the Treaty of Nijmegen, which ended the Dutch War.

As to SWEDEN, [though you consider all those Provinces she has conquered on the South side of the *Baltick Sea*],[a] yet she is not to be compared to [the rest of] *Germany* in Men or Monies: For whereas some
[simple-minded] men have been so much mis-led on the account of the
old Proverb, which called *Scandinavia,* now *Sweden, Vagina Gentium,*
the *Sheath of Nations*[8] (and on the score also of the late <168> great
Victories obtained by the *Swedes* in *Germany*[, under the Conduct of
Gustavus Adolphus their King][+]) as to think it is superiour, or at least
equal to *Germany* in Men; yet wise men do very well see and understand
[the true Reasons of those great Successes, and that they proceeded neither from the Numbers nor extraordinary Valour of the *Swedes*].[b] For
in the space of Eighteen years, there was not brought over out of *Sweden*
into *Germany,* above Seventy thousand men, [the far greatest part of
which][c] returned back [home] again, and yet, during that War, there was
scarce ever less than an Hundred thousand men[, indeed, often more,]
of the *Germans* [in pay];[d] so that the true cause of that [wonderful][+]
Progress was the Discord of the *Germans,* the opportunity of the Times
[situation], [which favoured the *Swedes,*][+] and because all the Protestants being oppressed [hard pressed] by the *Austrians,* looked upon *Gustavus Adolphus* as a Deliverer sent to them for their Preservation, from
Heaven.

But as to the now most flourishing Kingdom of FRANCE, we may with
greater probability doubt, whether it be not a Match for *Germany.* And
yet if the Forces of both Nations be well considered [in themselves],
[without their Advantages or Weaknesses, (*France* being the stronger for

a. Rather: despite the many German provinces it has lately acquired / This refers
mainly to western Pomerania and Bremen-Verden, which Sweden received through
the Westphalian settlement (1648), but also to various territories in the eastern Baltic
acquired before and after that date. [Ed.]
b. Rather: what is really the case
c. Rather: many of whom
d. Rather: under arms
8. Jordanes, a historian of the sixth century A.D., referred in his *De origine acti-
busque Getarum* [On the origin and deeds of the Goths], chapter 4, to Scandinavia
as *officina gentium, vagina nationum* (the workshop of races, the womb of nations).

being a regular Kingdom, and *Germany* the weaker for being a knot of Independent States)]ᵃ *Germany* is certainly the strongest of the two. For, (1.)ᵇ It is much greater [larger] than *France;* and though we should suppose it only equal to *France,* in <169> point of Fertility, yet even then it would [far] excell *France* as to its Minerals. (2.) It has more Men than *France,* and the *Germans* have on many occasions proved themselves the better Souldiers of the two. (3.) As to the quantity of Money, it is very difficult to determine on which side the Advantage lieth, for [it is not to be guessed how much Gold the present King of *France* has squeezed out of the old Horseleaches of his Kingdom, and how much he has encreased his [annual] Revenues, which is not to be taken into consideration without wonder]:ᶜ But then, at the same time, it is to be observed, that the [common] People of *France* are much more harass'd, oppress'd, and ruin'd by their excessive Taxes [and tolls], than the People of *Germany* are, and that all the Wealth of *France* runs in one Channel<, which would shrink considerably if outsiders stopped desiring French merchandise that they could easily do without>; whereas in *Germany* it is divided amongst many Princes, and so it will not so easily be computed or estimated[, as it might if it were paid all into one Prince] ⁺.

An Addition. //Since this Author wrote, there have been two Wars between *Germany* and *France,* and the second is now depending.⁹ In the first the *Germans* were ever too hard for the *French,* whilst they fought them in the Field, but the *French* drawing on the War, the *Germans* were at last worsted for want of Money, and much more worsted in the Treaty, and after it

a. Rather: apart from the advantages that arise for France from its regular monarchy and the illnesses that arise for Germany from its disjointed form of state,

b. Parentheses added to Bohun's enumeration. [Ed.]

c. Rather: we behold with admiration how much gold the current king of France has amassed, especially by squeezing those old sponges, and what he has in annual revenues / e.p.: we behold with admiration how much it [France] has in annual revenues

9. Probably a reference to the Dutch War (1672–78), which ended with the Peace of Nijmegen (1678–79), and to the War of the League of Augsburg (1688–97), which was concluded by the Treaty of Ryswick (1697). Note that the latter conflict went on at the same time as the war against the Turks (see note 6, p. 188, in this chapter).

by the Treachery of the *French*. But now the *Turks* are reduced to such an ebb, and all *Christendome* is united against *France*, <170> so that all their Trade is cut off: The *Germans* have apparently at present the Advantage, and it is not denied by the *French*, who do what they can to separate the Allies one from another; if they fail in this, another Summer may, by God's Blessing, shew the World, the *German* Nation is much superiour to the *French*, and force that King to disgorge *Lorrain*, *Strasburg*, both the *Alsatia*'s, and the *Franche Comte*, which have been got more by Purchace and Surprize, than by the Force of a generous and open War.\\

<It is evident, however, that beside the Turks, who have now been repulsed, no enemy threatens Germany more than France. In former times, when Burgundy, Lorraine, Luxemburg, and the still united Dutch provinces were arrayed before it like defensive outposts, it did not dare even to make a sound against Germany. But now that all of these have been subjugated, as well as Alsace (with [the cities of] Breisach and Straßburg) and a large part of the territory west of the Rhine, and it is surrounded by a strong line of fortifications, it is all the more threatening to the Germany east of the Rhine, [especially] because it seems to have lost all respect for treaties and trustworthiness. And unless the Germans force it back to its former limits and oppose it with equal fortifications, they will be exposed to its constant incursions and, perhaps, will [one day] be entirely subjected to it.>

6. But though we suppose *Germany* superiour to any of its Neighbours when singly taken, what may be the event, if they should unite against her? Here, in the first place we ought to consider, that Interest of State will not suffer many [some] of her Neighbours to [unite]ᵃ against her; and that the Forces of others are so much inferiour to *Germany*, that there is no reason for her to be concerned how they behave themselves: And lastly, it ought to be considered, that the other Princes [states] will not sit still, and suffer *Germany* to fall into the hands of any one

The Strength of Germany compared with its Neighbours, united against her.

a. Rather: conspire together

[Prince],[a] who would then be in a condition [to oppress and enslave the rest of the *European* Princes]:[b] So that there will [for ever be some Princes found, who will join with the *Germans,* and help them to preserve their Liberty for their own sakes].[c] So that |[there is in effect but three Princes in the World, who <171> at present are in capacity of subduing]|[d] *Germany, viz.* The *Turks,* the House of *Austria,* and the King of *France.*

|[Now, it is not probable any Christian Prince will openly join with the *Turks* against *Germany,* no, not [even] the King of *France;* for the old Leagues the *French* had with the *Turks* [during the previous century], were only for the curbing the over-great Forces of *Charles* V. who was then much too powerful for [*Francis* I. King of *France*].[e] But we are never to fear a League, in which these two Princes shall unite their Forces, and jointly at once invade *Germany,* to the end to make a Conquest of it; because it would be both wicked and foolish to promote the Affairs of that barbarous Prince [the Turk] to that degree, who bears an immortal hatred to all that is call'd *Christian.* Besides, as it is better for *France,* that *Germany* should continue as it is, than that any considerable share of it should fall into the hands of the *Turks;* so it is better too for the *Turks,* that it should continue in this divided [ill formed] state, which makes it unfit to wage a War for Conquest upon its Neighbors, rather than to have it [brought by the *French* into the state of a well-formed Monarchy];[f] because if [*France* and *Germany* were once throughly united in one Prince's hand],[g] the *Turk* would have too much reason to fear what Fortune might betide his *Constantinople.*]|[h]

a. Rather: or other
b. Rather: that he could easily prescribe laws to all of Europe
c. Rather: never be a lack of those who will strive to preserve Germany
d. Rather: there are three [states] deemed capable of leading or heading an alliance to attack / e.p.: before the Turks were crushed, [only] three states were deemed capable . . .
e. Rather: the French
f. Rather: joined together with France and reformed according to the laws of a monarchy
g. Rather: those two empires really coalesced into one great body [*massam*]
h. E.p.: As we know, no Christian prince has openly conspired with the Turks

Nor is it the Interest of any of [the *European* Princes],[a] to suffer the House of *Austria* to reduce the rest of *Germany* under their Dominion [monarchical rule]; and therefore I <172> cannot think any of them would be so mad, as to promote them in it, or lend their Assistance to it. And as the *Spaniard*[, who is under a Branch of this Family, might possibly be contented to do it, so the *French* would certainly oppose it with all their Power, with whom, in that Case, the *Swedes* and *Hollanders* would join][b] the more readily, because they never defended the *German* Liberty, but to their own very great advantage. Nor would the Pope [Supreme Shepherd] in this Case be over-forward to assist the House of *Austria,* because though it would be very glorious to him[, and profitable too,]+ to reduce [lead back] so many [myriads of] straying Sheep<, as he regards them,> into the Church's Fold; yet let the hazard or loss of Souls be what it will, he [is not to hazard the loss of the *Italian* Liberty, by making either the Emperor or the King of *Spain* Masters of that Country]:[c]

And if now the *French* should attempt the Conquest of *Germany; Spain, England, Italy,* and *Holland* would all [unite with the Empire

---

against Germany, except that France has secretly consulted with them on some occasions. The alliances made with the Turks by Francis I. in the previous century may perhaps be excused, since any enemy whatsoever had then to be raised against the overbearing Charles V., lest France succumb to him entirely, and since any reason is considered justified when it comes to furthering one's self-preservation [*salutis expediendae quaevis ratio honesta habeatur*]. However, Louis XIV. should have forfeited the title "most Christian" when, without necessity but merely desirous to expand his borders, he stirred up the Turks against the Emperor, resolved to attack Germany from the other side if they happened to overpower Vienna. After that hope had failed, he kept quiet until the north-German troops were far away and then unexpectedly poured [his armies] across the Rhine, not only to give the Turks—who otherwise seemed on the brink of being expelled from all of Europe—time to gather themselves, but also to bring whatever remained of Germany west of the Rhine under his control. Whether the treachery of this insatiably ambitious prince, who has been disturbing Europe for such a long time already, will remain unpunished, remains to be seen.

a. Rather: its neighbors

b. Rather: is on the side of the Austrians, so the French, the Swedes, and the Belgian Federation are openly opposed to them, all

c. Rather: will not allow such excessive power to give a German or a Spaniard any say over Italian affairs against him].ᵃ |[The *Danes* perhaps would not be much concerned at it, so be they might be delivered from the Terror of *Sweden,* though they for ever truckled under *France*]|:ᵇ But then [the assistance of the *Swedes* would in this case]ᶜ be very considerable, especially if that Nation happened to have then a Martial and a Warlike Prince. But then it has been long since observed [by the wiser sort], that [the *French* must pay the *Swedes* very well]ᵈ for their assistance; the *French* would also expect to be the only Gainers in the end <173> [of the War] ⁺; for the *French* would never be pleased to see the *Swedes* [enlarge their Conquests in *Germany,* with their Money],ᵉ to that degree especially, that they might ever after [despise the *French* Monarch].ᶠ And on the other side, the *Swedes* are very sensible how foolish it is to spend their Bloods [exert themselves] to the Advantage of the *French,* and not at all for their own Benefit. Nor are they so dull, but that they very well know and consider, that when the *French* are once Masters of [the greatest part of] ⁺ *Germany,*

a. Rather: openly oppose it, the latter being rightly mindful, perhaps, of the old saying that "one should be a friend of France, but not a neighbor" / See *Vita Caroli Magni, scriptore Eginhardo* [Einhard], in Johannes Joachimus Frantzius, *Historia Caroli Magni Imperatoris Romani: ex praecipuis scriptoribus eorum temporum concinnata* (Argentinae [Straßburg], 1644), cap. 16 (*Verfassung des deutschen Reiches,* ed. Denzer, 1994, 219, note 10; *Severinus,* ed. Salomon, 138, note 1). [Ed.]

b. Rather: The Danes would perhaps not be afraid to become a protectorate of France, so long as they could thereby dispel their constant fear of the hated Swedes / e.p.: It is evident, at any rate, that if Germany were ever somehow combined with France into one empire, all of Europe would be threatened by servitude. No prince, I should think, would want to contribute to this result, unless he is pleased to exchange his high rank for servitude. Of the nations capable of attacking Germany from the rear, the Poles, at least, do not seem easily induced to prefer French gold to the interests of their own state, [since] after Germany has been subjugated they too would share that vile servitude. For the same reason, I think, the Danes too would hardly provide much help to France, if it is evidently trying to subjugate Germany, especially since anyone seeking to become monarch of Europe [as such] would need above all to control the straits of the Baltic Sea.

c. Rather: a [French] alliance with Sweden would

d. Rather: though the French are willing to pay the *Swedes*

e. Rather: increase their own power by means of French gold,

f. Rather: be able to do without the friendship of France

they will then pretend to give Laws to the *Swedes,* as well as to [the *Germans*]:[a, 10]

|[And from this Consideration it is, that there has for some time been a very moderate and luke-warm Friendship between these two Nations [peoples],[b] [and] the *French* King growing weary of the distant *Swedes,* thought it more for his Interest, [before this,][+] to draw]|[c] some of the [neighboring] *German* Princes on the *Rhine* into Leagues with him, and <174> as the Report goes, [has not been sparing in his Pensions to them],[d] and upon all occasions shews himself very solicitous for [the

An Addition.

a. Rather: their other neighbors

b. //"which since the War in 1672. in which the *French* exposed the *Swedes* to all the Forces of the *Branden burgers,* and at the same time seized the Dukedom of *Deuxpont,* which belongs to the King of *Sweden,* though it lies on the Borders of *France,* is so much abated, that it is verily believed the *Swedes* will now heartily join with the *Germans,* to humble *France;* and it is certain, in this present War he [the king of Sweden] has done what was possible to prevent the *Danes* from embroiling the North parts of *Germany,* which the *French* passionately desired."\\ / Bohun's in-text elaboration interrupts Pufendorf's thought and thus appears in this note instead. [Ed.]

c. E.p.: And noble nations [such as Sweden] have good reason to disdain the reproach of being for sale, with which an insolent people [France] customarily insults allies that depend on its financial support.

Finally, since it is in the common interest [*bonum*] of all Princes that none of them be so superior that he can insult the rest as he wishes, but that the strength of all be in equilibrium as far as possible, one who for some peculiar or temporary gain contributes to the establishment of a power [*moles*] formidable to all, must be seen as betraying the common liberty. More than anything, Germans must be careful not to contribute to their own servitude by assisting France, as happens when they do not conjoin their counsels and strength to repulse the enemy that threatens them all, but either incline together to ruin their fatherland because they have been bought by French gold, or sit by quietly, corrupted by noxious bribes, without a care for the public good—even though others are struggling and they, too, will be devoured by Polyphemus after the rest have been consumed. Certainly, one would have to be blind not to grasp the French king's stratagems, whereby he initially presented himself in a milder fashion so as to have a pretext for interfering in German affairs, and then drew . . .

d. Rather: to bind them to himself by means of annual subsidies

10. Sweden's alliance with France (see III.3, note 6, p. 85; and VI.7, note 8, p. 171) lasted until 1682, when Charles XI established closer ties with Austria. This shift led Samuel's older brother, Esaias (i.e., "Laelius"), to leave Swedish employ in 1684, after a long and distinguished diplomatic career there.

general Liberty of]⁺ *Germany;* offering himself as a Mediator, to compose any Differences that happen to arise between one Prince and another, and is ever ready to send Money or Men to every one of them that desireth either of them; and in short, makes it his great business to shew them, that [if they need assistance of any sort,] they may certainly expect more [protection] from his Friendship than from the Emperor's, or from the Laws of the Empire.

|[Now, the man must be very stupid, who doth not see, that the End of all this Courtship is the opening a Way to the Ruin of the *German* Liberty, especially if the Male Line of the House of *Austria* should happen to fail.]|ª //And the *French* King should there upon obtain the Empire. When this Author wrote, the Emperor of *Germany* had no Son: The Princes of the *Rhine* he here hints at, are, the Elector of *Cologne,* and the Duke of *Bavaria,* to whose Sister he [Louis XIV] afterwards married the *Dauphin* his Son, to fix him for ever to *France;* but all would not do, that Prince has since seen his true Interest, as all the German Princes too by this time do; and now *France* finding the wheeling way will never do, has taken the way of Rage and Conquest, having disob-

An Addition.

a. E.p.: Soon, however, swelled by constant successes, he decided to seize whatever seemed opportune, either by treachery, absurd pretenses, or overt force, and adjoined to France the entire left side of the Rhine, securing it with awesome fortifications so that no army could make its way into France, though it remained open to him, as often as he pleased, to fall upon Germany and reduce it to a miserable condition. Given such designs, all those who take France's side do openly betray their fatherland, and those who do not join in removing the common danger would be most deserving of French servitude if their citizens would not become involved in the same disaster. Above all, German princes should refrain from abusing their right to make treaties to the detriment of their common fatherland, and one wishes it were possible to enter upon a resolution suitable for preventing that abuse. Of course, sensible people should deem it weighty enough that once the Empire's structure has been overturned, their own authority may also be hurled to the ground and trampled by French arrogance. And one should note well the statement of that French minister who said frankly to the envoy of a certain Elector negotiating a treaty with France, when he demanded an exclusionary clause acknowledging [his lord's] obligation and bond to the Empire, "What need is there for words? Unless your lord is an Elector of the Holy Roman Empire, he is nothing."

liged[a] the whole World, and what the event [outcome] will be, is in the Hand of God.\\[11] <175>

7. This bulky and formidable Body, which is thus united in the common Appellation of the *German* Empire, and if it were reduced under the Laws of a regular [*justi*] Monarchy, would be formidable to all *Europe,* is yet, by reason of its own Internal Diseases and Convulsions, so weakened, that it is scarce able to defend it self. //Nay, it is certain, if it were not powerfully assisted by its Neighbours, it is not able to defend it self against the *French*.\\ The principal Cause of this [Impuissance and Weakness][b] is its irregular [*inconcinna*] and [ill-compacted Constitution or Frame of Government].[c] The most numerous multitude of men is not stronger than one single man, as long as every man acts singly by himself and for himself; all [its extraordinary Strength is from its Union and][d] Conjunction. And [as][e] it is not possible that [many should join in][f] one natural Body, [so they may certainly be united into one Force, whilst they are governed by one Council as a common Soul].[g] By how much the closer and more regular this Union is, so much the stronger this Society or Body is: But on the contrary, Weakness and Diseases [ever follow upon a loose Conjunction and an ill-combined and irregular Union].[h]

Germany weak by reason of its irregular Constitution.

a. That is, set free from any obligation. [Ed.]

b. Rather: malady [*mali;* ill, *Übel*]

c. Rather: ill-composed form [*compage*] of state

d. Rather: strength is from

e. Rather: though

f. Rather: several should coalesce into

g. Rather: the strengths of many are united insofar as they are governed by one counsel [*consilio*] as by one soul / See VI.8 and note 11, p. 175, on sovereignty as the soul of the state. [Ed.]

h. Rather: necessarily accompany a loose and ill-composed union of members

11. Louis, dauphin of Viennois (1661–1711), was the eldest son and expected heir of Louis XIV, but he died four years before his father. In 1680 he married Maria Anna of Bavaria (1660–90), daughter of Elector Ferdinand Maria (1636–79). In 1671, for similar reasons, Liselotte (Elisabeth Charlotte) of the Palatinate, a daughter of Elector Karl Ludwig, had been married to Philippe I of Orleans, brother of Louis XIV.

Monarchy the best and most lasting Government.

A well [*rite*] composed Kingdom or Monarchy is certainly the most perfect Union, and the best fitted for duration or continuance; for as for *Aristocrasies,* besides that, they can scarce ever conveniently subsist, except when the [main] force of a Commonwealth is <176> collected into one single City, yet even then in their own nature they are much weaker [more fragile] than *Monarchies*{; for the serene Commonwealth of *Venice* is to be reputed amongst the Miracles of the World}.

A *System* of many Cities [states] united by a League, is much more loose in its conjunction, and may more easily be [disturbed and] dissolved[, (which is the Case of the States of *Holland*)] +. And here, that

Wherein the Strength of a System of States consisteth.

there may be some strength [firmness] in these kinds of *Systems,* it is in the first place necessary, that the Associated [Cities or] + States have the same form of Government, and be not overmuch disproportioned in their Strength, and that the same or equal Advantages may from the Union arise to every one of them. And lastly, It is necessary, in this case, that they have come together, upon [well weighed and great Reasons],[a] and associated upon well-considered Laws or Conditions; for they that unite in a Society rashly, and as it were [in a hurry],[b] without [first] bethinking themselves very seriously what their future state shall be, |[can no more form a [regular well compacted Society],[c] than a Taylor can make a beautiful Garment after he has cut his Cloth all into Shreds and small Pieces, before he has resolved whether he will form it into a Man's or a Woman's Garment]|:[d]

And it has long since been observed, that *Monarchs* very rarely enter into [a sincere friendship with *Commonwealths* [(v)] or *Free Cities*],[e] though it be for a short time: And it is yet much more difficult <177> to make a perpetual or lasting League, because [all] + Princes hate [abhor] Popular Liberty; and the People[, or Popular States,] + do equally detest the Pride

(v). *The Leagues between Kings and Commonwealths seldome lasting.*
a. Rather: mature consideration
b. Rather: by some impulse
c. Rather: well-ordered body
d. E.p.: must admit many things not because they are useful or appropriate, but because they cannot be corrected
e. Rather: alliances with free states in good faith

or Grandeur of Kings. And such is the Perverseness of Humane Nature, that no man doth willingly see one inferiour to himself in point of Power, live by him in an equal degree of Liberty; and Men very unwillingly [contribute to the Common Charges, if they reap nothing, or but a very little Advantage from the Common Profit].ᵃ

8. Now [the State of]⁺ *Germany* is so much the more deplorable, because all the Diseases of an ill-formed Kingdom, and of an ill digested [arranged] *System* of [associated] States, are conjunctly to be found in it; nay, it is to be reckon'd as the principal Calamity of *Germany,* that it is neither a Kingdom, nor a System of States. The outward Appearance and {vain} Images represent the Emperor as a King[, and the States as Subjects]⁺; and in the most ancient times he was without doubt a King, as he was call'd. After this, the Authority of the Emperor was from time to time diminished, and the Liberties and Riches of the States were encreased, till at last the Emperor had nothing but a shadow of the Kingly Power{, as at this day it is, and seems liker the General of an Association than a King}.ᵇ |[From hence proceeds a most pernicious Convulsion in the Body of the <178> Empire, whilst the Emperor and the States draw counter each to the other]|;ᶜ for he, with might and main, by all waies, endeavoureth to regain the old Regal Power, and they, on the other side, are as solicitous to preserve the [Liberties and Wealth]ᵈ they have got the possession of. From whence there must necessarily follow Suspicions, Distrust, and underhand Contrivances to [hinder each others Designs, and break each others Power]:ᵉ The [first]⁺ effect of this is, the rendering this otherwise strong and formidable Body unfit [powerless] to invade

The Diseases of Germany.

The Princes and the Emperor distrust each other.

a. Rather: bear common burdens if they perceive that there remains for them no part, or only a very small one, of the common advantages
b. Rather: , much like that discerned in leaders of an alliance
c. E.p.: Hence the Empire contains deep within itself the seeds of a most pernicious convulsion, in that the Emperor and the Estates are compelled to strive toward different objectives / The e.p. revision makes more clear that both sides are acting out the logic of their respective positions, and that the basic problem is a structural one. [Ed.]
d. Rather: might
e. Rather: keep the former's power from increasing, or to break that of the rest

others, or to make any Additions to its own bulk by Conquest, because the States are not willing that any thing should be added to the Emperor's Dominions, and yet it is not possible to distribute it equally amongst them. [This alone is monstrous, that the head [of the Empire] should confront its members in partisan disputes.]ᵃ

The States embroiled one with another.
And there are very many distracting [divisive] Differences between the States themselves, on divers accounts, [and this makes them less happy than a well united System of States might be].ᵇ The [States are under]ᶜ different forms of Government [*reipublicae*], some of them being Princes, and the rest Free Cities [*civitates*], and these are [not well] intermixed one with another. The Free Cities [*urbes*] drive, for the most part, a considerable Trade, and their Wealth excites the Envy of the Princes, but especially when a great part of their Trade and Wealth ariseth from any of the Princes Dominions. Nor can it be denied, but that some Cities, like the *Spleen,* have <179> swell'd too much to the damage of their Neighbour Princes, their Subjects being drained away, and their States impoverish'd to augment the Cities. The Nobility are [also] apt to despise the common People, and they [these] are as prone to value themselves on the account of their Money, [and to undervalue the Nobilities]ᵈ old Titles and exhausted Dominions. Lastly, some of the Princes look on these Cities as a reproach to their Government [absolute rule], and think their own Subjects would live more contentedly under their Command, if these Instances of Popular Liberty were removed, and all occasions of comparing their own Condition with that of their Neighbours in these Cities were taken away. From hence proceed Envy, Contemt, Mutual Insults, Suspicions, secret Contrivances against each other, all which Mischiefs are yet more manifest, and outragiously [vehemently] prosecuted between the Bishops and the Cities in which the

---

a. E.p.: This alone is irregular [in place of *monstrosum* (Ed.)], that the Empire's very form should put the interests [*rationes*] of its head and members completely at odds with one another. / This sentence was omitted by Bohun. [Ed.]

b. Rather: so that Germany cannot even be regarded as a well-ordered system of confederates

c. Rather: Estates utilize

d. Rather: as the former are on account of their

Cathedral Churches are fixed: Yea, [even] in the Diets the Princes do ever express a great Contemt of the [college of the] Cities, but the Emperor, on the contrary, doth alwaies cherish and protect them, because he finds them [generally] more observant of his Orders [authority] than the other States.

Nor do the [Princes themselves bear that mutual kindness each to other they ought, especially the *Secular* and the *Ecclesiastical Princes*].[a] [Though in the same class,] the *Spiritual Princes* have the Preheminence or Precedence of the *Temporal,* on the account of the <180> Sanctity of their Office [*muneris*], |[and also because their great Experience in the World and Learning is supposed to make them better able than the Laymen to advise, which in the barbarous times begat them a great Authority in the State]|.[b] But then the *Temporal Princes* are now very much concerned [annoyed] to see these Prelates, which are for the most part the Sons of meaner Families than themselves, in a few years time equal, yea, and mount above them as if they had more of the *Grace of God than themselves.* They are yet more aggrieved, because these men cannot transmit their Estates [dignity] to their Posterity, but [and] their Families continue in the same [low] estate it was before, but that many [of these Holy Fathers have learned from the Pope to enrich][c] their Kindred by Ecclesiastical Benefices and large Donations[, out of the Revenues of the Church] [+]: On the other side, the Prelates have [more] [+] reason to be offended with the Temporal Princes, [who have intercepted and cut off so many of their old Preferments][d]{; of which I shall say more hereafter}.[e]

Besides all these that I have represented, the [great] Inequality of their

a. Rather: secular and ecclesiastical princes regard one another with any favor

b. Rather: and also because the deity undoubtedly infuses itself more abundantly through bald pates than through unshorn heads, something that also accounts for their greater authority in the state [*respublica*] during the former, barbarian times [probably a reference to the Middle Ages (Ed.)] / e.p.: which has, according to its first institution and original function, nothing princely about it

c. Rather: bishops tend, according to the example of our Most Holy Father, to make very ample provision for / e.p.: . . . Pope . . .

d. Rather: because of whom they have started lacing up their bellies much more tightly

e. In VIII.8–10, which was also omitted from the e.p. [Ed.]

Estates and Riches is another [Fountain of Discontent betwixt them]:[a] For first, [as is common],[b] the more potent contemn [disdain] the weaker, and [are but too apt][c] to oppress them; and the weaker[, on the other hand,] are as ready to complain and suspect, and sometimes to boast unseasonably, that they are equally free with <181> the most powerful. The very exalting the *Electors* above the other Princes, is [also] a great cause of Discontent [disagreement]; whilst [in that] the other States [are displeased at their Dignity],[d] and charge them with usurping some things they have no Right to; and the *Electors* as stifly maintain what they have got as their Right and Due [*autoritate*].

The Differences of Religion cause great Disturbances and Disquiet.

9. [These would not be sufficient Principles of Disorder, if the most effectual active Ferment, which can possibly affect the Minds of Men, I mean the *Difference of Religion,* were not added to all I have mentioned, which at this day divides *Germany,* and distracts it more than all the rest.][e] Nor is the diversity of Opinions and the commonly practised, excluding [each other][f] out of the Kingdom of Heaven, (as Priests of diverse and contrary Opinions use to do) the only cause of their mutual hating each other: [The ROMAN CATHOLICKS charge the PROTESTANTS, That they have deprived them][g] of a great part of their Wealth and Riches, [and they (good men) are][h] night and day contriving how they shall recover what they have thus lost; and the other Party [are as well resolved to keep][i] what they have got: [Nay, they think they have still too much, and that the Revenues of the Church, at this day, are][j] a

a. Rather: source of division among many of the Estates
b. Rather: by a flaw of human character [*ingenii*]
c. Rather: desire
d. Rather: find it hard to bear such great display [*splendorem*]
e. Rather: As if these illnesses were not enough, religion, which is otherwise the most effective bond among spirits, divides Germany into parts severely at odds with one another.
f. Rather: those who have different beliefs
g. Rather: but also the fact that the Protestants have driven Catholic priests out
h. Rather: the desire for which has them
i. Rather: deems it cowardly to give up
j. Rather: Indeed, there are those who think that in general the excessive wealth [*opes*] of priests is

Burthen to the State, [especially] seeing the Priests and Monks depend upon another Head, who is no part of the *German Empire,* |[but a Foreigner, and an ever-<182>lasting Enemy to their Country, nay, to all the Laity in the World, which he would fain impoverish, that so his own Followers might flourish, and flant it with their Spoils]|.[a] [If he could bring this about, there would then be a State within the State, and an Head to each of them]:[b] |[And this, to those that love their Country more than the Church of *Rome,* seems the greatest Mischief that can betide any State.]|[c]

Nor is this a less [pernicious] Disorder than the last, *viz.* That [some of] the Princes [Estates] of *Germany* enter into [special] Leagues, not only one with another, but with [Foreign Princes][d] too, |[and the more securely, because they have reserved to themselves a Liberty to do so in the Treaty of *Westphalia,* which not only divides the Princes of *Germany* into Factions, but [also] gives]|[e] those [Strangers an opportunity][f] to mould *Germany* to their own particular Interest and Wills, and [ultimately, when given an appropriate opportunity,] by the assistance of

The Princes of *Germany* enter into Domestick and Foreign Leagues.

a. Rather: and who never had any genuine love for Germans, and would be willing to have all the laity perish so long as his own followers enjoyed the flourishing of their own affairs / e.p.: . . . Germans, and values the welfare of the laity only insofar as, through them, he may provide richly for his own followers

b. Rather: It is obvious that in this manner a special state [*statum*] is produced in the middle of the state [*Republica*], which then becomes two-headed

c. E.p.: Indeed, the power of truth even caused Pope Pius to write in his *Historia Australi* that no exceptional evil occurs in the Catholic Church whose first origin does not depend on the clergy, unless it comes about by some hidden counsel of God. (Pandolfo Collenucio, *Collectiones rerum Neapolitarum* [Dordrecht, 1618], l. 4, p.m. 185.) / Salomon and Denzer have "p. 184," though Dove and the e.p. have "p. 185" (*Severinus,* ed. Salomon, 143; *Verfassung des deutschen Reiches,* ed. Denzer, 1994, 231, note 17; *Verfassung des deutschen Reiches,* trans. Dove, 128). An Italian humanist, Collenuccio (1444–1504) was born in Pesaro, employed by Lorenzo the Magnificent, and wrote a number of works in Latin and Italian. [Ed.]

d. Rather: foreigners

e. Rather: . . . because it is expressly permitted by the Peace of Osnabrück, which . . . / e.p.: which leagues do not square well with the welfare of the Empire as a whole, since they give

f. Rather: foreign allies the ability

their [German] Allies, to [insult on all the rest of the Princes],[a] especially when [the Design of those Leagues is not levell'd against other Foreign Princes],[b] which might [somehow] be born, but [also] against the Members of the Empire [itself].

There are scarce any Footsteps or Trace of *Justice*[c] neither left in the Empire. For if any Controversie arise between the States themselves, (which must often happen where there is such a number of them, and their Dominions lie intermixed one with another) if they commence a Suit in the Chamber of *Spire,* it is an Age [century] before <183> they can hope to see an end of it. In that of *Vienna,* (the *Palace-Court*) [it is feared that] there is too much [opportunity for] Partiality and Bribery, and after all, it [i.e., the Court] is suspected to think more than is fit of the Place it is seated in: |[So that in *Germany* men for the most part right themselves by their Swords, and he that is strongest, has the best Cause, and feareth not to do his own business]|.[d]

The want of Justice, another cause of Disquiet.

The want of a Common Treasure.

Lastly, How weak must that Government [*societatem*][e] needs be, that has no common Stock or Treasure, nor any Army to resist the Invasions [attacks] of Strangers, or for the acquiring some Provinces to bear the publick Charge. And how much better were it for *Germany* to spend her valiant men, who cannot live in Peace, in her own Service, than to have them, as they now do, [run into foreign Countries, and there sell their Blood at cheap rates, to those who will employ them as mercenary Souldiers of Fortune].[f]

a. Rather: increase their power vis-à-vis the whole [of Germany]

b. Rather: such leagues with outsiders are sought not only against other outsiders

c. Rather: *Astraea* [the goddess of justice]

d. Rather: . . . and feareth not to carry out the judgment on his own / e.p.: Hence in Germany, one who is strong can enforce his own rights claims. But those who are not capable of war, even if they have the stronger case, are left with nothing but empty complaints against the more powerful

e. That is, Germany, understood as a collectivity or "association" that is weak because it is lame or "disjointed" [*elumbem*]. [Ed.]

f. Rather: sell their blood throughout almost all of Europe

10. There are also a vast number [*non paucae*] of Emulations and Controversies, between [the Inferiour]ᵃ States and Princes, which do much weaken the strength of the whole Body. {It will be enough for us here only to touch the principal of these Differences.

The House of *Austria* has raised a Spirit of Jealousie and Envy in all the other Princes of *Germany,* by its long Possession of the Imperial Dignity, and [the vast Dominions it has by that means acquired in the Empire and elsewhere]:ᵇ Besides the old Quarrel between the Houses of the Elector <184> *Palatine* and that of *Bavaria,* there is a new one concerning the *Administration of the Publick Affairs during the Vacancy of the Empire,*ᶜ which [will hardly]ᵈ be determin'd, the one House relying on its Power, and the other on its Right. In the House of *Saxony* [there is a Contest and Heart-burning between the Lines of *Ernest* and *Albert,* because the former stripp'd the latter of the Electoral Dignity, in the Reign of *Charles* V].ᵉ The Elector of *Brandenburg* will never [genuinely] forgive the *Swedes,* for their usurping from him the best part of *Pomerania.*¹² The Elector *Palatine* [is hated by many]ᶠ of his Neighbours,

a. Rather: individual [*singulis*]

b. Rather: its excessive power

c. That is, *vicariatu Imperii.* According to the Golden Bull (chapter 5), if the Emperor was a minor or incapacitated, as well as during an interregnum, imperial authority was exercised by two so-called vicars: the Saxon Elector and the Elector Palatine. The latter lost his vicariate and electoral status to Bavaria in 1623, but his restoration to electoral rank in 1648, by the addition of another (eighth) electorate, initiated an ongoing dispute with Bavaria over the vicarial role. This was complicated in 1659, when the Saxon Elector recognized Bavaria. Bohun's order of mention obscures the respective claims: the Palatinate appealed to ancient right, while Bavaria was more powerful. [Ed.]

d. Rather: no one knows how it will

e. Rather: the Ernestine line resents the Albertine because its electoral dignity was transferred to it / The (Protestant) Albertine line (i.e., Moritz of Saxony) received the Ernestine's (i.e., Johann Friedrich's) electoral status in 1547, as a reward for supporting Charles V against the Smalkaldic League. See IV.4, note 15, p. 102; and V.10, note 8, p. 129. Bohun's error here reflects the Latin. [Ed.]

f. Rather: has long been resented by some

12. The duchy of Pomerania was divided into western and eastern portions in 1648, with the former (including the important Oder River port of Stettin) going to Sweden for its role during the Thirty Years' War. See II.7 and III.3, note 6, p. 85.

on the account of some [disputed]$^+$ Rights he claims [has] in their Territories, [so that very lately they were for Arming against him to recover them].^{a} And I cannot believe the memory of that old Controversie is extinguished wholly, which [formerly] embroiled the Family of [*Nassaw,* with that of]$^+$ *Hesse,* for the Territory of *Marpurg.* Nor will there ever be a sincere Friendship [*fida pax*] between the Elector of *Brandenburg* and the [House]^b of *Newburg,* [(which, since our Author wrote, has succeeded in the Electorate of the *Lower Palatinate* of the *Rhine*)]$^+$ on the account of the Inheritance of [the Dukedom of]$^+$ *Juliers* [*Jülich*]. [Beside these,] who can number now the smaller Controversies depending [pending] between them? [The empty]^c vain Contests about Precedence have kindled lasting Hatred in the Hearts of some of the Princes against each other.}

To this vast Inundation [morass] of Diseases [in this <185> Politick Body]$^+$ we may add (although of less consequence) the tedious Proceedings [especially] in all Civil Causes, by which the most manifest and apparent Right is [disputed and deluded]^d for many years: And the great variety of Monies which is current in *Germany,* [which being neither of good allay or due weight],^{e} brings great damage to the Commerce or Trade of *Germany,* and [sinks the value of the Estates of private men very sensibly].^{f} {But then we are to ascribe the Luxury of some of our Princes, who being too much addicted to Hunting, take little or no care

a. Rather: on account of which they recently resorted to arms / Bohun's addition of "disputed" and use of "claims" both obscure Pufendorf's implied (and actual) support for the Palatinate position in the *Wildfangstreit* of the mid-1660s. See V.8 and Pufendorf's 1667 preface, p. 7, note 12. [Ed.]

b. Rather: Palatine Count

c. Rather: Indeed, even

d. Rather: eluded

e. Rather: despite the commendable modesty of their coins, whose shame at being so thin is openly reflected in their very color / That is, they are made of cheap [reddish] metal, probably copper, which emerges through repeated handling. [Ed.]

f. Rather: to the patrimonies of private individuals

of their [Estates and Subjects],[a] more to [the Men than to the Form of
that State];[b] and we [must grant, other States are as liable as *Germany*
to these kinds of Miscarriages, and we see them suffer as much by it].}[c]
<186>

a. Rather: public or private affairs
b. Rather: a fault of men than of the state [*reipublicae*]
c. Rather: see that other states [*civitates*] are clearly not immune to this evil [*malo*]

CHAPTER VIII

[*Of the* German *State-Interest.*] [a]

The Remedies of these Diseases enquired into.

1. |[I suppose by this time it is sufficiently shewn, how many and great the Diseases of *Germany* are; to assign the Remedies is a Work of [much] greater difficulty, and which will [would] not become a Stranger and a Traveller, if the Humanity of the *German* Nation were not so great, that she is apter to [trust and admire Foreigners than her own Natives].[b] I hope too all wise men will easily pardon the innocent [harmless] Freedom of a Man who has no Attachment to any of the contending Parties, and who, next the Prosperity [preservation] of his own Country, wisheth nothing more than [the Prosperity and Welfare of the honest *German* Nation].[c] But before I discover my mind in this Affair, I think it is fit [worthwhile] to consider [briefly] the Remedies proposed by [the aforementioned] *Hippolithus a Lapide,* [for the Cure of the *German* Calam-

---

a. Rather: *On the State-Interest of* the German Empire [*De ratione status Imperii Germanici*] / *Status* refers to both the political entity and the general condition of Germany. Denzer renders the term as *Verfassung* (constitution), which is ambiguous in the same way (*Verfassung des deutschen Reiches,* ed. Denzer, 1994, 235). [Ed.]

b. Rather: admire foreign things [opinions] more than her own / Compare VII.2 on the German imitation of foreigners, especially the French. The remark may also be an ironic reference to Pufendorf's cautious assumption of an Italian persona: that is, he has been speaking as the Italian, Monzambano, whom Germans can trust. [Ed.]

c. Rather: that the most upright of nations [*integerrima nationum*] should enjoy a most flourishing condition / *Integer* also means "whole" or "unimpaired," making its use here, in the superlative, ironic in light of the preceding account, which has shown Germany to be anything but whole or integral. [Ed.]

ities];[a] for though many men have admired his Prescriptions, yet I have ever thought they were ill contrived[, and not likely to contribute to her Cure]+.]|[b] <187>

2. In the first place he prescribes [announces] Six Laws,[1] which he calls the Interests of such a State, and saith, They ought [carefully]+ to be observed in a [form of] State like to that of *Germany,* that is, in an *Aristocrasie,* where the Supreme Soveraign Power is in the [States, or]+ great men [*optimates*], and nothing left to the Emperor [*principe*], but the Pomps and Images of a King: So (said he) they ought, (1.)[c] To study the waies and means of Concord, and to avoid Factions, (2.) Not to suffer the Imperial Dignity to continue long in any one Family, lest by the long use of these Pomps and Images, a desire of acquiring a solid and real Soveraignty should grow up in them. (3.) Though the [principate, and with it the] Power of directing and moderating the Offices [functions] of all the Parts to the Common Good is conferr'd upon a [Prince or]+ Single Person, for the greater union of the Commonwealth; yet the Nobility [*proceribus*] ought alwaies to keep the Stern [helm] of the State in their own hands, and the Power of directing and ordering the things of great moment, [is] to be exercised in the Diet, which ought [for this reason] to convene frequently; or at least they ought to appoint some Senate [or Counsel]+, which shall be perpetual; which kind of Regiment was in use in the beginning of the last Age [century] before this. (4.) That nothing but the Ensigns [symbols] of Royalty be left to

The Remedies of *Hyppolithus a Lapide* examined.

Six Rules by him prescribed to the Princes of *Germany.*

a. Rather: to an ailing Germany / The metaphor suggests offering a patient a medicinal drink. [Ed.]

b. E.p.: Although others have worked hard to provide remedies for Germany's ills, a certain personage under the pseudonym *Hippolithus a Lapide* formerly made special claims for himself in this regard. And even though many people initially admired those remedies, since they have nonetheless always seemed to me somehow badly devised, I decided some time ago that I would dismember them [tear them apart].

c. Parentheses have been added to Bohun's enumeration to distinguish it from Pufendorf's section numbers. [Ed.]

1. Lapide, *De ratione status,* part 2, chapters 1–3, 6, 9, 10 (*Verfassung des deutschen Reiches,* ed. Denzer, 1994, 235, note 2). See VI.7, note 6, p. 169.

the Prince, but that the [Regal Jurisdiction]ᵃ and Power be reserved entire to the Commonwealth [*Reipublicae*]. (5.) That neither the Life, Fortunes, <188> or Fames of [any of the Princes be trusted to the single Justice or]ᵇ Discretion of the Emperor. (6.) That neither the Army, Militia, or Forts, be under his single Jurisdiction or Government.

After this he takes great pains to shew in how many particulars these Laws are violated by the Emperor, and some of the States themselves, being very sharp in his Reflections on [criticism of] the House of *Austria,* and on some also of the Electors. Now, though these Laws were not wholly to be despised, yet seeing I have above [sufficiently] ⁺ proved, that *Germany* is no *Aristocrasie,* it is a folly to think the Safety of *Germany* is only to be found in the observation of these Laws.²

Six Remedies prescribed by that Author rejected.

3. The same Author [then] prescribes Six Remedies for the curing [all] ⁺ the Diseases of *Germany.* (1.)ᶜ [First,] he recommends the Study of [a striving after] Concord, and a General Pardon [amnesty], and a removing all Grievances by which mutual Hatreds are kept alive and nourished [in the minds of the Princes against each other] ⁺; and that they should not divide into Factions on the account of [differences of] Religion, and for that cause neglect the Publick Safety [welfare]. This Remedy affords a Copious Subject for a Scholastick Declamation, but can never be applied to the use of *Germany,* till all the Nobility [leading men] of that Nation {happen to be wise and good, and} <learn> to govern the Motions of their Minds [exactly] by Rules of Philosophy.

(2.) In the next place, he would have the House <189> of *Austria* extirpated, and their Estates [*bona*] brought into the Common [Imperial] Treasury. Now this is the Advice of a Hangman, and not of a Physician: As if every one that happeneth to be a little too rich[, for his Neighbour's advantage,] ⁺ were presently to be rooted out and destroyed

---

a. Rather: rights [*iura*]
b. Rather: the Estates of the Empire be subject to the sole
c. Parentheses have been added to the enumeration. [Ed.]
2. Pufendorf considered this totally unrealistic and worthy of dismissal, like other scholastic irrelevancies.

[from off the face of the Earth] [+]: But suppose we should obey [the Tyrannical Law], [a] who will dare to lay the Ax to the Root of a Tree, which has spread its Branches over so many Provinces [lands], [so that it is not for the Interest of *Europe* to have all its Territories added to those of any one or two other Princes]? [b] [Besides,] [+] a part of the Princes [leading men] of *Germany* are heartily united in their Interest and Affections to this House; a great many [of the rest neither love nor] [c] hate it; and the rest [of the Princes, when united, are not] [d] able to overthrow that vast Fabrick [colossus]. They must [then call Foreigners to their assistance], [e] and who, I pray, but the *French* and *Swedes?* For when *Hippolithus* wrote this Book, those Nations were zealously at work to do this, and the Ignorant much applauded them, because they craftily pretended to defend the *German* Liberty, which was oppress'd by the House of *Austria.* But [was it civil to expect they should take so much Pains, and spend so many Men, and so much Money for nothing?] [f] Nor [was there to] [g] be found any Lord Treasurer; who would faithfully bring this Prey [booty] into the Treasury. Wise men more rationally conceive [prophesy], <190> that if [they had prospered in their undertakings against the House of *Austria,* the Princes of *Germany* would have been forced to] [h] take up the old Complaint of [*Aesop's*] [+] Froggs, who instead of a *Block* had got a *Stork* for their *King:* [3]

a. Rather: that harsh decree [of Lapide]

b. Rather: and the addition of whose power to one or two others is against the interest of all of Europe

c. Rather: do not

d. Rather: are by no means

e. Rather: therefore acquire allies

f. Rather: it would be uncivil to demand from them [i.e., the French or Swedes] such great labor for free.

g. Rather: would there

h. Rather: the enemies of the house of Austria should succeed in their efforts, the Estates of the Empire would

3. In one of Aesop's fables the frogs had asked for a king from Zeus, who thereupon threw a log into their swamp. Dissatisfied with this, they complained to Zeus, who responded by sending a stork to rule (and devour) them. Martin Luther alludes to this passage in his *On Secular Authority* (1523), part 2, saying that frogs (wicked humans) require storks (stern rulers).

[And when the House of *Austria* had been ruined, *Germany* must have had][a] an Head, and therefore our Author would have another Emperor elected, whom from his common Place-book he adorns with the attendance and splendor of all the Virtues, [only that he might be trusted with][b] an empty Title, being destitute of all Regal Power, and appointed to be a meer Director [*directoris*] and a Magistrate. Now, there may be some use of such a President [*praeses*] or Director in some *Aristocratick* City [*civitate*], where the Nobility [leading men] all live within the Walls of the same Town [*urbe*]: But as for *Germany*, if he would have spoke [his mind out],[c] he ought to have said, that it has no need of any Emperor.

[Our Author, after all, has taken care to add as much to the Exchequer of his Emperor, as he has taken from his Power. It was great pity so great a Prince, so virtuous a Man, should live in want. But yet][d] the Dominions of the House of *Austria* were [are] to be employed as the Patrimony of the Empire, and if this was [is] not sufficient, then he would needs have the Electors restore what had been given [or assured] them by *Charles* IV.[4] But [in the mean time,][+] this Learned Gentleman seems to know nothing of the nature <191> and temper of Mankind, who thinks that a Prince [someone] who is possessed of so much Power [wealth] as these[e] are, will [in the turn of an Hand][+] be contentedly reduced to [the state of a private Gentleman];[f] and when the House of *Austria* is once dead and buried, [these Electors will be much less][g] disposed to part with what they have possessed [without challenge] above 300 years. For besides that, Princes are so dull, that they cannot possibly understand the

a. Rather: [3.] After the deposition of the house of Austria, he [Lapide] nonetheless does not wish Germany to be without

b. Rather: but so that he shines with only

c. Rather: more succinctly

d. Rather: Yet whatever Hippolithus subtracts from the Emperor's power he apparently wishes to add to his income, since it would be shameful for so great a prince to go hungry. Therefore,

e. That is, the Austrians, or the Austrian emperor (not the electors). [Ed.]

f. Rather: to such a small sphere of power

g. Rather: the Electors will not be easily

4. On Charles IV and the Golden Bull, see IV.3, note 10, p. 101.

Doctrine of their Confessors, when they prate to them about restoring ill-gotten Estates; the Electors have here something to say for themselves against all the other States;[a] for I will suppose that very many of them [the latter] must return to very mean Cottages [or Country-houses][+], if they be equally bound to give an exact account how they [and their Ancestors][+] got what they now enjoy. And therefore 'tis but just, that all men should possess what they [and their Predecessors][+] have a long time possessed.

In the 4th. place, *Hippolitus* would have a mutual Confidence restored amongst the States [and Princes][+], and all Distrust eradicated; which, he supposeth, would certainly follow, if all Grievances [and Injuries were taken away by a friendly Composition; and he thinks the greatest part of these Jealousies have arisen from the different Religions professed in the Empire].[b] |[Now, when these things had been considered in the first Article, what need was there to repeat them here?]|[c]

What he <192> further saith of [settling the Civil][d] Government, [of convoking diets for important matters,][e] of taking away the Chamber at *Vienna,* of maintaining a [considerable Army in perpetual Pay, of settling a Revenue for the Army and War, of employing the Annats to that purpose],[f] shall all of them be considered in the following Sections.

4. |[It is time now to produce our own Remedies [ointment jars], that it may be tried, whether we are more fortunate in discovering what may abate the *German* Feaver, and please them [the Germans] too at the same

The Author's own Remedies proposed.

a. That is, if the other estates favor the idea of having the electors give back a portion of their possessions, the latter can reply to them that . . . [Ed.]

b. Rather: , most of which originate in religious differences, were removed by a peaceful settlement approved by all sides

c. Rather (exploiting the medicinal analogy): But since these things were already contained in the first remedy, what need was there to fill a special jar with them? / e.p.: But those things were already contained in the first remedy.

d. Rather: establishing the Imperial

e. Omitted by Bohun. [Ed.]

f. Rather: standing army and setting up a military fund to be supported by annates

time. I know proffered Advice is seldom well resented [received],[a] and
wise men [undoubtedly] would never counsel any man to offer unasked
Remedies to those that are sick, because [they that are invited and hired
too for that purpose,][b] are often forced to endure the Reproaches of their
angry Patients. [Private men do very rarely meet with any other Reward
than that of Contempt and Scorn],[c] when they presume to give Advice
to [those that govern others].[d] [Besides, they will ever pretend],[e] when
the [state's] Disease is once found out, it is very easie to discover the
Cure also. Yet after all, lest this small Piece should end [abruptly and
imperfectly],[f] I will here subjoin a few things.

I lay this as a Foundation to all I shall propose, *viz. That the depraved
state of* Germany *is become so inveterate and remediless, that it cannot be
reduced back to the state of a Regular Monarchy, without the utter Ruin of
the Nation and Government* [*totius Reipublicae*]. But then, seeing it
comes very near to the \<193\> state [*status*] of a *System of several Independent States united by a League or Confederacy,* the safest course it can
possibly take [for its preservation], is to follow those methods which the
Writers of Politicks have prescribed for the [well-governing such Soci-
eties],[g] the first of which is, That they should rather be sollicitous to
preserve their own [possessions], than think of [taking any thing from
their Neighbors].[h]

[Their next greatest care][i] is to preserve Peace at home [internal con-
cord].][j] And to that end it is absolutely necessary to preserve every one

The German
Government
nearest to a
System of
States.

---

a. That is, is generally viewed with suspicion; Pufendorf's expression echoes Erasmus, *Adages,* I.9.53: *merx ultronea putet* (freely offered wares "smell"). [Ed.]

b. Rather: even hired physicians prescribing beneficial measures

c. Rather: Indeed, private individuals must become the laughing-stock of know-
it-alls / That is, of those who pretend to special expertise. [Ed.]

d. Rather: helmsmen of the state

e. Rather: But for those versed in civil science [*sapientiae*]

f. Rather: as a torso [without a head] / The analogy suggests that the following
sections were very important to Pufendorf. [Ed.]

g. Rather: observance of such allies [*sociis*]

h. Rather: acquiring those of others

i. Rather: Their greatest task [*labor*].

j. E.p.: To discover the true interests [*genuinas rationes*] of the German state [*reipublicae*] will be easy for those who have thoroughly examined its structure. It must

in the Possession of his own Rights, and not to suffer any of the stronger [Princes] + to oppress any of the weaker, that so, though they are, as to [other things],ᵃ not equal, yet in the point of Liberty they may be all equal each to other, and alike secured; that all old out-dated Pretences should be buried in eternal forgetfulness, and every one for the future be suffered quietly to enjoy what he now possesseth. |[That all new Controversies which may happen to arise, should be referr'd to the Arbitrement of the other Allies [in the League] +, who are neither byassed by Love nor Hatred; and those that refused to submit to their Judgment, should be compell'd to do it by all the rest of the Confederates.

And if it be thought fit to appoint a Prince over this System [of allies], great care must be taken, that he [doth not take into his Hands, or pretend at least to a direct]ᵇ Soveraignty over them. [That the]ᶜ best way to prevent this, is to take care <194> that neither the strong places nor the Souldiery may depend on that Prince. That he is not only to be bounded by certain and accurateᵈ Laws [in his Administration] +, but [a perpetual Council to be assigned him, which may represent the States, and govern those Affairs with him, which every day happen in the Administration of the Publick Affairs, according to the Laws enacted in the

---

be laid down as basic here that the present state [*status*] of Germany is so firmly established in public law and popular custom that it cannot be altered without the greatest convulsions and, perhaps, the overthrow of the Empire. Hence the Emperor must forgo efforts to return that state [*respublica*] to the exact form of a kingdom, and the Estates must patiently bear the chain by which they are now bound, and not seek a full and independent liberty that will bring servitude, at least to most of them. For if the present bond is broken, the weaker Orders would undoubtedly become the prey of the stronger ones, or of outsiders. And in this consists that harmony between head and members which Germans ordinarily say should be observed.

Now just as it behooves states in which there is some irregularity to be more concerned with preserving their own possessions than with acquiring those of others, so their greatest task is to maintain internal concord among so many who have far surpassed the condition [*sortem*] of ordinary citizens.

a. Rather: power [*opes*]
b. Rather: cannot aspire to
c. Rather: The
d. That is, clear and precise [*certis et accuratis*]. [Ed.]

Diets].[a] That all Foreign Affairs, which concern the whole Body of the Empire [state], should be likewise committed to this Council, who shall [give an account of them to their Principals, that at last they may be determined by the general Consent of all the Parties].[b] And when any difficult Affairs arise, let this Council have a Power to summon extraordinary Diets, which to the end they may be held with the less expences, and dispatch business the more quickly, [there ought to be a new and more certain form of Proceedings thought of]:[c]

But then it doth not seem very probable, that the Family of *Austria* will suffer such a Council to be introduced, because they [will ever labour to keep their Power above controul].[d] Nor will the Present State of *Germany* [*res Germanicae*] permit the transferring the Imperial Dignity into another House, as long as there is any Male [offspring] in that of *Austria*. Therefore their Modesty is to be wrought on, to perswade them to be content with their present Grandeur [might], and not to labour to establish a Soveraign <195> Authority over the [rest of the States and Princes].[e] And it will become the Princes [Estates] manfully, and with united Hands and Hearts, to oppose and resist all such Encroachments, which tend to their prejudice, and in the first place, to take care that none may league with one another, or with [the Princes of the Empire],[f] against any of the Members of it; [and if they do so, to render all such Combinations ineffectual; and if any Princes have any Controversie

The Empire cannot be transferred to another Family.

a. Rather: also surrounded by a permanent council representing the allies, to which the enactment of daily affairs concerning the entire state [*rempublicam*] is committed, according to the previous determination of all the allies

b. Rather: , after first examining them, refer them to the individual allies, so that at last a general conclusion may be reached

c. Rather: should have a certain procedure prescribed for them [by the council]

d. Rather: are loath to have their power reduced to the level of a private citizen [*ad civilem modum*]

e. Rather: Estates

f. Rather: [external] Estates [*Ordinibus*] / Bohun's translation is broadly in line with the Latin, but renditions such as "external powers" or "other states" are contextually more accurate. "Estates" seems even more apt, however, because the thought surely includes the Catholic clergy and their religious ties to Rome. [Ed.]

with each other],[a] to take all the Care [that] is possible, that *Germany* may not be by that means involved in a War:

But in the first place, Care ought to be taken]|,[b] that Foreigners may not intermeddle with the Affairs of *Germany,* nor [possess themselves of the least][c] Particle of it; [to that end all waies that are possible are to be considered, that they that border on *Germany* may not have the opportunity of enlarging their Kingdoms which they so passionately desire, by ravishing its Provinces from it one after another, till their Conquests, like a *Gangreen,* creep into the very Bowels of the Empire].[d] If any thing of this nature happen [appears] to be attempted, let *Germany* presently take the Alarm, provide her Defences, and seek the Alliance and Assis-

---

a. Rather: but if those leagues are directed toward others [outside the Empire]

b. E.p.: New quarrels should be settled by the intervention of common friends rather than by legal action.

In order that the so-called head of the Empire cannot undermine the liberty of the Estates, precautions should be taken that the common military and the fortresses of the Estates are not dependent on his will [alone]. It also seems necessary in a state [*republica*] where the supreme authority [*summa rerum*] does not belong to one person, that there should be a standing [*perpetuum*] council composed of those who are called to share in the sovereignty [*partem Imperii*], and that the main domestic affairs, as well as those arising with outsiders, be brought before it, and a common verdict issued after it has first been discussed with the individual [Estates]. The Diets begun in the year 1663, and continued for so many years since then, have now almost taken the place of such a council; and it seems much in Germany's interest that they acquire the character of a constant gathering, to maintain the common bond of the Empire and facilitate the discussion of public affairs. [See VI.5, note b, p. 165, on the contingent nature of the Diet even after 1663.]

Above all, precautions must be taken to prevent a certain few from entering into treaties directed against a member of the Empire, either among themselves or with outsiders. And if such treaties are directed against others [outsiders], one must take care not to involve Germany in a war on such occasions. Once a war with outsiders has begun, it is by no means allowable that one or other [of the Estates] be able to consult its special interest or remain neutral; rather, any member of the Empire, when attacked by someone else, must be protected by the strength of all, including those who, because of their more remote position, do not consider themselves endangered.

Provision must also be made. . . .

c. Rather: break off any further

d. Rather: and, indeed, one must prevent more powerful enemies eager to enlarge their borders from absorbing one or other of the neighboring regions, whence the contagion can spread into Germany itself

tance of those whose Interest it [also] is to keep [any one Kingdom]ᵃ from mounting to too great and exorbitant a Power.⁵

|[And then [Besides], as long as *Germany* is contented with the defending what is her own, she will <196> have no [great] need to maintain any [standing or, especially,] very numerous Armies, yet she ought in due time to concert [agree about] the Numbers that every one shall send, in case of necessity: And *Germany* may, from her Neighbour the *Swedes,* learn the methods of maintaining an Army in the times of Peace with [very] small Expence, which yet shall be ready when occasion serves, at short warning, to draw into the Field for her defence.]|ᵇ

[END OF *EDITIO POSTHUMA*]⁶

The Opinions of some great men, the different

5. [Now it were very easie for wise and good men to find out all I have said, and all besides which can be necessary for the Safety of *Germany,* if they pleased calmly to apply their minds to it, who have the chief

a. Rather: certain kingdoms

b. E.p.: And depending on the military situation of its [Germany's] neighbors, appropriate military forces that can be set in opposition must be prepared in time, lest recruitment begin only after an incursion has already taken place, which is a remedy too late for border areas already widely devastated.

Finally, lest those who disagree in their opinions about sacred matters disturb the peace [*concordia*] of Germany through their importunate religious zeal, the provisions established by public law [particularly the Westphalian settlement of 1648] regarding such matters must be exactly observed. Those especially who follow the Roman [Catholic] rites must not take it ill that Protestants enjoy the same right as they, and should deem it impious [*profanum*] and harmful to subvert by force or stealth those who are no less eager [than they] to equip and defend the common fatherland; for they may be sure that once the Protestants have been suppressed, the rest will also be brought into servitude.

[Notably, this final paragraph of the *editio posthuma* returns to the theme of religious disagreement as a serious threat to civil order and, thus, human affairs in general, even though that edition omits the extended discussion of Germany's religious situation (in §§5–10, below) that concluded the work in 1667. (Ed.)]

5. See *On the Law of Nature and of Nations,* II.5.3–9, on the limits to self-defense and preemptive violence.

6. See the introduction, p. x, and the Note on the Text, p. xxx.

hand in the Government:]ᵃ But then, seeing the greatest part of the World think the Differences of Religion the principal Causes of the Distraction and Division of the Empire [Germany], it will well become the Liberty I have taken in this [small] piece to shew [in a few words] what [certain] wise men have said of this thing in my company; for I am not so well acquainted with Church-affairs [theological matters], as to [be able to] interpose my own Judgment [thereon], and therefore I think it will be less [liable to Exception],ᵇ to represent the Thoughts of others than my own, [which I submit, &c.]ᶜ

When I was once at *Cologne,* with the most Reverend and Illustrious [Apostolic] *Nuncio* [of the *Holy See*]⁺, [whom I had come to see with several others] to pay him my respects, I happened [among other things] to say, That I could not [yet sufficiently] understand the [true]⁺ reason of the great Dissentions in *Germany,* on the Subject of Religion, whereas [since] in *Holland* [the Belgian confederation],ᵈ <197> where I had lately been,⁷ there was no such thing, and yet there men had the utmost liberty to think and believe as they themselves pleased. For there every man was intent upon his own Trade and Business, and not at all concern'd of what Religion his Neighbour was.

Upon this an Illustrious Person, who had spent a great part of his Life in the Courts [of several Princes]⁺, but was now retired to live a very private life [*otium*], begged the *Nuncio*'s Leave to speak his own mind freely, which being granted: "Since (said he) that travelling Gentleman

a. Rather: All these and any other things required for Germany's welfare would be very easy to discern and apply in practice if those who sit at the state's helm were well and favorably disposed [thereto].

b. Rather: of an infraction

c. Rather: especially since I most humbly submit myself to the judgment of Holy Mother Catholic Church.

d. Literal translation matters here, since Pufendorf has just (see pp. 216–20) recommended the view of Germany as a confederation. [Ed.]

7. Pufendorf was in Leiden (in the province of Holland) from early 1660 till the fall of 1661, when he assumed his university post in Heidelberg.

has mentioned a thing I have very long and seriously thought on, I will now discover what I take to be the most probable cause of this thing, we being now at good leisure, and I am well resolved not to approve my own former Thoughts on this Affair, [if your *Eminence* should happen to dislike them]."[a] After this beginning, [at a distance from our present times, he][b] shewed how many Heresies had, from the beginning, afflicted and distracted [fragmented] the Church of Christ [*res Christiana*], the greatest part of which, in process of time, vanished of their own accord. But then[, he said,] there had hardly happened any *Schism,* that had [spread so far, and ruin'd so many private Families and][c] whole Kingdoms as this, which in the last Century arose here in *Germany;* and was occasion'd by some few Doctors [of that Nation][+]: There were great Wits on both sides, and [but] <198> they [also] contended against each other with the most furious Passions [hatreds], and to this day there [is not the least][d] hope of putting an end to this [dreadful] Quarrel. It is [to no purpose][e] to enquire into the secret causes of this Affair, as far as Fate or Providence are concern'd; but it will [did] not misbecome my [his] Profession [*ordinis*], [he said,] to discourse of the Nature and Temper of Mankind[, as far as the condition of reason allows].

Contempt and *Loss* exasperates men greatly.

6. "It is (saith he)[f] apparent, that two things above all others exasperate and enrage the Minds of Men, *Contempt* and *Loss* [deprivation of advantages]. As to the first of these, I would not be understood here to

---

a. Rather: unless they have also been approved by minds as refined as I take all of yours to be

b. Rather: he entered deeply [into the matter] and

c. Rather: torn apart the Church as deeply, and ruined not only private individuals but also

d. Rather: appears to be no

e. Rather: not possible for us

f. The quotation continues through §8, p. 237. Even though he has already assumed the persona of an Italian Catholic (i.e., Monzambano) throughout the work, here Pufendorf adds a second layer of distance between himself and the following (critical) remarks by putting them into the mouth of a supposed personage at the papal nuncio's court, albeit one who had retired from active service and thus posed no threat to actual affairs. [Ed.]

speak of that Contempt by which the Reputation [*existimatio*] and Good Name of a Man is directly [oppressed and]⁺ trodden under foot, but of that which every [ordinary man]ª thinks is thrown upon him, when another shall but presume to differ from him in any thing; for the Minds of Men are generally infected with this [foolish and unreasonable Distemper]:ᵇ And it is hateful to them, to find another disposed not only to contradict, but even to disagree with them in any thing; for he that doth not [presently]⁺ consent to what another saith, [doth tacitely accuse]ᶜ him of being[, as to that particular,]⁺ in an Error; and he that differeth [vigorously] in many things from any man, seems to insinuate that he is a Fool.⁸

This Disease [haunts the sedentary]ᵈ part of Mankind, above all others, who are [educated in the Schools, and wholly taken up <199> with solitary Speculations, and consequently not overwell acquainted with the *World*].ᵉ He that shall not reverence all this melancholy man has embraced as an Oracle, is presently his deadly Enemy. Nor was the War between the *Romans* and *Carthaginians,* for the Empire of the World, managed [waged] with greater heat than that which we have [often] seen between some of the Learned World [*literatos*], about some few Syllables or [other] small Distinctions.

An equal, nay, a greater Fury [has taken possession of the Churchmen],ᶠ (the *Nuncio* having [in the beginning of his Discourse promised him the utmost Freedom].)ᵍ For whilst [since] every Sect of them [*singuli*] believes it has God on their side, if any man differeth from them

a. Rather: hothead [*cerebrosissimus*]
b. Rather: defect [*labe*]
c. Rather: is thought to be tacitly accusing
d. Rather: afflicts the shadowy [*umbraticos*] / That is, those who spend their time in dark study halls. [Ed.]
e. Rather: nourished by the dust of the schools and have leisure to pursue their solitary speculations / Bohun's extrapolation is correct, given Pufendorf's frequent references to the uselessness of scholasticism and the importance of practical knowledge. [Ed.]
f. Rather: stirs up the nation of priests [*Sacerdotum nationem*]
g. Rather: nodded quietly when he had asked leave to speak freely
8. See Hobbes, *On the Citizen* (1642), I.5, and *Leviathan* (1651), I.10.

[their opinions] in any thing, besides the affront [*injuriam*] offered to their [spurned] Authority, they are [also] for accusing him forthwith of Impiety, [Contempt of the Heavenly Truth, Obstinacy, and Unwillingness to be brought over by another from a manifest Error]:[a] And yet, [in the mean time,][+] it is a wonder, that they which [pretend to][+] teach others the utmost Clemency and Goodness [kindliness] of the Christian Religion, should [not observe what horrid Passions they carry about them].[b] Or, let them shew me some other sort of men, more ambitious, covetous, envious, angry, stubborn, and [selfish than they, if this is possible,][+] who [make so much of themselves and their opinions that,] so soon as ever they meet a man that differeth a little from them, presently damn him to the Pit of Hell [eternal flames], and will not [suffer <200> God himself][c] to reverse their outragious [harsh] Sentence.

But then, for men to [be a little more than ordinarily warm, when they find their beloved Wealth like to be diminished, that (*though not often mentioned for good Causes*)][d] is not altogether so irrational.

The Tempers of the Three Religions in Germ[any].

7. But for the more accurate knowledg of the Causes of our Dissentions, it is [also] necessary here to make a close reflection on the Tempers of the three Religions which are now allowed a publick Liberty in *Germany*. [I shall not trouble my self with a curious Enquiry][e] how well each of them can prove their respective Doctrins by the [Authority of the][+] Sacred Scriptures, because we [are only allowed the use of them][f] for the

---

a. Rather: as if, because of contempt for heavenly truth or from a profane stubbornness, he refused to put aside even manifest error merely in order to avoid the appearance of having learned something from others

b. Rather: carry about dispositions teeming with such horrid passions

c. Rather: leave even God the ability [*facultas*]

d. Rather: take it ill, when their advantages are taken away by others,

e. Rather: It is not our business to examine

f. Rather: deal with such matters only / Pufendorf's point is twofold: (1) laypersons like him are concerned with doctrinal questions only because of their implications for religious practice; (2) the current discussion does not concern personal religiosity, so there is no need to examine the scriptural foundations of the respective Christian denominations. That task occupied Pufendorf in *The Divine Feudal Law,* which compares Lutheranism and Calvinism. [Ed.]

Improvement of our private Piety, and [so are not allowed to suppose we can understand them, and are besides bound to think our Church loves us too well to destroy us by false Doctrine].[a] Yet we [may be allowed to see and consider how far the way they teach us of going to Heaven will agree with our other Temporal][b] Interests; for I cannot think the [all-gracious] Deity ever intended his Worship should [embroil and disquiet the World].[c]

[That therefore I may begin regularly,][+] I will consider the *Lutherans* in the first place, because they first deserted our [Holy Roman][+] Catholick Church: And I say, I could never yet find any thing in their Doctrine [*religione*] which was contrary to the Principles of [Civil Prudence and Government]:[d] <201> [The Power they ascribe to Princes, for the governing [of] Religion, is indeed not so favourable to the excessive Grandeur of the Priests; so where it has prevail'd, their Wealth is little, but the Commonwealth has the benefit of that Abatement]:[e] The People [*plebi*] are taught by them to reverence their Magistrates [and Princes][+], as [the Ministers of God],[f] and [finally] that all the good works expected from them, is to do the Duties of Good men: Nor [am I displeased],[g] that they have retained [so much of the Ceremonial Part and the Pomp

The Temper of the *Lutherans* considered.

a. Rather: must not attribute to Holy Mother Church a malice so great that she would willingly serve up fatal errors to those who venerate her so obediently

b. Rather: are permitted [*fas est*] to investigate how far the way to eternal salvation, about which priests are occupied, agrees with our political

c. Rather: disturb the tranquillity of civil life / On the compatibility of religion and the state, and the normative importance of the latter, see *On the Law of Nature and of Nations,* VII.4.8; and Pufendorf's dissertation *De concordia verae politicae cum religione Christiana* [On the concord between true politics and the Christian religion] (1673), §2. The latter work is contained in *Dissertationes academicae selectiores* (see note 2 in the introduction). [Ed.]

d. Rather: politics [*doctrinae civilis*]

e. Rather: They attribute authority [*potestas*] over sacred matters to princes and reduce the wealth of priests to a bare minimum (which you regard as grim), for the great good of the state [*reipublicae*] / The comment in parentheses, omitted by Bohun, is directed to the Catholic clerics surrounding the nuncio, and the Italian Monzambano. [Ed.]

f. Rather: God's representatives on earth

g. Rather: is it displeasing

of Religion, which serves]ᵃ to divert [guide] the minds of the [simple]
People, who have not sence enough to contemplate [the Beauty of]⁺
simple undress'd Piety: [So that though]ᵇ their Religious Mysteries are
not adorned to the frightful height of Superstition, [yet they are in a
decent and grave Dress, and adapted to teach Mankind, that the Divine
Wisdom and Power is able to effect that which we are not able thoroughly to comprehend];ᶜ [indeed,] the very Rusticity and Simplicity
that appears in the Professors of [those who profess] that Religion, and
which is so much blamed by some, [is to me a sign and a testimony of
their]ᵈ Sincerity and Uprightness:

So that as it is not possible to imagine a Religion that can be more
serviceable and useful to the Princes of *Germany,* [than that of the *Lutherans,*]⁺ we may from hence conclude, that this is [generally] the best
[suited] for a *Monarchy* of any in the World.⁹ And[, in fact,] if *Charles
V.* <202> had not been diverted by the consideration of his other States
and Kingdoms,¹⁰ he must, as Emperor of *Germany,* have been thought
[blind and impolitick],ᵉ in not taking the opportunity [the Reforma-

a. Rather: certain empty ceremonies and [external] trappings in their public
worship,

b. Rather: Moreover, just as

c. Rather: so they deem it proper for human subtlety to posit no more divine
wisdom and power than supports the belief that the latter can fashion something
more sublime than the former is able to grasp / That is, they are theological mini-
malists. [Ed.]

d. Rather: contributes to their reputation for

e. Rather: very simple-minded

9. Pufendorf was generally suspicious of the political intentions of Calvinism
(which he associated with its monarchomach past) and thought Lutheranism more
compatible with civil authority. See his dissertation *De concordia verae politicae cum
religione Christiana* [On the concord between true politics and the Christian religion]
(1673), §17, contained in *Dissertationes academicae selectiores* (see note 2 in the introduction). Yet he served Calvinist ruling families in Heidelberg and Berlin and strongly
criticized the Danish court preacher and theologian, Hector Gottfried Masius (1653–
1709), for maintaining that only Lutheranism (not Calvinism or Catholicism) was
compatible with civil peace. See his letter to Christian Thomasius (on November 1,
1690), in *Briefwechsel,* letter 192, pp. 289–90.

10. Beside Germany, the territories of Charles V (1500–1558) included Spain, Austria, and parts of Italy, which were mostly Catholic.

tion]⁺ offered him, to enrich the Patrimony of the Empire [from sacred holdings], when so many of the Princes and Free Cities had before shewed him the way, and would very gladly have permitted him to have shared in the Prey, and the People were [generally so]ᵃ taken with their new Preachers [teachers][, that he needed not to have feared them]⁺.

As to the [CALVINISTS, or *Presbyterians*],ᵇ it differeth very little from the *Lutheran*, but only in their great Zeal for sweeping out all [remainders of] the Roman Catholick Rites and Ceremonies [with the Dust of their Churches],ᶜ and in a design to [new-polish the *Lutheran Doctrine*, and to make it more subtile];ᵈ neither of which Intentions are accommodated or suited to the Minds of the meaner People [*plebis*], for they are apt to fall asleep [lose interest], when the whole [worship] Service of God [in publick]⁺ is reduced to a [paltry] *Psalm* and a *Sermon*. And when it is once [made a fashionable thing, to have the meanest of men exercise their Curiosity upon the most Sacred Parts of Religion],ᵉ the most perverse and ignorant will soon catch the Itch of Innovating and Inventing [many things], and when they have once started a new Opinion, they will persist in and defend it with invincible stubbornness:[11] Yea, some of them have faln into lamentable <203> Follies, and with them it was a great Sin to have a comely Head of Hair: And it has long since been observed by wise men, *That the Genius [Spirit] of this Religion [is purely Democratick, and adapted to Popular Liberty and a Commonwealth]*:ᶠ For when the People [*plebe*] once are [admitted to a share in

The Temper of the Calvinists.

---

a. Rather: very
b. Rather: Calvinist religion, as it is called
c. Rather: , no matter how small
d. Rather: hone the new doctrines more finely than the Lutherans had done
e. Rather: considered a virtue to exercise one's curiosity upon sacred matters
f. Rather: generally inclines toward democratic liberty
11. Though Pufendorf frowned on theological innovation (see *On the Law of Nature and of Nations,* preface), he welcomed it in philosophy; see *Specimen controversiarum circa jus naturale ipsi nuper motarum* [Sampler of recent controversies over natural law] (1678), chapter 2, on "philosophical innovation." Despite this passage, he supported lay theology and did not see religious interpretation as the sole province of clerics.

the Government and Discipline of the Church],[a] it will presently seem very unreasonable [unfair] to them, that one Prince should [without them govern the great Affairs of the State].[b, 12]

The extent of these two Religions.

These two [new] Religions having spread themselves over a great part of *Germany,* by their mutual Enmity each to [the] other, [gave Opportunities to the *Roman Catholicks* to destroy them both].[c, 13] Now what Reason can any [sensible] man assign for this, but [the one we just spoke about, that is,] the Perverseness of their Ministers [clergy], who were [are] on both sides more concern'd to maintain their Reputations than their Doctrine, and they thought [think] that they should certainly much sink in the esteem of Men, if they should [tamely submit their Judgments to such as explained things better than they could, or taught

The Differences destructive.

them more Humility and Modesty than they had occasion for]?[d] For as for these two Parties, there is no Contest between them, which is attended with any Gain or Loss,[e] it being equally mischievous to both of them, to be forced again to submit to the Church of *Rome.*

And therefore seeing the Ministers could [clergy can] never be perswaded to [sacrifice their Obstinacy to the Peace of the Publick],[f] it had <204> been the Duty of the Princes, by degrees to have laid these Controversies asleep, not by violent methods, [(which commonly ex-

a. Rather: allowed a vote on sacred matters and moral standards [*censuram morum*]

b. Rather: decide about all civil affairs

c. Rather: have increased the strength of their common adversaries

d. Rather: yield in the slightest to those who teach things more plainly or urge them more moderately [than they]

e. That is, their empty disputes are not about anything practically significant, or as important as their common interest of remaining independent of Rome. [Ed.]

f. Rather: subordinate their obstinacy to the advantage of the state [*reipublicae*]

12. See note 9 in this chapter. Pufendorf also associated Calvinism with democracy and attributed the midcentury political turmoils in England to the democratical excesses of the Reformed religion. See *Introduction to the History,* chap. 12, §27, pp. 420–21, and §24, p. 150.

13. Pufendorf attempted a theological reconciliation of Lutheranism and Calvinism in his *Divine Feudal Law.*

asperate Dissenters) but by oblique ways and Artifice]:[a] For if Princes, in chusing their Ministers,[b] would [for the future][+] not regard the Names of Mens Parties [*sectarum*], but the [Abilities and Endowments of their Minds];[c] and if [the Subjects were inured to bear an equal regard to both the Religions];[d] if the Ministers [clergy] were forbidden [all Disputes][e] in their Sermons, and [especially to anger the opposite side by sharp Reflections];[f] and [if, finally,] none were suffered to teach in the [public] Schools but moderate and prudent men, I doubt not but, in a few years, all these Debates [*lites*] would end of themselves: But I believe, [at the same time,][+] he would deserve very ill of the Church of *Rome,* who should give this [wholesome][g] Advice to [her Enemies].[h, 14]

//And I believe this Advice would certainly end in the ruin of the Reformation in *Germany;* for by that time any Parish had been *Lutheran*   An Addition.

    a. Rather: to be sure, which stir up dissensions rather than quiet them, but in softer and, as it were, more oblique ways

    b. That is, *ministris* in general, not only the clergy, as below. [Ed.]

    c. Rather: endowments of their hearts [*animi*] and minds [*ingenii*] / As Denzer has it, a distinction between dispositional and intellectual components is suggested (*Verfassung des deutschen Reiches,* ed. Denzer, 1994, 255). [Ed.]

    d. Rather: the adherents of both religions were considered citizens in equal measure / Bohun obscures Pufendorf's distinction between religious and secular interests. [Ed.]

    e. Rather: to stir up those controversies

    f. Rather: to criticize [i.e., "put down"] the other party with sharp words [*nominibus*] / That is, name-calling. [Ed.]

    g. Denzer and Salomon read *sana* (wholesome, healthy) (*Verfassung des deutschen Reiches,* ed. Denzer, 1994, 254; *Severinus,* ed. Salomon, 156). However, some printings have *profana* (profane) instead: for example, *Severini . . . De statu Imperii Germanici,* 1667, which is no. 4 in Salomon, "Literaturverzeichnis," 11. Either reading works, though *profana* is more apt for the cautious Monzambano, while the bolder *sana* fits the general frankness of the current speaker. The variation is probably an example of the uncontrolled printing of the first edition by different publishers throughout Germany. [Ed.]

    h. Rather: those men

    14. On the sovereign's civil management of religion for the benefit of the state, see *On the Law of Nature and of Nations,* VII.4.8, and *Of the Nature and Qualification of Religion,* §7, pp. 20–21, and §49, pp. 104–7. Monzambano's view is an ironic (and distinctively modern) reversal of the medieval church's attempts (see I.14 and IV.1) to wield secular power through its religious authority.

and *Calvinist* in their Worship by turns, two or three times backward and forward, as the Ministers changed, they would care for neither of them, but divide and hate each other mortally; some would persist in one way, and others in the other, and the major part would think this fickle unconstancy in Religion an Argument of the uncertainty of it, and without ever enquiring which were the best, reject < 205 > both, and sit down in Atheism. Were the difference only in point of Doctrin and Speculation, like that of Predestination amongst us, both Parties might be tolerated; but different waies of Worship can never be allowed in the same Congregations without Heart-burning Envy, Hatred, and Detraction, which would break them into Factions at first, and at last destroy all Religion, the Modes of Worship being visible, and extreamly loved or disgusted.\\¹⁵

The Temper of the *Roman Catholicks*.

8. But now the Temper of our *Roman Catholick* Religion is extreamly different from these new Religions. For their Clergy own themselves the Servants (Ministers) of the Magistrates and People, that their Souls being [here below] [by their Care and Pains]⁺ endowed with good holy Principles and Manners, they may, after Death, be [fitted to be]⁺ translated into Eternal Life [salvation]: [In the mean time, the great Care of the Roman Catholick Priests is spent in enlarging their own Wealth, Power, and Authority, and not in forming the Minds of the People committed to their Care to Piety and Honesty.]ᵃ And in truth, I have a great while admired [wondered at] the Folly of our Priests, in pretending to decide the Controversies depending between them and the [Protestants],ᵇ by the Sacred Scriptures, when they might have taken another course, that for certainty and plainness would have been equal to a Math-

a. Rather: The Catholic religion is less concerned about forming morally upright minds than about the boundless increase of the clergy's wealth, power, and authority.
    b. Rather: heretics (as they call them)
    15. Bohun clearly disapproves here of Pufendorf's deemphasis of religious differences and his implicit advocacy of mutual toleration and political equality. For Pufendorf's view on religious toleration and conciliation, see *Divine Feudal Law* (2002), §§3–12, pp. 14–37; Palladini, "Stato, chiesa e tolleranza"; and Seidler, "Pufendorf and the Politics of Recognition."

ematical Proposition: For if[, according to the Use and Custom of <206> the Church of *Rome,* the great design and principal end of all Religion be to promote]ᵃ the Riches and Authority of the Priests, our Adversaries are mad if ever they write one word more in a Controversie that has spent [already consumed] such innumerable number of Tuns of Paper, to no purpose. For example sake, let us propose a few Instances.

It is pretended the Sacred Scriptures are very obscure, and all Laymen are forbidden to read them [on that pretence] ⁺, that so the Priests may have the sole Power [right] of interpreting them, and that the Laymen may not from thence pick out any thing that shall be contrary to the Priests Interest. *Traditions* are added [by the latter] to the Sacred Scriptures, that if any thing has happened to be omitted in the Scriptures, which is necessary to the former great Design, it may from thence be conveniently supplied: Nay, that whole Religion is adorned with so many [gaudy] ⁺ Ceremonies, that the Splendor and Pomp of them, as well as the excessive number, [may amuse]ᵇ the Minds of the common People, that like men in an amazement and wonder, they may never so much as think on [searching for] solid Piety.

To leave the remission [and forgiveness] ⁺ of Sin only to God, were a thing that would yield no profit [to the Priest] ⁺, and therefore [the Priests challenge that, and know wondrously well how to improve it to the best advantage, for they will not dispense so profitable and gainful <207> an Office, upon]ᶜ a general Confession, [to a whole Congregation at once,] ⁺ and then be contented with some mean Present or Salary, as the Parties concerned [penitents] shall freely give: No, [they have taken order] ⁺ there shall be an exact Enumeration of [individual] Sins, and the Taxing [assessing] them is then left to the Discretion of the Priest. And now, if the Party confessing is rich, [Paradise will go at a good price],ᵈ though the Sins be freely remitted[, as they pretend] ⁺; for, Who

a. Rather: one accepts as an established principle that the end of the Catholic religion is to magnify

b. Rather: so overcome

c. Rather: that power has been claimed by the priests, who are by no means willing to waste such a useful right by acquiescing in

d. Rather: the gain is readily available [*paratissimum*]

[can be so hard-hearted, as not to]ᵃ give liberally to so good [kind] a
Father? And if the Party is poor, then the Priest will exercise his
[Ghostly]⁺ Authority with the greater severity [confidence].ᵇ And [in
the mean time,]⁺ what a vast Advantage it is [to the Church and
Clergy]⁺ to know all mens Secrets? And who would not revere the Mas-
terᶜ of his Soul and Heart?

[And in short, the Wit of Man can never invent a thing that shall
turn more to]ᵈ the Gain and Authority of the Priests than the *Mass;* for,
Who can deny the man that performs this saving Office [service] a good
Reward? And who can forbear worshipping him that can by a secret
whisperᵉ produce so venerable a Victim or Sacrifice? It is fit to deny the
Laity the use of the Cup to the utmost extremity [bitter end], that they
may think the Church [clergy] never did, or can err.ᶠ The number of
the Sacraments was not encreased for nothing, but to the intent men
might the oftner need the assistance of their Priests. <208>

Who can tell what profit the Ecclesiastical Courts have drawn from
Matrimonial Cases [alone], all which have been brought under their cognizance, only on the pretence Marriage was a Sacrament? Yet [apart from
this doctrine,] one would think married men should [understand all
these Cases]ᵍ full as well as they.

[The vast Force they ascribe to the Merit of Good Works, as it excites,
like a Spur, the ambitious and vain-glorious Piety of Men; so on the
other hand, they have craftily taken care to give us such a Catalogue of
Good Works, as for the most part tends to the enriching of the Clergy,
and doth most incomparably well agree with the rest of their Theological

a. Rather: would not
b. That is, rich penitents are likely to donate on their own, while the clergy can
more easily pressure poor ones to do so. [Ed.]
c. *Arbiter* (one who sees and passes judgment). [Ed.]
d. Rather: Now, nothing is more suited to promoting
e. In the act of consecration. [Ed.]
f. The restriction is unjustified on scriptural grounds, but this should never be
admitted. [Ed.]
g. Rather: be able to understand the nature of marriage

System.]ᵃ Nor can I think the Fire of *Purgatory* was kindled for any other purpose, but only to lay, on that pretence, a Tax upon those who by Death had [escaped all other Jurisdictions, (and to make the separate Souls a Merchandable Commodity, which was never dreamt on before.)]ᵇ The Invocation of Saints encreaseth very much the Gaity [*splendorem*] of their Religion, [and the Authority of their Clergy, who by their Vote advance whom they please to be Nobles]ᶜ in the Court of Heaven. To add more [to those who so well know them, were troublesome and needless, and in truth, whoever tries the whole by this Rule, will see this was the only thing that all is levell'd at].ᵈ

The [*Hierarchy* or *Ecclesiastick Commonwealth* or *Government,* as they have ordered it, is a <209> wonderful artificial Contrivance, so compacted, so knit, closed, and fixed together],ᵉ that I think I may truly say, since the Creation of the World, there never was any [Politick]⁺ Body so well formed and disposed, and which had such strong Foundations as this has. For it is form'd into a most exact Monarchy; and the King [*principi*] of the Priests has an Authority given him equal to that of God. This Vicar of God cannot err; and administreth the Function of a Turn-key to the Gates of *Heaven* and *Hell,* with an Authority above controul, and from which there lies no Appeal. And in the better and more fortunate Ages [of this Church]⁺, it was [most firmly]⁺ believed too, that this King was the Disposer of all Kingdoms; that he could depose Kings, and set others up in their steads; but now, [alas!]⁺ the new Doctors have [so traduced this most useful Doctrin, that it is become

a. Rather: The meritorious force ascribed to good works, though notably stimulating men's pious ambitions, also squares quite well with the rest of their theological system, in that those works are almost all defined in terms of things that enrich the clergy.

b. Rather: been otherwise removed from human affairs.

c. Rather: and it also makes us admire the authority of the clergy, when we reflect on the fact that their decrees create nobles [*proceres*]

d. Rather: would be tiresome for those well acquainted [with these things], and anyone who has time to probe them more thoroughly will find the rest to be like this sample

e. Rather: The commonwealth [*respublica*] of priests is so artfully contrived, and all its parts so closely interconnected

hateful and invidious to the very Catholick Princes themselves, and they are fain, in some Kingdoms, to deny they ever taught any such thing]:[a] And because the Majesty of this King [principate] depends only [mainly] on the Opinion of his [its] Sanctity, [they have wisely contrived, that it should pass][b] by Election, [for fear this Royal Blood should degenerate, and that this Throne may ever be filled with a person free from the defects of Youth, and to the end he might be more intent upon the Good of the Church, <210> than the enriching his Family].[c] [For this last reason they have denied Marriage to all the Members of this Society (the Priests and Clergy) that their Family-concerns might not divert them, (or Wife and Children make them subject to the Wills of their Princes.)][d]

The multitude and variety of their Religious Orders is [so] very great, that there might [be many in every place, to take care of their Affairs],[e] and spread their Nets, and bait their Hooks to catch the Estates and Goods of the Laity. Nor has any Temporal Prince [in the whole World][+] so great and profound a Respect and Obedience paid to him by all his Subjects [citizens], [as this Ecclesiastick Monarch][+]; and although there [are many furious Emulations between his Subjects],[f] yet the *Pope* wisely takes such care to moderate and govern them [these], that they never bring any Damage or Disturbance to his Kingdom [*reipublicae*]. Thus [all][+] the old Orders look very discontentedly on the new company of the *Jesuits,* because [they believe that] it has much abated the Esteem they enjoy'd before. For after [it appeared that] this wanton Age would no longer be bridled by the simple [ignorant][+] Sanctity of the [old]

The reason of inventing the Jesuits Order.

a. Rather: discredited this notion, which they regard as very odious / That is, the Lutherans and Calvinists. [Ed.]

b. Rather: it is passed on

c. Rather: so that, given the frequent degeneration of royal offspring, that place lies open only to the most worthy individuals, who are beyond the reach of youthful passions and, as well, more intent on the good of the church than that of their family

d. Rather: For the same reasons, celibacy is imposed on all members of this commonwealth [*reipublicae*], so that private considerations do not divert their concerns toward different ends [*alio*].

e. Rather: thereby be more to watch out for the Church's affairs

f. Rather: is no lack of emulation among them

Monks, that holy Society was invented, to the great good of the Church, which [at first with great Art]^a supported this falling Fabrick, by undertaking the Instruction of Youth, [Confession of Penitents, and a cunning Scrutiny into the Secrets of all men].^b So that many think <211> [all that *Job* hath said of the *Leviathan,* may, in a mystick sence, be very aptly]^c applied to this Priestly [sacred] Empire:[16]

No doubt can reasonably be made however, that the Religion is the very best of all others which heaps most Riches and Honours on all its Votaries, and is furnished with the best means of shearing the Sheep to the very Skin, and at the same time keeping them [as quiet, and more obedient than those that have all their Wool left on them to keep them warm].^d [I think by this time I have sufficiently proved, that they have hitherto managed the Disputes between the Catholicks and the new Teachers very ignorantly].^e For these Catholicks [*nostri*] have ranged their Antagonists amongst the Hereticks, and raised brutish Cries against them [in all places]⁺, that they ought to be extirpated by Fire and Sword, by which they have made all sincere and hearty reconciliation desperate [hopeless] and impossible.[17] This has again forced the Hereticks to take the utmost care for their own safety and security; and when they had once possessed the Laity with a Suspicion of the [Catholic] Priests Sanctity; it was a very easie step, by shewing them the Priests Wealth [would

a. Rather: successfully [*felicissime*]

b. Rather: and by ascertaining all men's secrets through confession and, as well, by refined conversation

c. Rather: that most things said in a mystic sense about the *Leviathan* in the book of *Job,* can be

d. Rather: obedient

e. Rather: Even so, I think it apparent from these things that up to now, the religious controversies between Catholics and the new teachers plainly have been dealt with in a dimwitted manner / An ironic tribute followed by a conditional criticism. [Ed.]

16. Job 40:20–28 and 41:1–25. Compare Hobbes, *Leviathan,* I.1 and II.17, on the state as an artificial man and a mortal god, whose role it is to tame proud men. Pufendorf's use of Hobbes's secularized biblical metaphor to refer back to the so-called empire of priests is a piece of provocative irony.

17. See note 13 in this chapter and the corresponding text on p. 228.

be their reward] [+], to [draw them on their side, and] [+] engage them to be their Defenders:

But if at first their [the Catholics] Brains had lain right, there might have been means found out to have sweetned the Minds of the Laity, [before they embraced <212> that side]; [a] and that small *Saxon Monk* [*(Luther)*] [+] might more easily have been won to a reconciliation with the *Pope* [*Pontifice Maximo*], by presenting him with a good fat Benefice, [18] than by [all the Thunders of the *Vatican*], [b] the force of which, by the [great] distance of the place, and the coldness of the *German* Air, was so much abated[, that by that time it reached the Monk, the noise, the heat, and the terror of it was wholly lost] [+]. And on the other side we cannot enough admire [wonder at] the folly [naivete] of the [modern Protestant Doctors], [c] that they should, without blushing, perswade [urge] those of the Church of *Rome* [*nostratibus*] to leave their present state [*conditione*], and renounce all their vast Wealth, and to come over to them, that they may there be reduced into the mean condition of the vulgar people, and work hard for a Living, or starve: For [they have some reason for what they say, when they offer the Lay-people more Liberty, and the Princes the Spoils of the Priests]. [d] Yet [to give the *Roman Catholicks* their due; after the Terror of the first Defection, and the Heat of the first Reformers was abated, they recollected the Remains of their broken Forces with all the Industry and Care that was possible; and they have ever since managed their affairs with more order and subtilty than the Reformed have theirs]. [e] For, to the best of my remembrance, in this present Century none of our [*Roman Catholick*] [+] *Princes* have [become

a. Rather: who [still] embraced different sides
b. Rather: attacking him with bans [of excommunication]
c. Rather: new teachers
d. Rather: it would have been much more reasonable to draw the people over to themselves with the promise [*obtentu*] of freedom, and princes with the allure of gain
e. Rather: once the intensity of that first attack [*impetus*] subsided and our side [*nostri*], following its unanticipated defeat, arrayed its forces more carefully, it has clearly done a better job in managing its affairs than those others [Protestants] have theirs
18. See V.9.

Protestants],[a] <213> but some of theirs have returned into the Bosom of our [Catholic] Church;" // *Christina* Queen of *Sweden,* the House of *Newburg* now Elector *Palatine,* and *James* II. late King of *Great Britain.*\\[19]

An Addition.

This Gentleman was going on, when the [*Pope's*] *Nuncio* put an end to his Discourse, by saying, *Sir, you have sufficiently shewed us what Skill you have in Church* [*theological*] *affairs, and were you to preach* [*teach*] *these things in the publick, you would seldom want Auditors* [*and Approvers*][+], *though I think* [*the Protestants would not approve of*][b] *them.* Then looking upon me, he said, [*It was not convenient to have thus on a sudden admitted this Lay-Gent, to the knowledge of a Secret which many thousands make it their business to conceal from the most cunning and accomplished Men the World has*].[c]

9. [These things were once][d] discoursed with this liberty [I have represented them][+], in the presence of the [*Pope's*][e] *Nuncio,* who seemed to approve the Candour of this old Minister of State, [and gave me such encouragement and insight into things, that from thenceforward I be-

Some Considerations on the excessive Revenues of the Church.

a. Rather: gone over to them

b. Rather: that novices [*novitiorum*] would not be able to grasp them / Protestants like Pufendorf would surely approve many of them. Rather, the nuncio softens the preceding comments by suggesting that there is more to such matters than novices or noninitiates like Monzambano (who is addressed in the next sentence) can grasp. [Ed.]

c. Rather: and it would not be proper [*fas*] for you to be admitted in one short hour to a knowledge of mysteries which thousands of very clever men labor with great care to keep from the common people [*plebe*]

d. Rather: Once these things were

e. Rather: *Apostolic*

19. The first speaker's discourse ends here, followed by Bohun's short insertion. Christina of Sweden (1626–89) converted to Catholicism in 1654, after abdicating. The line of Pfalz-Neuburg became Catholic in 1613 by the conversion of Wolfgang Wilhelm (1578–1653); his son Philipp Wilhelm (1615–90) inherited the Palatinate (*Kurpfalz*) in 1685, after Elector Karl II (1651–85), son of Karl Ludwig (1618–80), died without issue. James II of England converted to Catholicism in 1672 and inherited the throne after his brother, Charles II, died in 1685. He fled to France in 1688 during the invasion by his brother-in-law, William III (of Orange), also called the Glorious Revolution.

came less scrupulous to converse freely with men of the contrary per-
swasion, whose Hearts are more open than those of our own party are].ᵃ
Not long after, I met with a man who was well acquainted with [the
German]ᵇ Affairs, and seem'd not very averse to the *Protestant* [new]
Religion, ([which I speak by way of Apology]ᶜ for what I am going to
relate, that you may not think I do approve of all he said).

And giving <214> him [by chance]⁺ an account of what I had heard
in the fore-recited Conference, he began [a little higher],ᵈ and added,
That in a well-constituted Government [state] there ought to be some
men [*personas*] set apart, for the [celebration of the Holy Offices of
Religion],ᵉ who ought to have no other Employment, and yet should
be competently [decently] maintained. That it was also fit, that
Churches should be built on the publick charge, whose [external beauty
and magnificence might create in the Minds of Men an awful regard to
Religion,]ᶠ for the kindling the Devotion of the Common People. "But
then[, he said,] I think no wise man will deny, that those men who [are
no way necessary to the Service of God nor employed in his Worship,
ought not to be called or thought Churchmen, or of the Clergy],ᵍ and
that what was employed in the maintaining such men, has nothing of
Sanctity in it. But in *Germany* the Clergy [clerical Estate] were so vastly
enriched by the liberality of the [old]⁺ Emperors, [and] the Princes, and

a. Rather: it so encouraged me that I was less afraid thereafter to listen to men
willing to speak their minds

b. Rather: his country's [*patriae*]

c. Rather: I must speak somewhat cautiously here, apologizing

d. Rather: to elaborate / The following quotation continues almost to the end of
§10, p. 246. A new speaker explicitly sympathetic to Protestants has been introduced
because the ideas expressed are even more personal and controversial than the preceding ones. Indeed, Pufendorf demonstrates here some of same sharp wit that is
the hallmark of his notorious polemic in *Eris Scandica* [The Scandinavian quarrel]
(1678). [Ed.]

e. Rather: public performance of divine worship

f. Rather: beauty lends religion a certain external majesty useful

g. Rather: contribute nothing to the cultivation of religion cannot rightly [*jure*]
be called holy

the [Common People],[a] that [at least] one half, if not more, of [the *Lands* of that *Nation*][b] was in their hands, which [was never heard of in any other];[c] and an innumerable shole [swarm] of lazy useless men [have] made it their business to live upon and devour [this vast Wealth];[d] which was neither agreeable to [the Rules of the Christian Religion, nor of sound Policy].[e]

The Holy Scriptures do indeed command us to provide decently and liberally for <215> the Clergy, and that we should not muzzle the mouth of the Ox that treadeth out the Corn;[20] but then they never give that name to those who have no share in the [Ministry of the Church]:[f] Nor do they any where exempt the Persons of the Clergy, or their Revenues [goods], from [the Jurisdiction of the Civil Magistrate, or disable them to attemperate the same in such manner as may be consistent with the Publick Good].[g] And your *Venetian* [(vi)] Republick understands none better, that [the Revenues and Riches of the Church are not to be excessively encreased to the damage of the State],[h] and she has accordingly [wisely put a stop to that leak, the Pope and Court of *Rome* opposing her in this Design in vain, and without any success].[i] In truth, [she saw her self wasted by this means, and as it were brought into a Consumption, whilst her Riches and Lands were engrossed by a sort of men who acknowledge no Authority but that of an Head without their State, and

(vi). *The Author pretends to be a* Venetian.

a. Rather: devotion of private individuals

b. Rather: Germany

c. Rather: is an example unheard-of among all other nations [*gentes*]

d. Rather: the fruits of those holdings [*bonorum*]

e. Rather: theology, nor to the principles of politics [*civilis prudentiae*]

f. Rather: sacred ministry / That is, the name "clergy" (*sacerdotum*). [Ed.]

g. Rather: oversight [*inspectione*] by the supreme civil power, or prevent the latter from moderating them for the state's [*reipublicae*] welfare / See III.6, note 8, p. 88, on the sovereign's right of inspection. [Ed.]

h. Rather: an excessive amount of sacred holdings is of no use to the state

i. Rather: imposed a limit on their increase, the Pope's rancour [at this] being in vain

20. Deuteronomy 25:4.

pretended at the same time they were exempted by the Divine Laws from contributing to the publick Burthens].[a]

As to the number of Bishops, *Germany* has no reason to complain, except that, considering the extent of the Nation [region], they are [far] too few to discharge their [sacred] Office as they ought, if they were otherwise well disposed to do it: But to what purpose serves the vast Revenues belonging to these few Sees? You <216> will perhaps say they are [also] Princes of the Empire, [as well as Bishops][+], and take their share in the Care of the State [with the other Princes][+]: Why then let them abstain from the Sacred Title of *Bishops,* because that [holy][+] Office is inconsistent with the vast burthen of secular business[, which is necessarily attending on the Office of a Secular Prince][+]; [let them lay by the first; and stick wholly to the last Title].[b] For I think the Christian Religion would suffer no detriment if [they did not celebrate one or two Masses in a year, attended with a vast number of their Guards and Retinue in rich Garbs, and with great pomp, as if they designed nothing by it but to reproach the Poverty and mean Circumstances of the first settlers of the Christian Religion].[c] So let the Bishop of *Mentz* [(if he will)][+] possess his [great Revenues],[d] to enable him to sustain the Dignity and Charge of his Office of Chancellor of *Germany;* but then there is no apparent cause can be given why he should have a Bishop's See assigned to him, when the other Princes of the Empire, who have as great zeal for the welfare of their Country as he, have been contented to take none but Temporal Titles.[e]

a. Rather: states [*civitates*] must waste away to nothing, as it were, when such great riches are acquired by men who acknowledge another head outside the state [*rempublicam*] and take themselves to be exempt from public burdens by virtue of a divine right

b. Rather: and let them wish to be called [only] what they really are

c. Rather: some German bishop failed to celebrate his (at most) one or two Masses a year, while surrounded by a superb retinue and reproaching with his own poverty the first disseminators of the Christian religion / The comment is clearly sarcastic. See II.10, p. 69. [Ed.]

d. Rather: domain

e. There is a verbal play on the contrast between a holy [*sancta*] "chair" (i.e., see) and an ordinary [*vulgari*] one. [Ed.]

Now what shall I say of the Canons of the Cathedral Churches, which are the Blocks they hew into Bishops? They [perform none of the Sacred Offices];[a] and this they are not ashamed to own to all the World, <217> by calling themselves *Irregular Canons,* and [they too, to spare their own precious Lungs, fill their Churches with Noises, made by their mercenary Curates].[b] And such of them as are not employed in Secular Affairs, are meer useless Burthens of the Earth, serving their Bellies and their Lusts [groins]. Now as to those that are [wholly] + employed in Worldly Concerns, why are they called Holy men? Why are they maintained by the Revenues of the Church?

And what shall I say of the excessive [immense] Riches of the Monasteries, and of the [wonderful][c] swarms of shaven Crowns that hover about them? It is certainly necessary [expedient], that there should be Colleges[d] for the fitting your Youth for the Service of the Church and State; [and I should be well pleased to suffer some few men to spend all their daies in them too, in profound Contemplation, for which only Nature has fitted them; and besides, if they were brought on the stage, the world would lose the benefit of those advantages it might reap from their Studies; so that, as to these men, the State would have no great reason to complain, because at one time or other they would recompence the Charges of maintaining them with good Interest]:[e] Yet then both these sorts of men are [most happy],[f] when they have sober and competent Provisions made for them; overgreat ones load them with fat,

a. Rather: do no work of any relevance to sacred matters

b. Rather: , to spare their own throats, disturbing the church vaults with the noise of their vicars [instead of their own]

c. Rather: endless

d. Associated with monasteries. [Ed.]

e. Rather: and I would not deny that monasteries can be of use to men fitted only for profound speculation, the fruits of whose minds, whereby the state could benefit, are [otherwise] lost in the turbulence of civil life. When these men have been provided with a quiet retreat, they cannot complain that their sensitive nature [*ingenii*] has been given to them as a punishment, and what the state spends on them is often repaid with much interest / That is, both they and the state benefit. [Ed.]

f. Rather: best maintained / That is, the teachers and the sheltered intellectuals. [Ed.]

which stifles and obstructs both their *Vigour* and <218> *Industry.* But
then there doth not seem to be any good Reason [that can possibly be
given by the Wit of Man]⁺, why the Publick should be at the charge of
fatting up [a vast number of lubbarly]⁺ lazy fellows, who have betaken
themselves to their ugly [shapeless] Cowles out of pure desperation, and
are good for nothing but to fill the Church[es] with sensless noises, or
Prayers repeated with such cold and unconcerned affections, that they
are fain to [must] keep the account of them by their Beads.²¹

[The only pretence worth the regarding, that is made for the excessive
Riches of the Church],ª is, *That the illustrious and noble-Families [of*
Germany *have a means to provide for their younger Children, who being]*ᵇ
promoted to Ecclesiastical Benefices, are kept from being a Burthen to their
own Families, by which means Estates [patrimonies] *are kept from being*
crumbled into small Particles, [by dividing and subdividing them in every
Descent,]⁺ *and the Riches and Splendor of Families is* [better] *upholden,*
*nay, sometimes encreased; [the younger Brother],*ᶜ *who must otherwise have*
struggled with Want and Penury at home, being advanced to [considerable
*and rich Dignities in the Church].*ᵈ And I confess [it was a good Fetch
and a crafty Policy in the Church of *Rome,* thus to chain the noblest
Families to her Interest, and purchase their Favour].ᵉ

But then, though [it is worth our care to consider how we may preserve the Families of our Nobility and Gentry; yet in all probability, they
that first gave these Lands to the Church never dreamt of any such thing,
<219> and it is most certain this has nothing of Religion in it].ᶠ And as

a. Rather: Some think that the main argument for the great mass of sacred holdings [*bonorum*]
b. Rather: are thereby provided for, in that those
c. Rather: with those
d. Rather: the highest dignities
e. Rather: that for this reason alone, the Roman Church is able to assure itself of
the favor of illustrious families
f. Rather: it is perhaps an excellent thing to preserve the splendor of noble families,
those from whom the sacred holdings came undoubtedly never thought of procuring
such an outcome through them, even in their sleep, nor can we find anything sacred
in that end
21. A reference to praying the rosary.

to these younger Children [descendants], if they are men of spirit and courage, they have other means enough to raise their Fortunes, and improve their Estates and Reputations [at home or abroad]⁺, in times of Peace or War: But then, if they are useful to no body [in neither of these],^a it were fit to make them understand [they cannot reasonably expect their Sloth should be rewarded with an Entertainment at the Charge of the Publick, in the same manner the *Athenians* did their most deserving Citizens].^b If they will still insist, that at least, by this means, the over-great number of the Nobility is kept from becoming contemptible by their poverty; I reply, That if [they are men of truly noble Endowments],^c their multitude can bring no dishonour or disesteem to their Order, or to the State, because Virtue can never want a Station and a [suitable]⁺ Reward: But then, if they fear they[, having been produced by an age worse than that of their grandparents,] should fill the World with a degenerate Posterity worse than themselves, [I think this is true, and they ought to be kept]^d from Marriage, that they may not stock the World with useless Drones: [But then others, that are not in Holy Orders, abstain from the use of Women]:^e But if they [will not do that, I think the good old men, who gave these Lands to the Church, out of a belief, that whilst they lessened the Inheritances of their Children, <220> they promoted the Glory of God, and the Salvation of their Souls, are now miserably abused in their Graves, to have them now consigned only to the maintenance of a parcel of publick Stallions].^f

a. Rather: , either at home or in the military

b. Rather: that it would cause too much resentment if they were rewarded for their sloth by being maintained as in a public prytaneum / The Prytaneum in ancient Athens was a public hall where benefactors of the state such as Olympic victors were maintained. At *Apology* 36, Socrates suggests lifelong privileges there as a more suitable punishment than the death penalty demanded by his accusers. [Ed.]

c. Rather: the nobility generates descendants worthy of its name,

d. Rather: it is certainly right [*recte*] for them to abstain

e. Rather: For those outside Holy Orders are also permitted to abstain from women

f. Rather: cannot abate their lust without whores, it seems that one can only pity those good old men who believed they were looking out for their souls by keeping back some of their goods from the state and their heirs, in that they have [merely] provided fodder for black-robed breeding stallions

The Protestant
Princes fairly
vindicated.

10. This being [however the truth of] + the case, I for my part think the *Protestant Princes* will [easily] be able to give a very good and rational account to God and all wise [reasonable] men, why they [have taken that care they have to employ the Revenues of the Church, which lay within their Dominions, and so was properly under their Jurisdictions, to the education of Youth in Piety and good Arts, and to the maintenance of such Ministers as were truly and in good earnest employed in the Service of God, and what was overplus, to the Service of the State; whereas before the whole was spent in Luxury and Sloth].[a] And if the Emperor and the rest of the Catholick Princes had [taken the same care in their States, they had disburthened *Germany* of a number of ill Humours, which now oppress it].[b] Nor could the Pope [Most Holy Father] have resented it without shewing himself openly [more a Friend to the Vices of the Times than is consistent with his Honour].[c] Nor was there any necessity that [they should have ever the more changed their Faith in other particulars, though they had retrenched the number of their Clergy, and <221> reduced their Revenues to a narrower Scantling, for the publick good of their States].[d] For their Christian Ancestors[, too, still] finding Poverty and Piety united [in their days] +, long before the Priviledges of the See of *Rome* were thought of, agreed with the [same] Church of *Rome* in matters of Faith.

The greatest difficulty, as some [have] thought, [lay in the Bishopricks, which are still extant, because it was not for the Interest of *Germany* that those large Dominions should be added to the Emperor or

a. Rather: , who exercise the remaining parts of supreme sovereignty in their own domains, have also claimed for themselves the care of sacred matters; at least if they have so restrained themselves as [only] to take the things that previously did nothing but produce fat [*lardum*] and assign them for the use of those who actively contribute in some way to the real business of the Church, or instruct the youth in piety and wholesome learning [*bonis literis*], designating for the state whatever is left over

b. Rather: imitated them, they would have purged a great source of illnesses from the body of Germany

c. Rather: a patron of vices

d. Rather: compelled them to change their faith, in whatever way the clergy and their goods were brought a bit more closely into agreement with the good of the state

any of the other Princes].[a] [But then this is owing only to the ill constitution of the *German* State, which][b] is subject to very great Commotions on the least change. Let then those Bishopricks continue, and enjoy their large Revenues and Territories; only in the mean time let these Bishops remember that they are *German* Princes, and that they owe their Dominions to [the Liberality of the *Germans*],[c] and therefore ought to love [their Country more than the Pope]:[d] And let them [genuinely] put an end to their longing desires after [those Bishopricks][e] they have lost, and never more think of regaining them, for fear in the attempt they should also lose [what is left them];[f] [and however, it becomes them not to embroil their native Country [*patriam*] in any more destructive Wars and Quarrels].[g]

In truth, [it seems that] in the last Age [century] it would not have been so difficult to have brought the Bishopricks of *Germany* <222> into a [better state][h] than now they are, if either the Archbishop [Elector] of *Cologne* had not miscarried in his design, or if [more of the *German* Bishops had conspired with him in the same intention]:[i] For after the Reverence of the See of *Rome* was sunk to so low an ebb, it would not have been difficult to have turned the Bishopricks into Hereditary Principalities, [and to have assigned the other Revenues to the Chapters or Prebends];[j] or if this had not pleased them, these Principalities [digni-

---

a. Rather: concerns the bishoprics that still remain, whose addition to the Emperor or the other princes is not in the interest of the German state

b. Rather: Indeed, it is readily apparent what [alterations] the diseased condition of Germany can bear, since it

c. Rather: Germany

d. Rather: Germany more than Rome

e. Rather: the things

f. Rather: their present possessions

g. Rather: at least, let them refrain from embroiling their fatherland in any more turmoils

h. Rather: different form

i. Rather: other bishops had been moved by the desire to attempt something similar / See V.11 and note 10, p. 131. [Ed.]

j. Rather: if [some] benefices [*praebendis*] had been transferred to the cathedral chapters as well / That is, to gain their support for the change. [Ed.]

ties] might have still^a passed from one to another by Election. Nor are
the Protestants [of such small and contemptible Parts or Understand-
ings],^b as that they could not have employed these Revenues [goods] to
the same uses [the *Roman Catholicks* do, if they had thought fit to have
so continued them].^c It had been more also for the Peace of *Germany*
to have had [the whole Nation embraced the Protestant Religion, than
it was to have a part continue in the old, to distract the People by a
diversity in their Faith].^d And [could any man drive out of the Empire
those lazy Drones the Monks, and the cunning Companions of the Society of the Jesuites, *Germany* would thereby be delivered from a Sett
of dangerous Spies; and the Revenues they wastefully devour, would be
sufficient to maintain an Army that would defend *Germany* against both
the *Eastern* and *Western Turk*]."^e <223>

When I had heard this Discourse out, I [was in an horrible fright for
the *Roman Catholick Religion* in *Germany,* but that I considered it was
understood in vain by private men, who could indeed please themselves
with specious Counsels],^f and assume great Courages under the Covert
of their private Walls: [But then, as long as those that were born to *command* and *govern* others were for the most part beholden *to* their Des-
tinies, for giving them more Wealth than Wisdom, I thought again their
Ignorance of what was their true Interest, and for their good, would still
secure it].^g

a. As in the former bishoprics. [Ed.]
b. Rather: so dull-witted
c. Rather: they are intended for by Catholics
d. Rather: everyone enroll in the new religion, than to split up into parties [*partes*]
on account of differences in belief
e. Rather: if Germany could somehow expell that lazy flock of monks and the
devious [*prave solertes*] Jesuits, it would simultaneously rid itself of very clever spies
and have sufficient resources, even in the goods devoured by them alone, to maintain
an army formidable to all its neighbors / Though not in Pufendorf, the designation
of France as "western Turk" was current in the 1670s and 1680s. See Wrede, "Kaiser,"
108–9. [Ed.]
f. Rather: began to fear for the fortunes of the Catholic Church in Germany, until
it occurred to me that it is futile for private men to invent attractive schemes [*speciosa
consilia*]
g. Rather: as long as those who are placed at the state's helm by lot of birth—

This[, Sir,]⁺ is what I have in my Travels observed, concerning the Empire of *Germany*, and having thought fit to set it down in writing, I perswade my self, that if [I miss of Praise and Applause, yet at least the Candor and Sincerity of my Relations will deserve pardon].[a]

FINIS.

---

which is more likely to bestow undeserved wealth than wisdom—do not recognize their own interests [*bona*] / That is, the Catholic Church is safe so long as only private persons (like Monzambano—thus, the "fear") understand what is in Protestantism's true interest. [Ed.]

a. Rather: its professed candor does not merit praise among the judicious [*cordatos*], it will at least deserve pardon

BIBLIOGRAPHY

Sources

Editions of "De Statu Imperii Germanici"

Samuelis L.B. [*liber baron*= Freiherr = baron] *de Pufendorf De statu Imperii Germanici liber unus.* . . . Edited by Jakob Paul Gundling, with a preface. . . . Editio posthuma. Cölln: Johann Andreas Rüdiger, 1706.

Samuelis L.B. *de Pufendorf, sive antea Severini de Monzambano, De statu Imperii Germanici liber unus.* Edited by Gottlieb Gerhard Titius. Leipzig: Thomas Fritsch, 1708.

Severini de Monzambano Veronensis De statu Imperii Germanici liber. Enlarged and corrected ed. with notes and index by Christian Thomasius. 1695. Reprinted Halle: Christian Salfeld's Widow, 1714.

Severini de Monzambano Veronensis, De statu Imperii Germanici ad Laelium fratrem, dominum Trezolani, liber unus. Geneva: Petrus Columesius [The Hague: Adrian Vlacq], 1667.

Severini de Monzambano Veronensis, De statu Imperii Germanici, ad Laelium fratrem, dominum Trezolani, liber unus. 1667. Reprinted in *Staatslehre der frühen Neuzeit,* edited by Notker Hammerstein, 568–931. Bibliothek der Geschichte und Politik 16. Frankfurt am Main: Deutscher Klassiker Verlag, 1995. Based on *Severinus de Monzambano . . . De statu Imperii Germanici,* edited by Fritz Salomon (see below). The 1667 Latin original and the 1669 German translation are printed in parallel format.

Severinus de Monzambano (Samuel von Pufendorf), *De statu Imperii Germanici.* Edited by Fritz Salomon. Weimar: Hermann Böhlaus Nachfolger, 1910.

Translations of "De Statu Imperii Germanici"

L'Estat de l'empire d'Allemagne de Monzambane. Translated by Sieur François-Savinien d'Alquié. Amsterdam: J. J. Shipper, 1669.

Monzambano, Severinus von [Samuel von Pufendorf]. *Über die Verfassung des deutschen Reiches.* Translated by Harry Breßlau. Berlin: L. Heimann, 1870.

Monzambano, eines Veronesers ungescheuter offenherziger Discurs, oder Gründlicher Bericht von der wahren Beschafenheit und Zustand des Teutschen Reichs. Geschrieben an seinen Bruder Laelium von Monzambano. Herrn zu Trezolan . . . ins teutsche übersezet durch ein ungenantes Glied der hochlöblichen Fruchtbringenden Gesellschaft. 1669. Reprinted in *Staatslehre der frühen Neuzeit,* edited by Notker Hammerstein, 568–931. Bibliothek der Geschichte und Politik 16. Frankfurt am Main: Deutscher Klassiker Verlag, 1995.

The Present State of Germany; or, An Account of the Extent, Rise, Form, Wealth, Strength, Weaknesses and Interests of that Empire. The Prerogatives of the Emperor, and the Priviledges of the Electors, Princes, and Free Cities. Adapted to the present Circumstances of that Nation. By a Person of Quality. London: Printed for Richard Chiswel, at the Rose and Crown in St. Paul's Church-Yard, 1690.

The Present State of Germany. Written in Latin by the Learned Samuel Puffendorff, under the name of Severinus de Monzambano Veronensis; made English and continued by Edmund Bohun, Esq; London: Printed for Richard Chiswell, at the Rose and Crown in St. Paul's Church-Yard, 1696.

Samuels Freyhrn. von Puffendorff kurtzer doch gründlicher Bericht von dem Zustande des H.R. Reichs Teutscher Nation: Vormahls in Lateinischer Sprache unter dem Titel Severin von Monzambano herausgegeben. Anietzo aber ins Teutsche übersetzet [by Petronius Harteviggus Adlemansthal, or P(eter) Dahlmann] . . . Ingleichen mit . . . Anmerckungen der . . . Publicisten, nicht weniger mit gantz neuen Remarquen und nützlichen Registern versehen. Deme noch beygefüget (1.) *Die Historie von dem wunderlichen Lärmen und Tumult welcher in der gelehrten Welt dieses Buchs wegen entstanden.* (2.) *Des Hrn. Autoris Untersuchung von der Beschaffenheit eines irregulieren Staats* [= *De republica irregulari*]. (3.) *Vita, Fama, et Fata Literaria Pufendorfiana, oder denckwürdige Lebens-Memoire des weltberuffenen Herrn Autoris.* Leipzig: Weidmann, 1710.

Die Verfassung des deutschen Reiches. Edited and translated by Horst Denzer. Bibliothek des deutschen Staatswesens 4. Frankfurt: Insel Verlag, 1994. Parallel edition.

Die Verfassung des deutschen Reiches von Samuel von Pufendorf. Translated by Horst Denzer. Stuttgart: Philipp Reclam, 1976. Translation only.

Die Verfassung des deutschen Reiches von Samuel von Pufendorf. Translated by Heinrich Dove. Leipzig: Philipp Reclam [1877].

Other Works by Pufendorf

Briefwechsel. Edited by Detlef Döring. Vol. 1 of *Gesammelte Werke.* Edited by Wilhelm Schmidt-Biggemann. Berlin: Akademie Verlag, 1996.

Dissertationes academicae selectiores. Lund, 1675.

The Divine Feudal Law: Or, Covenants with Mankind, Represented. Translated by Theophilus Dorrington. 1703. Edited by Simone Zurbuchen. Indianapolis: Liberty Fund, 2002. Originally published as *Jus feciale divinum, sive de consensu et dissensu Protestantium* (Lubeck, 1695).

Elementa jurisprudentiae universalis libri duo [Elements of Universal Jurisprudence, Two Books]. The Hague: Adrian Vlacq, 1660.

Eris Scandica und andere polemische Schriften über das Naturrecht. Edited by Fiammetta Palladini. Vol. 5 of *Gesammelte Werke.* Edited by Wilhelm Schmidt-Biggemann. Berlin: Akademie Verlag, 2002.

The History of Popedom: Containing the Rise, Progress and Decay Thereof. Translated by John Chamberlayne. London: Joseph Hindmarsh, 1691. Originally published as *Basilii Hyperetae Historische und politische Beschreibung der geistlichen Monarchie des Stuhls zu Rom* (Leipzig and Franckfurt, 1679).

An Introduction to the History of the Principal Kingdoms and States of Europe. Translated by Jodocus Crull. London: Gilliflower, 1695. Originally published as *Einleitung zu der Historie der vornehmsten Reiche und Staaten, so itziger Zeit in Europa sich befinden* (Frankfurt, 1682).

Kleine Vorträge und Schriften. Edited by Detlef Döring. Frankfurt am Main: V. Klostermann, 1995.

Of the Nature and Qualification of Religion in Reference to Civil Society. Translated by Jodocus Crull. 1698. Edited by Simone Zurbuchen. Indianapolis: Liberty Fund, 2002. Originally published as *De habitu religionis christianae ad vitam civilem* (Bremen, 1687).

On the Law of Nature and of Nations. Vol. 2, *The Translation of the Edition of 1688.* Translated by C. H. Oldfather and W. A. Oldfather. Oxford: Clarendon Press, 1934. Originally published as *De Jure Naturae et Gentium* (Lund, 1672).

The Political Writings of Samuel Pufendorf. Edited by Craig L. Carr. Translated by Michael J. Seidler. New York: Oxford University Press, 1994.

The Whole Duty of Man, According to the Law of Nature. Translated by Benjamin Tooke. 1735. Edited by Ian Hunter and David Saunders. Indianapolis: Liberty Fund, 2003. Originally published as *De officio hominis et civis juxta legem naturalem* (Lund, 1673).

Studies

Asch, Ronald G. *The Thirty Years' War: The Holy Roman Empire and Europe, 1618–48.* New York: St. Martin's Press, 1997.

Bérenger, Jean. "Un diplomate Suédois ami de la France: Esaias Pufendorf (1628–1687)." *XVIIe Siècle* 45 (1993): 223–46.

Bohun, Edmund. *A defence of Sir Robert Filmer, against the mistakes and misrepresentations of Algernon Sidney, esq. in a paper delivered by him to the sheriffs upon the scaffold on Tower-Hill, on Fryday December the 7th 1683 before his execution there.* London: W. Kettilby, 1684.

———. *The Diary and Autobiography of Edmund Bohun, Esq.* With an introductory memoir, notes, and illustrations by Samuel Wilton Rix. Beccles: Read Crisp, 1853.

Bosbach, Franz. "The European Debate on Universal Monarchy." In *Theories of Empire, 1450–1800,* edited by David Armitage, 81–98. Aldershot: Ashgate, 1998.

Boucher, David. "Pufendorf and the Person of the State." In *Political Theories of International Relations,* 223–53. Oxford: Oxford University Press, 1998.

———. "Resurrecting Pufendorf and Capturing the Westphalian Moment." *Review of International Studies* 27 (2001): 557–77.

Breßlau, Harry. "Einleitung." In *Über die Verfassung des deutschen Reiches,* by Severinus von Monzambano [Samuel von Pufendorf], translated by Harry Breßlau, 5–14. Berlin: L. Heimann, 1870.

Bretone, Mario. *Geschichte des Römischen Rechts: Von den Anfängen bis zu Justinian.* Translated by Brigitte Galsterer. 2nd ed. München: C. H. Beck, 1998.

Conring, Hermann. *New Discourse on the Roman-German Emperor.* Edited and translated by Constantin Fasolt. Vol. 282 of Medieval and Renaissance Texts and Studies. Tempe, Ariz.: Arizona Center for Medieval and Renaissance Studies, 2005.

De Angelis, Simone. "Pufendorf und der Cartesianismus." *Internationales Archiv für Sozialgeschichte der deutschen Literatur* 29, no. 1 (2004): 129–72.

Denzer, Horst. "Samuel Pufendorf und die Verfassungsgeschichte." In *Die Verfassung des deutschen Reiches,* by Samuel Pufendorf, edited and translated by Horst Denzer, 279–327. Frankfurt: Insel Verlag, 1994.

Döring, Detlef. "Das Heilige Römische Reich Deutscher Nation in der Beurteilung Samuel von Pufendorfs." In *Samuel Pufendorf: Filosofo del diritto e della politica,* edited by Vanda Fiorillo, 73–106. Napoli: Istituto Italiano per gli Studi Filosofici, 1996.

———. "Der Westfälische Frieden in der Sicht Samuel von Pufendorfs." *Zeitschrift für historische Forschung* 26 no. 3 (1999): 349–64.

———. *Pufendorf-Studien: Beiträge zur Biographie Samuel von Pufendorfs und zu seiner Entwicklung als historiker und theologischer Schriftsteller.* Berlin: Duncker & Humblot, 1992. *Monzambano* bibliography, 255–58.

———. "Untersuchungen zur Entstehungsgeschichte der Reichsverfassungsschrift Samuel Pufendorfs (Severinus de Monzambano)." *Der Staat* 33 no. 2 (1994): 185–206.

Dotzauer, Winfried. "Der Kurpfälzische Wildfangstreit und seine Auswirkungen im Rheinhessisch-Pfälzischen Raum." In *Regionale Amts- und Verwaltungsstrukturen im Rheinhessisch-Pfälzischen Raum, 14. bis 18. Jh.,* 84–105. Geschichtliche Landeskunde 25. Stuttgart: Franz Steiner Verlag Wiesbaden, 1984.

Dove, Heinrich. "Einleitung." In *Die Verfassung des deutschen Reiches von Samuel Pufendorf,* translated by Heinrich Dove, 3–11. Leipzig: Philipp Reclam, 1877.

Dreitzel, Horst. "Samuel Pufendorf." In *Das Heilige Römische Reich Deutscher Nation: Nord- und Ostmittel-Europa,* edited by Helmut Holzhey, Wilhelm Schmidt-Biggemann, and Vilem Mudroch. Basel: Schwabe, 2001. 2:757–812. Vol. 4 of Friedrich Ueberweg, *Grundriss der Geschichte der Philosophie: Die Philosophie des 17. Jahrhunderts,* edited by Helmut Holzhey.

———. "Zehn Jahre 'Patria' in der politischen Theorie in Deutschland: Prasch, Pufendorf, Leibniz, Becher 1662 bis 1672." In *"Patria" und "Patrioten" vor dem Patriotismus. Pflichten, Rechte, Glauben und die Rekonfigurierung europäischer Gemeinwesen im 17. Jahrhundert,* edited by Robert von Friedeburg, 367–534. Wolfenbütteler Arbeiten zur Barockforschung, vol. 41. Wiesbaden: Harrassowitz Verlag, 2005.

Duchhardt, Heinz. "Pufendorf in England: Eine unbekannte Übersetzung von Pufendorfs Reichsverfassungsschrift aus dem Jahre 1690." *Archiv für Kulturgeschichte* 72 no. 1 (1990): 143–52.

Dufour, Alfred. "Federalisme et raison d'état dans la pensée politique pufendorfienne." In *Samuel Pufendorf: Filosofo del diritto e della politica,* edited by Vanda Fiorillo, 107–38. Naples: La Città del Sole, 1996.

———. "Pufendorfs föderalistisches Denken und die Staatsräsonlehre." In *Samuel Pufendorf und die europäische Frühaufklärung,* edited by Fiammetta Palladini and Gerald Hartung, 105–22. Berlin: Akademie Verlag, 1996.

Fagelson, David. "Two Concepts of Sovereignty: From Westphalia to the Law of Peoples." *International Politics* 38 (2001): 499–514.

Glafey, Adam Friedrich. *Vollständige Geschichte des Rechts der Venunft . . . , nebst einer Bibliotheca Juris Naturae et Gentium.* Neudruck der Ausgabe Leipzig 1739. Aalen: Scientia Verlag, 1965. §§121–42, pp. 201–16, esp. §125, pp. 203–4.

Goldie, Mark. "Edmund Bohun and *Jus Gentium* in the Revolution Debate, 1689–1693." *Historical Journal* 20 no. 3 (1977): 569–86.

Haakonssen, Knud. "Protestant Natural Law Theory: A General Interpretation." In *New Essays on the History of Autonomy: A Collection Honoring J. B. Schneewind,* edited by Natalie Brender and Larry Krasnoff, 92–109. New York: Cambridge University Press, 2004.

Haberkern, Eugen, and Joseph Friedrich Wallach, eds. *Hilfswörterbuch für Historiker: Mittelalter und Neuzeit.* 9th ed. 2 vols. Tübingen: A. Francke, 2001.

Hammerstein, Notker. "Kommentar." In *Staatslehre der frühen Neuzeit,* edited by Notker Hammerstein, 1013–1209; on Pufendorf see 1179–92. Bibliothek der Geschichte und Politik, 16. Frankfurt am Main: Deutscher Klassiker Verlag, 1995.

Haug-Moritz, Gabriele. "Kaisertum und Parität: Reichspolitik und Konfessionen nach dem Westfälischen Frieden." *Zeitschrift für historische Forschung* 19 no. 4 (1992): 445–82.

Hettne, Björn. "The Fate of Citizenship in Post-Westphalia." *Citizenship Studies* 4 no. 1 (2000): 35–46.

Hochstrasser, T. J. *Natural Law Theories in the Early Enlightenment.* Cambridge: Cambridge University Press, 2000.

Hoke, Rudolf. "Hippolithus a Lapide." In *Staatsdenker im 17. und 18. Jahrhundert,* edited by Michael Stolleis, 118–28. Frankfurt am Main: Alfred Metzner, 1977.

Hont, Istvan. "The Permanent Crisis of a Divided Mankind: 'Contemporary Crisis of the Nation State' in Historical Perspective." *Political Studies* 42 (1994): 166–231.

Hunter, Ian. "Natural Law." In *Encyclopedia of the Enlightenment,* edited by Alan Charles Kors, 4 vols., 3:130–34. Oxford: Oxford University Press, 2003.

———. *Rival Enlightenments: Civil and Metaphysical Philosophy in Early Modern Germany.* Cambridge: Cambridge University Press, 2001.

Jastrow, J. "Pufendorfs Lehre von der Monstrosität der Reichsverfassung." *Zeitschrift für Preußische Geschichte und Landeskunde* 19 (1882): 333–406.

Kemp, Geoff. "Bohun, Edmund (1645–1699)." In *Oxford Dictionary of National Biography,* edited by H. C. G. Matthew and Brian Harrison, 61 vols., 6:440–41. Oxford: Oxford University Press, 2004.

Kitson, Frank. *Prince Rupert: Admiral and General-at-Sea.* London: Constable, 1998.

———. *Prince Rupert: Portrait of a Soldier.* London: Constable, 1994.

Knoppers, Laura Lunger, and Joan B. Landes, eds. *Monstrous Bodies/Political Monstrosities in Early Modern Europe.* Ithaca: Cornell University Press, 2004.

Koch, Klaus. *Europa, Rom under der Kaiser vor dem Hintergrund von zwei Jahrtausenden Rezeption des Buches Daniel.* Hamburg: Vandenhoeck & Ruprecht, 1997.

Lenz, Georg. "Hermann Conring und die deutsche Staatslehre des 17. Jahrhunderts." *Zeitschrift für die gesammte Staatswissenschaft* 81 (1926): 128–53.

Lübbe-Wolff, Gertrude. "Die Bedeutung der Lehre von den vier Weltreichen für das Staatsrecht des Römisch-Deutschen Reiches." *Der Staat* 23 (1984): 369–89.

Modéer, Kjell Å. "From Samuel Pufendorf to the Raoul Wallenberg Institute: Lund University Law School During Three Centuries." *International Journal of Legal Information* 25 (1995): 5–16.

Moore, James, and Michael Silverthorne. "Protestant Theologies, Limited Sovereignties: Natural Law and the Conditions of Union in the German Empire, the Netherlands and Great Britain." In *A Union for Empire. Political Thought and the British Union of 1707,* edited by John Robertson, 171–97. Cambridge: Cambridge University Press, 1995.

Moser, Johann Jacob. *Bibliotheca juris publici S.R. German. Imperii.* Stuttgardt, 1729.

Mühlen, Patrick von der. "Die Reichstheorien in der deutschen Historiographie des frühen 18. Jahrhunderts." *Zeitschrift der Savigny-Stiftung für Rechtsgeschichte, Germanistische Abteilung* 89 (1972): 118–46.

Müller-Mertens, E. "Römisches Reich im Besitz der Deutschen, der König an Stelle des Augustus. Recherche zur Frage: seit wann wird das mittelalterlich-frühneuzeitliche Reich von den Zeitgenossen als römisch-deutsch begriffen?" *Historische Zeitschrift* 282, no. 1 (2006): 1–56.

Palladini, Fiammetta. "Discussioni sul *Monzambano*." Parte seconda, chap. 2, pp. 111–62, in *Discussioni seicentesche su Samuel Pufendorf: Scritti latini: 1663–1700*. Mulino: Societa' Editrice, 1978.

———. "Stato, chiesa e tolleranza nel pensiero di S. Pufendorf." *Rivista storica italiana* 109 no. 2 (1997): 436–82.

———. "Un nemico di S. Pufendorf: Johann Heinrich Böcler (1611–1672)." *Ius Commune: Zeitschrift für europäische Rechtsgeschichte* 24 (1997): 133–52.

Press, Volker. "Das Heilige Römische Reich in der deutschen Geschichte." In *Das alte Reich: Ausgewählte Aufsätze,* edited by Volker Press, Stephanie Blankenhorn, and Johannes Kunisch, 42–66. Berlin: Duncker & Humblot, 1997.

———. *Kriege und Krisen: Deutschland 1600–1715.* München: C. H. Beck, 1991.

———. "Zwischen Versailles und Wien: Die Pfälzer Kurfürsten in der deutschen Geschichte der Barockzeit." *Zeitschrift für die Geschichte des Oberrheins* 130 (1982): 207–62, esp. 223–62.

Prietzel, Malte. *Das Heilige Römische Reich im Spätmittelalter.* Darmstadt: Wissenschaftliche Buchgesellschaft, 2004.

Pursell, Brennan C. *The Winter King: Frederick V of the Palatinate and the Coming of the Thirty Years' War.* Aldershot: Ashgate, 2003.

Rebitsch, Robert. *Rupert von der Pfalz (1610–82): ein deutscher Fürstensohn im Dienst der Stuarts.* Innsbruck: Studien Verlag, 2005.

Reinhard, Wolfgang. "Frühmoderner Staat und Deutsches Monstrum: Die Entstehung des modernen Staates und das Alte Reich." *Zeitschrift für historische Forschung* 29 no. 3 (2002): 339–57.

Riklin, Alois. "Gemischte oder monströse Verfassung? Althusius, Limnaeus und Pufendorf über das Römisch-deutsche Reich." *Beiträge und Berichte* (St. Gallen: Institut für Politikwissenschaft, Hochschule St. Gallen) 190 (1992): 1–36.

Robertson, John. "Empire and Union: Two Concepts of the Early Modern European Political Order." In *A Union for Empire: Political Thought and the British Union of 1707,* edited by John Robertson, 3–36. Cambridge: Cambridge University, 1995.

Roeck, Bernd. *Reichssystem und Reichsherkommen: Die Diskussion über die*

Staatlichkeit des Reiches in der politischen Publizistik des 17. und 18. Jahrhunderts, 24–74. Wiesbaden: Franz Steiner, 1984.

Salomon, Fritz. "Einleitung." In Severinus de Monzambano (Samuel von Pufendorf), *De Statu Imperii Germanici,* edited by Fritz Salomon, 1–10. Weimar: Hermann Böhlaus Nachfolger, 1910.

———. "Literaturverzeichnis." In Severinus de Monzambano (Samuel von Pufendorf), *De Statu Imperii Germanici,* edited by Fritz Salomon, 11–23. Weimar: Hermann Böhlaus Nachfolger, 1910.

Saunders, David, and Ian Hunter. "Bringing the State to England: Andrew Tooke's Translation of Samuel Pufendorf's *De officio hominis et civis.*" *History of Political Thought* 24 no. 2 (2003): 218–34.

Schindling, Anton. "The Development of the Eternal Diet in Regensburg." *Journal of Modern History* 58, suppl. (1958): 64–75.

Schmidt, Georg. *Geschichte des Alten Reiches: Staat und Nation in der frühen Neuzeit 1495–1806.* München: C. H. Beck, 1999.

Schröder, Peter. "The Constitution of the Holy Roman Empire After 1648: Samuel Pufendorf's Assessment in His *Monzambano.*" *Historical Journal* 42 no. 4 (1999): 961–83.

———. "Reich versus Territorien? Zum Problem der Souveranität im Heiligen Römischen Reich nach dem Westfälischen Frieden." In *Altes Reich, Frankreich und Europa,* edited by Olaf Asbach, Klaus Malettke, and Sven Externbrink, 123–43. Berlin: Duncker & Humblot, 2001.

Seidler, Michael J. "Pufendorf and the Politics of Recognition." In *Natural Law and Civil Sovereignty: Moral Right and State Authority in Early Modern Political Thought,* edited by Ian Hunter and David Saunders, 235–51. New York: Palgrave Macmillan, 2002.

———. "'Wer mir gutes thut, den liebe ich': Pufendorf on Patriotism and Political Loyalty." In *"Patria" und "Patrioten" vor dem Patriotismus. Pflichten, Rechte, Glauben und die Rekonfigurierung europäischer Gemeinwesen im 17. Jahrhundert,* edited by Robert von Friedeburg, 335–65. Wolfenbütteler Arbeiten zur Barockforschung, vol. 41. Wiesbaden: Harrassowitz Verlag, 2005.

Stephen, Leslie. "Bohun, Edmund (1645–1699)." In *Dictionary of National Biography,* edited by Leslie Stephen and Sidney Lee, 22 vols., 2:768–69. Oxford: Oxford University Press, 1993. Originally published by Smith, Elder & Co., 1885–1901.

Stolleis, Michael. "Textor und Pufendorf über die *Ratio Status Imperii* im

Jahre 1667." In *Staatsräson. Studien zur Geschichte eines politischen Begriffs,* edited by Roman Schnur, 441–63. Berlin: Duncker & Humblot, 1975.

Thompson, Martyn P. "Bohun, Edmund (1645–99)." In *The Dictionary of Seventeenth-Century British Philosophers,* edited by Andrew Pyle, 4 vols., 1: 105–7. London: Thoemmes, 2000.

Treitschke, Heinrich von. "Samuel Pufendorf." In *Historische und politische Aufsätze,* 4 vols. Vol. 4, *Biographische und historische Abhandlungen,* 202–303. Leipzig: S. Hirzel, 1897.

Tuck, Richard. "The 'Modern' Theory of Natural Law." In *The Languages of Political Theory in Early-Modern Europe,* edited by Anthony Pagden, 99–119. Cambridge: Cambridge University Press, 1987.

Willoweit, Dietmar. "Hermann Conring." In *Staatsdenker im 17. und 18. Jahrhundert,* edited by Michael Stolleis, 129–47. Frankfurt on Main: Alfred Metzner, 1977.

Wilson, Peter H. "Still a Monstrosity? Some Reflections on Early Modern German Statehood." *The Historical Journal* 49 no. 2 (2006): 565–76.

Wrede, M. "Der Kaiser, das Reich, die Deutsche Nation—und ihre 'Feinde': Natiogenese, Reichsidee und der 'Durchbruch des Politischen' im Jahrhundert nach dem Westfälischen Frieden." *Historische Zeitschrift* 280 no. 1 (2005): 83–116.

Wright, Martin. *Systems of States.* Edited by Hedley Bull. Leicester: Leicester University Press, 1977.

INDEX

This book is set in Adobe Garamond, a modern adaptation by Robert Slimbach of the typeface originally cut around 1540 by the French typographer and printer Claude Garamond. The Garamond face, with its small lowercase height and restrained contrast between thick and thin strokes, is a classic "old-style" face and has long been one of the most influential and widely used typefaces.

Printed on paper that is acid-free and meets the requirements of the American National Standard for Permanence of Paper for Printed Library Materials, z39.48-1992. ∞

Book design by Louise OFarrell
Gainesville, Florida
Typography by Apex Publishing, LLC
Madison, Wisconsin
Printed and bound by Edwards Brothers, Inc.
Ann Arbor, Michigan